No Messing –
The Story of an Essex Man

The Autobiography of
John Castelfranc Cheveley
1795-1870

VOLUME TWO

Edited by
C.C. THORNBURN

Crosswave Publishing

First published in 2012

Crosswave Publishing
1 Victoria Road
Chichester
West Sussex
PO19 7HY

ISBN 978-0-9565561-2-7

Set in Copperplate Gothic Light and Times New Roman

Printed in Great Britain by SS Media Limited (ss-media.co.uk)
Cardinal Point, Park Road, Rickmansworth, Hertfordshire, WD3 1RE

To the Cheveley family:
past, present and future;
and to my own family.

Watercolour by JCC: maybe around Prescot? – Unlikely to be flat Essex! (Courtesy Mrs J. Cheveley)

Contents

Illustrations

Acknowledgements

I am very grateful to the following for their help with Volume 2: particularly, again, Mrs J. Cheveley, for so kindly making JCC's notebooks freely available to me, also for JCC's watercolour, the portrait of George, and the black shade profiles.

My (distant) cousins Mrs J. Shapiro, for material relating to the Castelfranc family, and Mrs M. Timmington, for the photograph of JCC himself, and his pencil sketch.

Ms R. Lloyd, who has taken the Cheveley family tree back another two generations.

My late friend Mr M. Meadows of Birmingham, who told me about his boyhood escapades.

Mr N.A. Draper, for information about Sir Barnard Turner and 'Brother Jonathan'.

Dr B. Crosby, Durham, for information about hymns.

Rev T.M. Steel, former Vicar of Prescot, for information and the picture of Rev Driffield.

Mr R.C. Brunning, Messing, for the picture of the church east window.

The Curator of Maps of the Royal Geographical Society, Mr F. Herbert, for various maps.

Mr A. Higham and especially Mr J. Vinter for assistance with the publication – which, owing to something of a let-down and family problems, necessitated a change of publisher from Volume 1.

Introduction

During researches into my family history, I was lucky enough to enjoy one of those totally-unexpected pieces of good fortune that come only occasionally: the discovery of the autobiography of John Castelfranc Cheveley (JCC), my three-times great-uncle, held by a distant cousin on my paternal grandmother's side, who very kindly loaned it to me. It comprises eleven thick notebooks, plus a fragment from another, and a supplementary one about British Guiana. They provided not only family information, but a wealth of detail about life a couple of centuries ago, in a very significant period of history, which I felt deserved a wider audience. Accordingly, I made a full extract: and the present work is the result. John's life-history falls naturally into four parts of roughly similar length: Volume 1 (ISBN 1 84104 024X) covered the first two, Volume 2 now deals with the latter.

John and his brother George, my great-great-grandfather, were second and third of a family of eight, six boys then two girls; all were born and spent their formative years in rural Essex, in the village of Messing, near Colchester, where their father was a tenant farmer. It seemed an idyllic existence, but after experiencing the delights of London, John tired of the sleepy countryside with an increasing sense of frustration as he longed to get away to something more exciting; but the termination of the Napoleonic wars had thrown multitudes out of employment, and jobs were simply not to be had. However, he did escape the monotony of life in Essex, though not in the way he would have desired, when in 1816 his father's farming failure brought a rude awakening to the reality that they would all have to leave their home.

John and George were lucky enough to obtain places as midshipmen with the East India Company on a voyage to China. John then went out again with a free-trader to India, whence he returned to the family, now residing near Messing, at Tiptree; a period there was broken by a winter's experience as a commercial traveller. A further decline in fortunes finally dispersed the family in 1821. An old friend, the Rev George Driffield, now Vicar of Prescot in Lancashire, kindly offered to take John in, with a view to finding employment in Liverpool. Volume 1 left him at this point, and the present Volume 2 rejoins him as he prepares to go north into the unknown.

Sadly, his career was not very successful materially, dogged by disappointment, misfortune and trouble, the first three parts each ending with him having to re-start in some way (somewhat mirrored in the preparation of the present volume). But in 1821 occurred the most significant event of his life, his religious conversion, and from then on he was buoyed up by his faith, which became central to his attitudes and outlook. His views, though, were somewhat narrow, and coloured his writing in the form of judgemental comments in his notebooks about, for example, his fellow-men's enjoyment of earthly pleasures rather than things spiritual. These I have cut out, as they rapidly become tedious and do not really advance his story.

As was typical of the nineteenth century, John tends to verbosity, sometimes to excess, and to make him readable, he has had to be significantly condensed. His grand total word count for the material of the present volume was some 236,000, represented here by about 87,000 (which includes headings), a reduction to 37% of the original. I have tried to retain the flavour of the original, avoiding paraphrasing, by using his own words wherever possible with minimal alteration: for after all, it is his story and he should tell it. The language (and the spelling) is thus his, not mine, and readers should bear in mind that words can shift in meaning with the passage of time; what was perfectly normal the best part of two centuries ago may nowadays be considered vulgar, impolite, or 'unacceptable' – and vice versa, of course, when words formerly taboo in anything like polite society are now bandied around all too freely. John's son (who had the same name) added some marginal remarks to the original; these, and my editorial notes and additions, are in square brackets. He did several thumbnail sketches to illustrate China and India, but not for British Guiana – a pity!

Outline of the Story

IV – Essex Man in Liverpool

Part 13: Escape to England, 1826

Part 14: Restart, 1826-31

Part 15: Widower, 1831-37

Addenda and Corrigenda to Volume 1

The Cheveleys

A likely, although not absolutely confirmed, Cheveley line has been put together going back two generations earlier than 'William of Coopersale' (* below), who began the family tree:

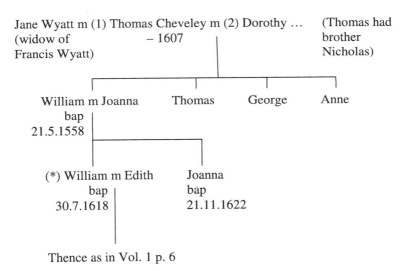

Jane Wyatt m (1) Thomas Cheveley m (2) Dorothy … (Thomas had
(widow of   – 1607   brother
Francis Wyatt)   Nicholas)

William m Joanna   Thomas   George   Anne
bap
21.5.1558

(*) William m Edith   Joanna
bap   bap
30.7.1618   21.11.1622

Thence as in Vol. 1 p. 6

JCC mentions his grandfather John Stokes Cheveley: The origin of the latter's middle name is now known; his mother Elisabeth Lagdon was the daughter of Jeremiah Lagdon (b. ca. 1673) and Johanna Stoake(r)s (b. ca. 1677-1732).

JCC's son (JCC II) wrote a 'Pedigree' on the end-papers of his father's Books 1 and 2, which his father also refers to, though he cannot vouch for its authenticity. It outlines his descent back to William of Coopersale, and continues: '– From whom we have a genealogy back to the Norman Conquest [Wouldn't it be great to have it now! What happened to it, one wonders?], to William de Cheveley, Knight to King William the Conqueror – whose life he saved at the Battle of Hastings by giving him his horse when in danger of being taken prisoner by Edwin, Earl of Mercia. For which service he received 46 manors in Leicestershire and 4 in Essex, including Hatfield Peveril, and bore arms: Gules – a Cock Or – Combed and Wattled Sable – Motto 'Dum vigilem vincam'. He married Alicia, daughter of William Earl of Warren – whose wife was the Lady Gundrada, daughter of William the Conqueror. Both were buried in Lewes Castle, Sussex. Sir Gulielmus de Cheveley was a famous Knight of the Emperor Charlemagne's Court.'

This is far from proven, and may well be only legend and hearsay, but a nice thought! Reference books disagree about the Arms: *Dictionary of British Arms* (ed. Woodcock, Grant, Graham) 2 356, has: Cheveley, Gu chev Arg between in chf 2 boar's heads erased Sa tusked Arg each holding in mouth apple or acorn Or and in base 3foil slipped Az. Whereas Papworth's *Ordinary of British Armorials,* p. 295, gives: Cheeke, Cheevely, Chiefly: Gu a cock Arg.

The Castelfrancs

I regret a spelling error of the name Nautonnier in the Castelfranc family tree (p. 10), due to a transcription error. According to 'Protestant Exiles from France' by D. Agnew (1866), the estate of this old Huguenot family was not far from La Rochelle. Castelfranc village, however, is far distant, on the river Lot, near Albi, between Cahors and Villeneuve. The château of the same name is further south, near Montredon-Labessonnié in Tarn département; near-ruinous at one time, it has now been taken over by the 'Dandelion Trust' and is being restored to use as a home for respite holidays, though much work still remains to be done on the older part. (How did the village and the château acquire their names when they are so far from the family estate?)

The family's patronymic was De Nautonnier, and they were Seigneurs of Castelfranc. Their coat of arms is described as: Nautonnier de Castelfranc: Armes: D'azur un navire d'argent, au chef d'or chargé de trois croisettes tréflées botonées de gueule; Support: Un lion et un ours rampant – casque panaché d'écuyer –

ours se pourléchant de mièle; Devise: Spes Mea Christus. (Blue with ship in silver, in chief gold with three red trefoil upright crosses; Supporters a lion and a bear rampant, knight's helmet, and a bear licking a honeycomb; Motto Spes Mea Christus).

Castelfranc Coat of Arms (Courtesy Mrs J. Shapiro)

Further information on the family has come to light: a revised diagram is attached. Two notable ancestors are worthy of mention: First, Daniel Chamier (known as 'The Great Chamier'), Minister of the Reformed Church in Montélimar and Professor of Theology at Montauban Academy (inter alia). He is chiefly known as the architect of the Edict of Nantes, negotiated under Henry IV, which guaranteed freedom of worship for Protestants. He was killed on October 17th 1621 by a chance cannon-shot during the siege of Montauban by the Roman Catholic forces of King Louis 13th (one of only 10 Protestant casualties, compared with heavy Royalist losses). He was said to be tall, somewhat corpulent, of a fair ruddy complexion, grave and serious; a most zealous preacher, invincible in argument, temptation-proof and altogether inflexible, so that his adversaries hated him.

The Castelfrancs

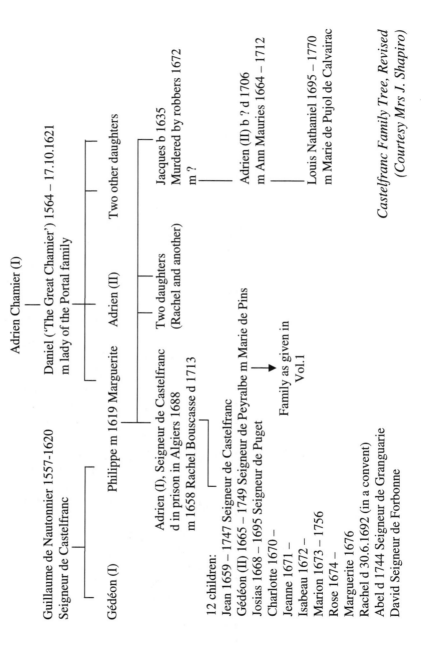

Castelfranc Family Tree, Revised
(Courtesy Mrs J. Shapiro)

PART 9

Sojourn at Prescot, 1821

Northbound

I prepared to go north to Prescot; on this journey hung the future, as afterwards revealed, for time and eternity, both of myself and others. I took with me to London my poor mother's jewellery, which she consented, with some tears at this last sacrifice of old family relics, to part with; and sold them for about £40, which served for present exigencies at home. I had much anxious thought with the thorough break-up of our domestic circle. I had seen enough to shock my hopes for four unemployed young men: I had called on everybody I could think of in London. At the Jerusalem Coffee House I met Midshipman Burt, the little evil-minded hard-faced never-give-in, who had been another voyage and chuckled at having cost his father 'a heap of money'; and Johnny Hood, the picture of half starvation, who had not been in employ since he had left *Hugh Inglis*. I felt somewhat terrified at this image of the world's neglect. I called on Eastgate at his lodgings in Salters Hall Court, but he looked grave, shook his head, and talked about hundreds out of employ. He was then in command of a fine East India ship, the *Fame*, and doing well; he was afterwards appointed Harbourmaster at Diamond Harbour in Calcutta.

The 'Royal Umpire' stage to Prescot, owned by Bartholomew Brotherton & Co, started from the Swan With Two Necks in Ladd Lane, now swallowed up in the enormous premises of Pickford & Co in Gresham Street which has absorbed as well Cateaton Street and others. I left London about the beginning of February 1821 on a Friday [the 2nd], about 2 in the afternoon. I recollect the half dozings, noddings, and tumblings to and fro of a night on top of a stage in the depth of winter. A quarter hour proclaimed for tea and supper, and a vast relief to get off, cramped, cold, scarce in possession of legs or senses, to a cheerful fire and well-spread table.

In marvellous quick time, the 'Now gentlemen!' of the guard, and back to 'roost' again on the stage top. Roused to consciousness only by a town or place to change horses, and the sure accompaniment 'Please to remember the coachman!' Was day ever going to break! And when it did, sufficient light to shew what a dreary unwashed set we were, the deplorable condition of those who have travelled all night. Breakfast done perfect justice to, as rather more time was allowed for our ham and eggs, tea and toast. Of all meals I have taken, the old stagecoach breakfasts hold the most grateful place in my remembrance, mainly I imagine because I was too seriously cold and hungry to be fastidious.

All next day on, on, through Leicestershire, Staffordshire, the Potteries and Cheshire, dining lastly at Knutsford. Towards evening the guard shewed me Prescot Church spire. I began to pick up my scattered thoughts; I confess that my anticipations were not agreeable. What was I to do in a family so dissimilar in their views, decidedly methodistical, which I held in abhorrence? I came to the politic conclusion that it was my duty to fall in with the customs of the house while preserving my own 'proper sense of religion' (like the Samaritans (2 Kings 17 33) who feared the Lord and served their own gods.). We entered Prescot about dusk: a straggling black dirty-looking town, the Vicarage a striking contrast, being light and cheerful. My reception corresponded, and I was made to feel as much at home as Mr and Mrs Driffield could devise. I met their family of three boys, Townshend (about 4), Wren, and infant Vero; also residing with them was a cousin of Mr Driffield's, Miss Jane Lisum, of indifferent health. Tired with the long journey, I was glad to retire early; my snug room at the top of the house had every comfort a young fellow could wish for, certainly greater than I had any right to expect.

The Church and Vicarage

Next morning, I was only just awaking at 8, the breakfast hour, but I had a dispensation on the grounds of fatigue, and appeared a little after 9. Being Sunday, the bells were ringing for morning service. From the garden by a wicket gate across the churchyard, I entered the church by the chancel door. The introductory hymn was 'Again the day returns of holy rest, Which when he made the world Jehovah blest.' The Psalms were the old version, which the Vicar preferred to the new as more scriptural, though not so adorned with the grace of poetry, and was using until the 'respectabilities' could be brought to tolerate the innovation of the Hymn Book.

[The complete hymn is as follows, taken from a printed version, headed 'Morning Hymn' to indicate when it should be used; its second line is '... when God made the world, Jehovah blest', implying that God and Jehovah are two separate entities, but how JCC has it makes more sense. There is an extra syllable in the last line of verse 2, but the 'and' can be cut out without affecting the sense. The words may be considered somewhat old-fashioned nowadays, possibly why it has fallen out of use. Its tune is pleasant and quite lively, and deserves an airing; it is unnamed, but would fit anything in metre 10.10.10.10. It is now rather pleasing to know exactly how Morning Service began at St Mary's Prescot on Sunday February 4th 1821!

> Again the day returns, of holy rest,
> Which, when He made the world, Jehovah blest.
> When, like His own, he bade our labours cease,
> And all be piety, and all be peace.
>
> While impious men despise the sage decree,
> From vain deceit and false philosophy;
> Let us its blessings own, its blessings feel,
> Receive with gratitude, and perform with zeal.
>
> So shall the God of mercy pleas'd receive,
> That only tribute man has power to give;
> So shall He hear, while fervently we raise,
> Our choral harmony, in hymns of praise.

It is not altogether clear what JCC means by the 'old version' of the Psalms. His remark in Vol.1 (p.40) suggests the form in the Book of Common Prayer, pointed for chanting and closely following the Authorised Version of the Bible, therefore truly 'scriptural', which,

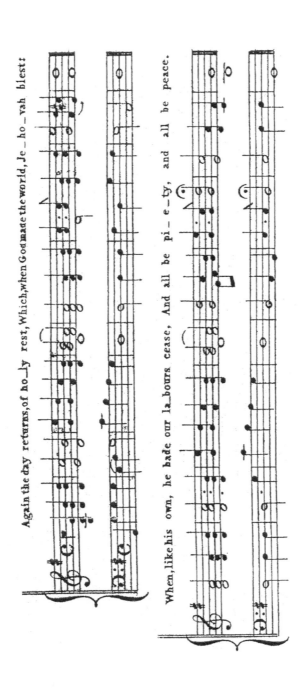

Tune for 'Again the Day Returns'
(Courtesy Dr B. Crosby)

side to discover that the resistance was equal – a one-sided argument truly! And it would be costly, and a failure. However it was done at last and was no failure.

We passed through Knotty Ash and Old Swan, with its three public houses (all Swans, with one, two, and three necks), Edge Lane [near where his great-niece Mary ('Polly') lived around a century later] and Edge Hill. I had heard of Liverpool as a large dirty seaport, and as we entered by the better neighborhood of Bold, Church, and Lord Streets, it appeared more sightly than I had anticipated. The ladies began their shopping, and Mr Driffield took me to the Exchange and the Docks, Queens on the south, Princes, not quite complete, on the north, and the 'Old Dock', now all filled up, obtruding into the town. The changes of the past 40 or 50 years are well-known: Liverpool people, next to the Yankees the greatest braggers in creation, have taken care that the world shall know what a wonderful town theirs is. Water, Castle and Lord Streets were then narrow, the roadway just wide enough for two carriages and a footway scarcely sufficient to allow two passengers to pass: all paved with pebbles, like the roads.

We found the ladies at Mr Cheshire linen draper's shop in Pool Lane, then a place for all sorts of good articles. Finally we had veal pies at Horridge the pastrycook's in Castle Street; and so home by London Road, Low Hill, and Kensington. Here lived a Dr Solomon who invented a medicinal liqueur, 'Balm of Gilead' [sarsaparilla extract – JCC II]. Some dinner guests wished to sample it, and he obliged – then gave each a bill for 5/-! [five shillings]: 'Dinner and wine you are welcome to, but I sell my balm!' [Chambers' Dictionary states that Balm of Gilead is the resin of a tree Balsamodendron gileadense, formerly esteemed as an antiseptic, the name coming from a biblical reference. I have also seen the name applied to a herb, Cedronella triphylla. Sarsaparilla is an extract from plants of the genus Smilax, known as cat-brier, from Central and South America.]

Religious Gatherings

Following receipt of a letter from Mr Roger Wilson vicar of Preston and his brother Rev William Carus Wilson of Kirkby Lonsdale, Mr

Driffield invited all the neighboring evangelical clergy for a few days: Messrs Buddicom of Everton, Rawson of Seaforth, Alix of Latchford, Bowstead of St Philips Liverpool, Parry of Eastham, Powell curate of Wigan, Pigot of St Helens, Hall of Billinge, our curate, and some others I forget. Their conversation turned entirely on spiritual things – what a contrast to the clergy I had been accustomed to meet, whose whole talk was earthly, over the bottle after dinner, and then an evening of card playing. This gathering of 1821 served as the nucleus of many more, which became regular at Prescot Vicarage for many years and served as a rallying point for all the evangelical clergy for many miles around Liverpool. I had never seen anything like it before. At Mr Driffield's request I took profiles of them with my camera lucida, and they were long preserved as a memento of this gathering.

In those days before photography, profiles done in black shade with the camera lucida were much prized as the easiest attainable approach to a likeness. I had long used mine for this purpose, and wherever I went I generally hit off the whole family. At the Vicarage, the one which most interested Mama was a full length of Baby seated on the table, frock turned up to shew his little fat legs and bare feet; more to the life than the face, which was too chubby and infantile to be very clearly shown. 'Mite' the tiny spaniel I depicted curled up asleep on the hearthrug before the fire. I sketched the Vicarage and the church; such a crowd of children squeezing to see 'what the strange mon was agait on' that all view of the church was blocked out by a mass of heads, to which I in vain appealed until Mr Driffield, greatly amused at my fix, settled the matter.

A deputation from the Bible Society came from London to Liverpool later in the spring for their auxilliary meetings. From its foundation in 1804, this Society had been a test between the Evangelical clergy and those who adhered to the dry dull lifeless state of things from the Georgian period up to the days of Whitfield and Wesley: who called themselves Orthodox, which means opposed to any progress, and preferring to drag the country back into the great dismal swamp of Papistry than to real vital godliness. The Society was thus accustomed to being stigmatized as the focus of all mischief. Mr Driffield had staying with him his cousin Guy Brian, rector of Woodham Ferrers in Essex, and we all went to the public meeting to hear Rev Owen, the travelling Secretary of the Society, speak. I was rivetted as he and others unfolded the nature of the Society, embracing all classes for the distribution of the word of God without note or comment. My prejudices and misconceptions vanished, and it seemed marvellous [= incredible] how an objection could be raised against this noble Society.

Rev Charles George Thomas Driffield, a seminal figure in JCC's life. From a daguerreotype, date unknown, authenticated by his grand-daughter. (Courtesy Rev T.M. Steel)

Driffield Road, named after Rev C.G.T. Driffield, some 200 yards from the church. (Author)

A New Creature

I have already said that my confidence in my own religious opinions had been considerably shaken, and my dislike of 'Methodism' modified. I increasingly felt a conviction that true religion went deeper than I had imagined, and was not a shallow surface sort of thing based on the Ten Commandments and the Sermon on the Mount as the sole rule of faith, with little or no reference to the salvation of Jesus Christ as the Way, the Truth, and the Life. I had had no idea of taking Scripture as the sole authoritative rule of faith and practice [Which it is under the teaching of the Catholick Church, the pillar and ground of the Faith and the witness and keeper of Holy Writ – JCC II (Suggesting that JCC II had Roman leanings? – CCT)], and looked on it as antiquated and not applicable to modern times. But light was breaking in on my mind, wonderfully opening it to Divine truth; Scripture became to me the only foundation of knowledge, wisdom, and virtue, and the New Testament a book of wonders. A great change had indeed come over me, and Mrs Sach's prediction had been remarkably fulfilled; I was now a new creature in Jesus Christ.

I was desirous for definite views about worldly amusements. Dancing and card playing I was not reluctant to surrender as detrimental to Christian life and progress; however, the theatre had been the greatest pleasure I could enjoy, and I was some time in concluding this could not coexist with a close walk with God. I appealed to Mr Driffield, who disapproved of the evil tendency of the performances, their debasing effect on the actors, and the atmosphere of vice and profligacy around these places of amusement. The forsaking of all to follow Christ now determined my views.

I had all this time been corresponding with my family. Father, again relieved from pressure, was comparatively easy in his new position; to my poor mother the change was not so pleasant, the society was not to her taste, and she felt the removal like a banishment. Richard went on with his mole plough and savings bank clerkship. Charles had been invited to stay with Mr Brewster, a surgeon at Tolleshunt D'Arcy, but had to look elsewhere for something permanent. He assisted Richard for some time, then stayed with Father's cousin George at Boyton Hall farm; and lastly, through a friend of the Laurences [another of Father's cousins], was procured a place with Barber Beaumont at the County Fire and Provident Life office in Regent Street in London, where he earned his living for a time, although not comfortable with Beaumont, a scheming unpleasant man. George remained at Blundeston with Nathaniel Rix; we shall see what was found for him.

To my family, I could but speak 'of the things which I had seen and heard', my new views and feelings. I wrote to George, who spoke of the change wrought in his own heart. He avowed himself a 'Protestant Dissenter', a term new to me, and we had an active correspondence in which neither of us were disposed to yield. I did believe his feelings were genuine, yet he was highly emotional, and likely to be severely tested by the first shock to his earthly hopes. Charles I found much interested in the subject now uppermost in my heart; I rejoiced at an expression or two from Richard, but which died away to nought. To Father and Mother and my sisters, the change in me, though not distinctly adverted to, shewed itself in my mode of expressing myself. Father wrote decorously, but in his usual offhand manner when he wished to cut short a matter not pleasant to him. My mother thought I had always been so good! that she could scarcely imagine I could want to be better, and hoped 'her dear boy's love for religion would not lead him to adopt severe opinions so contrary to those of our Saviour'.

New Opportunities

All this time, Mr Driffield had not lost sight of my temporal interests, and had mentioned my case wherever it was likely to serve to obtain employment. Mr Buddicom, the incumbent of St George's, Everton, where the elite of the Liverpool merchants resided, had come to pass a few days at Prescot; he had a well-stocked mind, and his conversation was pleasing and profitable. A member of his congregation, Mr John Pattinson, who was in the West India trade, wanted someone to go out for a term of years to assist his brother and partner in Demerara; and would be glad to see me. He was from Westmorland, a handsome man, with a frank manner which gave us confidence in his right-mindedness, of which Mr Buddicom had expressed a high opinion. His office did not exhibit signs of much business, but he had only recently begun as a commission merchant, and his brother had more than he could attend to. We left with the understanding we should hear more in due time, as I should not be wanted before the beginning or middle of June. Another interview with Mr Pattinson settled the preliminaries, an agreement for three years with a salary of £100, £150, and £200, board, lodging, washing, and medical attendance, with the prospect of a partnership at the end if all went well. I felt a comforting and happy assurance that the Lord's hand was in it; whether worldly prosperity might result remained to be seen.

Our kind friends now turned to George, and to my great joy proposed he be invited to the Vicarage that something might be done for him in his sailor's capacity. Mr Driffield was on most friendly terms with Mr (afterwards Sir John) Gladstone, father of Mr W.E. Gladstone; he was a Scotchman, the head of John Gladstone Grant & Wilson, the leading Liverpool merchant, and founder of his own fortune and those of his three brothers, who were ship and anchor smiths, ropemakers, and chandlers, and to whom he threw a great deal of business by means of his shipping property: so that they had become the richest family in Liverpool (Mr Gladstone was instrumental in building several Liverpool churches, such as St

Mary's Edge Hill, St Andrews Renshaw Street, and Seaforth – and took care they should be served by Evangelical ministers.). Mr Gladstone promised an appointment in one of his ships in the Demerara trade for George; and he was forthwith a guest at the Vicarage. I found him much more sturdy in his assertion as a 'Protestant Dissenter', and much more disposed to parade his views, than I liked. Mrs Driffield replied quietly and calmly; and in time he became less pertinacious. His proclivities were strongly Dissenting, mine towards the Church of England, but on all the vital points, we were quite agreed.

Preparation for Departure

Summer approached, and I found Mr Pattinson was expecting the *Thalia* home from Demerara very shortly, and was sending out another, *Sir John Cameron*, to succeed her; the *Ann* was already on her way out, and *Ardent* was conveying lumber (deal boards) from St John's New Brunswick to Demerara for sale there. These vessels were all chartered, i.e. hired, for the voyage, to make a profit either by goods or freight. Mr Pattinson wished me to go in *Sir John Cameron*; I was to pay my passage, which I thought did not seem very liberal. [One leaf cut out here in the original. 'Goods' are the actual articles, 'freight' refers more to their carriage.].

My sea chest and bedding were had down to Prescot and all things packed ready; a large parcel of tracts was added: alas! we little thought how little call there would be for them. I had an introductory letter from Mr Gladstone to his agents in Demerara, McDonald Edmonstone & Co, and one from the Rev Ambrose Dawson to his younger brother Edward, who was agent for the estates of his uncle Mr John Bolton, a great name there. A third was from Mr Samuel Sanbach [sic], of Sandbach Tinné & Co to the Demerara firm of McInroy Sandbach & Co, in which I recognized the kind but too partial colouring of good Mr Buddicom. Thus I was furnished with commercial ammunition which it was considered would benefit my future progress.

I had come almost face to face with the idea of expatriation for a term of years, and had shrunk a little from it; however, familiarity with something reconciles it, and duty, if nothing more, had its proper influence. My mother had the same feeling; but my parents could not object to what appeared so advantageous, and by degrees were reconciled to my expatriation. I had made some remarks about my views, but Father did not think I should trouble them with discussing religious opinions when I knew their minds must be much occupied with the trial of my departure. Dick wrote me a farewell letter, and sent me 'The Pleasures of Memory', the first book he had ever had given him, saying 'accept it as all I have to offer'. George and Tom corresponded, for Tom had been the depository of George's inmost thoughts relative to Sarah Rix. When he came to Prescot, he was fully determined, whenever he was in a position to do so, to come forward as the affiancé; however, matters turned out differently.

At the beginning of June, we received notice of when *Sir John Cameron* would be ready. Mr Driffield drove me over to Liverpool; he thought indulging my disposition to procrastinate and my love of a quiet life might be against my success in life, and he gave me a text, 'Be not weary in well doing, for in due season you shall reap if you faint not', which served to nerve and cheer me in many trials.

PART 10

Expatriate: First Half, 1821-23

Sir John Cameron

Oh the uncertainty of everything connected with those uncertain elements, the winds and the waves! At Mr Pattinson's office in Drury Lane/Water Street we found the time of sailing had been put off several days, and we must go back again. I could not feel sorry for this reprieve, who does? yet it was painful to do all the leavetaking again. This time George and I arranged to go by one of the coaches that ran through Prescot, but we waited in the wrong place and missed it; nothing for it but to hire a chaise (half a guinea) and drive as hard as we could go! Rushed to the office, vessel gone? Oh no, wind did not suit, all our bustle and money for nothing. So we waited! waited! waited! Mr Pattinson was out, looking after the *Thalia* which had just arrived.

The day closed; he came, gave us the news that *Sir John Cameron* was ready to sail early next morning, and took us to his home in Juvenal Street for the evening. Mrs Pattinson had just been confined with her fourth child, named Frances after her aunt Miss Barry, whom we found doing the honors of the tea table in her sister's absence. I found her well informed and very conversible; we were at one on religious subjects, and I felt quite at home with this young lady. Mr Pattinson's other children were William, a flaxen-haired boy of 5 or 6, taking after his father; Eliza 4 or 5, dark like her mother; and Daniel, like the other boy, 2 or 3. There was also a mulatto girl with negro features, of 6 or 7, daughter of a brother of Mrs Pattinson's, whom she had brought over from Demerara where her brother lived. Who her mother was did not transpire, but she was probably a slave of his.

Mr Pattinson had left his brother James, a deformed lad of 15 or 16, to send up and let us know when to go on board: which he did around 9 o'clock, to go off in about half an hour; George was to go with me and return with the Pilot the next day. We made for Georges Dock and got into the boat; the Captain, Lillie, was a Scotchman of the most disagreeable type, dark and ugly, swearing and abusing the men at the oars. Two passengers had evidently had too much drink, another kept silence.

The ship, a brig of some 300 or 400 tons, was lying at anchor off Bootle Bay, and we had a long pull down river to get to her. At length, about 11 at night, we got on board and went below. What a cabin! If my heart had sunk on the way to the ship, I felt at zero when I found myself in this scene of confusion, dirt, misrule, disorder and hubbub. The Captain called for the 'Steheward', abused him for not being there, and ordered the 'Sperrits' – clearly what neither he nor his companions wanted [= needed]. One was a young man, Mr Irish, with a very quarrelsome deportment, a native of British North America, a people who are exceedingly sensitive about nationality, or were so then: besides, he had been taking more than would do him good. He proved to be one who with the brain once excited by strong drink, acts like a madman. A pleasant prospect for the voyage. A little old man, Captain Dowdall, was a retired shipmaster friend of the Captain's; he had also taken in as much grog as he knew how to carry, but was just in a friendly and affectionate state.

The third gentleman appeared to take little notice of what was going on. George and I retreated to his corner and entered into conversation. He was Mr Benjamin James Hopkinson, an old and well known family amongst the Demerara cotton planters, himself the owner of two estates on the East coast which he was going out to superintend and improve during an intended three years' residence. He was of very agreeable manners, and surveyed the scene with considerable surprise and apprehension. He exhibited unqualified disgust with all his surroundings; to be consigned to such a 'Pigstye' and the society of such a 'Ruffian' was what he had never had the least idea of. He had not been prepared for what he saw; his passage had been engaged for him, he had left it all to his agents Nicholas Waterhouse & Sons of Liverpool. It appeared to me very strange that they should have selected such a conveyance for someone like him. However, he seemed disposed to make the best of it, and hoped matters would sober down at sea. It was a relief to find I should have one companion of intelligence and gentlemanly feeling.

The cabin was by no means spacious. On either side of the 'companion' or entrance were two 'state rooms', whose dignity and splendor, in a Liverpool merchant brig whose object is cargo not passengers, meant a strip partitioned off, about 8 feet wide and 6 or 7 long, with a shelf on one side called a standing bed place. Here the Captain reposed, under it all the precious things required to be taken care of, such as butter, cheese, fine biscuit, soap and candles, whose combined odours composed an atmosphere peculiar to such apartments. The room on the other side held the delicacies of the steward's pantry, whose odours fell not far short of the others. At one end of the cabin, shut in by press doors during the day, were two shelves, or bedplaces, one my birth, the lower one Mr Irish's. George took up his birth on the stern lockers, or bunkers as they are termed in Liverpool. So after a while the confusion subsided.

Westward Ho

The early dawn of a June morning peeped through the dismal skylight, and the voice of our commander roused me, calling for the Steheward. The first morning waking 'on board' is never agreeable; reminiscence of what you have left and consciousness of what is before you dart into the mind, and if I ever did feel disposed to turn back, it was now. Unable to sleep any longer, George and I strolled on deck. Our noble commander was in red-hot wrath with the Pilot, whom he was ordering to up anchor and make sail, and who was trying to make him understand that it was too early for wind and tide. Little Dowdall tried to convince him, but the man was wild; flying at the Pilot, he kicked and pummelled him so unmercifully, that the man jumped into the boat alongside, and told him he would go ashore and report his conduct. Hopkinson did not relish, any more than me, the appearance of things, but no help for it now.

There were hen-coops on the narrow and confined quarterdeck, stuffed full of unhappy fowls, ducks and geese, without food or water, stretching their necks through the bars to get at the puddles of salt water with which the men were sluicing the decks, which added only mockery to their misery, and a few pigs were running about for what they could pick up. The Captain was roaring at the mate, Mr Drummond, for not looking after things in general; at his own brother Jock, the second mate, who always appeared to come in for his most wrathful execrations, for not looking after things in particular; and at the Steheward for neglecting the pigs and fowls, while he, poor fellow, was at his wits end to get the cabins [sic] cleared and breakfast set. Such a breakfast table! A foul cloth begrimed with daubings and sloppings of many previous meals, and all else corresponding in cleanliness – faugh! Who could eat the salt beef, stale eggs or fusty biscuit with a stomach anticipating its sea exercise? Captain Dowdall urged the steward to 'decorate his table' by placing things in more order, but he did not coax our appetites, which were as jaded as we felt ourselves, so we went on deck again.

We were by this time under sail, with a fresh pilot, and rounding the 'Black Rock.'. We should soon be through the channel, and I must find myself again thrown on the world. Recollection of what I had exchanged in the past twenty four hours for what I had now before me, pressed on me so vividly that I burst into tears; and when it came to the leave taking with George, I could with difficulty restrain my feelings. So we parted. [It seems Capt Dowdall must also have gone ashore: he is not mentioned again.]

I was all this day maukish and miserable. Dinner was a greasy mess of boiled fresh beef and cabbage; but even seasoned as I had been to sea life, the dirt and foetid odours of the cabin and the greasy food turned my stomach. Poor Hopkinson was already tucked up under the horrors of incipient sea sickness, as the weather was somewhat rough, which kept us a good deal to the cabin.

I felt I must at once openly but quietly shew I was on the Lord's side; I had no privacy, and I therefore, in a matter of course sort of way, sat down at the table for about half an hour every evening before turning in, to read my Bible. By the time we got out to sea, the Sabbath had arrived: alas! it augured ill for a day of rest. The Captain commenced an investigation of the cabin stores with the steward, and a hot one it became. After matters settled, I went below again. I was agreeably surprised to find the steward a simple-minded young fellow who was well-acquainted with many of my tracts, which he had had at Sabbath school, and he promised to distribute a selection amongst the men after dinner. Hopkinson shewed by some sarcastic remarks that he cared for none of those things and did not believe in them. I found that he had been educated at Cambridge University and had spent a good deal of time in France and on the Continent since the peace; he had associated with refined intellectual people, and had read a great deal.

Mr Irish was now in a more settled state of mind, but I found him a shallow-pated fellow, with no directing principle but his own whim and caprice. He was a native of Halifax, Nova Scotia, where his business as a shipping agent had failed, *he* said through the fault of his partner. He had a wife, though why he had separated did not come out. Her family had lived at Kelvedon, and we had known something of them, but they had left the neighborhood on account of something to do with this daughter, now become Mrs Irish, who was reputed to be a wild one. As Mr Irish appeared a very wild one too, I was not surprised that he had been unsuccessful both in business and in matrimony; he was now on his way to patch up his broken fortunes and wasted life wherever he might.

A Navigational Problem
After about a fortnight we were drawing towards the latitude of Madeira, our first destination. Now Latitude is so easily settled every day, by a meridian altitude of the Sun, that few even of the greatest bunglers in navigation have not learned by a few figures in chalk how to determine it (see Vol. 1 p. 189). But the problem with these captains who might be good seamen, but on account of being very bad navigators were sure to make long passages, was Longitude: a different and difficult matter, being determinable by the difference of time at the ship's place and at a given point of departure, which in English navigation is always the meridian of Greenwich. Ship time can always be found by an altitude of the Sun or a fixed star, but the corresponding time at Greenwich is the difficulty: which can only be determined by a chronometer set to Greenwich time at starting, and keeping a correct rate of going, or by Lunar observations [which required complex calculations]. The first Captain Lillie did not possess, and could not have used if he had; the second, he knew nothing about.

Now the captain knew very well when he was in the latitude of the place, or near it; he ran on in latitude till the change in the colour of the water, or some other indication, told him he was within sufficiently safe distance. Then if he knew he had kept his ship well to the eastward he put her head westward and began to run down his longitude. But drawing near Madeira, our predicament was, were we east or west? One was as likely as the other; nay, we might be 200 or 300 miles either side for anything that Captain Lillie could possibly tell. By dead reckoning, miles sailed and courses steered, he opined we were eastward; but as evening came on, he declared indications in that quarter must be land, so 'bout ship and stand to the east. At daylight the land had retreated, and nothing for it but to retrace our course west. After a run of two days more, we saw Porto Cristo looming in the distance, and on the third came into Madeira roads where we anchored. This is a fair specimen of the navigation of common merchant ships in those days, especially those out of Liverpool; how they blundered their way out and home was marvellous.

[Jumping ahead, he talks about the same topic again and includes a thumbnail sketch; the occasion is the approach to Demerara. Out of interest: determining latitude was very accurate in skilled hands, but what was the error? 1° is 60 nautical miles, about 69 'land' miles – could it be determined to 1 second of arc?]

On this occasion we were thus
E ~~~~~~~~~~~~~~~ W
                    Demerara
'bout ship
300 miles to the Eastw.
If the Captain had known his longitude
he would have been here NBB 'bout ship
from this spot

Madeira: Awkward Situations

The vessel was under my direction as the charterer's agent, to regulate proceedings at Madeira. We had brought out some goods for Page Phelps & Co, from whom we were to receive some wine, in which all payments were made, and some besides for consignees in Demerara. We had to find lodgings; and having been so miserably mauled at an hotel previously, I counselled a private boarding house. Of course our passengers must have some of the best wine, and Mr Irish and the Captain soon became exhilarated; then brandy and water, and loud talk: Hopkinson, most heartily ashamed of the noise in a respectable house, prevailed on them to go out, while we remained quietly – but what they met with on their rambles sent them home noisier than ever. The Captain went on board, but Mr Irish insisted on staying; what a hubbub half the night with this drunken blockhead! It was a counterpart of the night with the *bugs* on the first occasion.

In the morning, I called at the office of our consignees. In conversation with Mr Joseph Phelps, the junior partner, I mentioned my friend William Cantley; on finding the nature of the friendship between Cantley's family and mine, he asked me to take up my quarters with him, of which I very gladly availed myself, as I was really so disgusted with the conduct of Irish and the Captain that I was only too pleased to get away from it. I was introduced to his partner Mr Page. I called on Mr Blackburn, whom I had seen before, and he asked me to dine with him; but Mr Doran was again in England.

Mr Phelps told me one morning that I would have to dine by myself that evening, but said 'As you will be very solitary, go to the theatre where there is a favorite actress performing'. What did I do? Tell him my religious principles were opposed to it? This obvious and honest course would have saved me from a world of embarrassment and painful afterthought; but I could not bring myself up to it, for I was taken by surprise. My other defences were knocked down as fast as I raised them: I did not care about the theatre, it would be all in Portuguese, &c, &c. Nothing for it; like a cur going to be whipped, I straggled away, wishing myself a hundred miles off. I entered the pit: and what a sight! Hopkinson, Irish and the Captain, all laughing, such a triumph! 'Glad to see you have been converted since you came to Madeira!' They had chosen their place to afford the best view of the danseuse's legs! and there sat I, ashamed to be there, yet ashamed to move. This was the last time I ever witnessed a theatrical performance.

Next day I went to dine with Mr Blackburn. I mentioned having been at the theatre the night before; he observed it was a place he never went to, having strong objections on religious grounds, but I felt too humbled to wish to prolong the conversation on that subject. In the afternoon, Mr Blackburn had to go to Porto Praya, a watering place where his family were staying, and left me with one of the young men who had dined with us, Mr Henry R. Laird. It was not long before it became quite apparent that he was a well-instructed Christian, so I told him my trial and trouble of the night before, and he gave me delicate and wise counsel. His family came from Glasgow, where his elder brother William had failed in business, and was now in Liverpool as agent for the Glasgow and Liverpool steamboats; being himself in ill health, he had sought a milder climate in Madeira (He was the uncle of William's son Mr John Laird, the founder of the great steamship works and member for Birkenhead.).

I thought it proper to call on Mr Ruffey, with whom Lutey had business four years before and had treated disgracefully in the matter of the wine he had taken; I considered he should understand I had no other hand in it than as Lutey's supercargo. He said he was glad I had explained, as it had been no better than a swindle on Lutey's part, whom they had trusted on the strength of a recommendatory letter, and he had felt exceedingly provoked to be taken in 'by a villain like that'. He concluded by asking me to dine with him, and all was right as far as I was concerned.

A Pleasant Sunday
On Sunday during my stay, Mr Phelps invited me to his country residence. At an early hour, I found a poney at the door and a man to act as guide. We soon got clear of the town; the ascent then became so steep that I had great difficulty to avoid slipping over the back of the saddle. Over the white stuccoed walls of the vineyards could be

seen the vines trailing luxuriantly over horizontal trellices supported by underprops, about 5 or 6 feet from the ground, and forming the most delicious arcades of half-grown bunches of grapes hanging in great profusion, suggesting a still more delicious scene a few weeks hence when the luscious fruit was ripe. A most enchanting picture: the higher I ascended the more the scene unfolded in extent and beauty. Eventually I came to a part overshadowed with large luxuriant trees, mostly Spanish chestnuts, from amongst which peeped pretty villas or ornamental cottages; over low stuccoed walls, hedges of fuschia [sic] in full bloom formed a beautiful frame to the picture of gardens laid out in English taste with lawns and flower beds. Enormous hydrangeas with azure-tinted masses of blossom broke the outline and gave variety and additional luxuriance.

After about four miles, which from the steepness of the road seemed twice as many, I reached Mr Phelps' villa, in time for their late breakfast. Mr Phelps read the church service, and we then took a walk to see the neighborhood; truly it was an enchanting spot, hill and dale beautifully wooded. How the rest of the day went on I forget; we took another walk towards the end of it, and I took my leave about 8 o'clock. I toddled downhill much faster than I had come up, and very pleasantly, as it was a lovely night, till I came to the vineyards. Then began such a hubbub of dogs as I never heard. At every gate a cur was yelping, but as I proceeded, the plot thickened: one roused up others, which speedily found their way to my heels, at which they followed. I stumped along, and at length got rid of them, only to encounter a succession at every vineyard I passed. But their bark was, to use a Scotch saying, 'waur than their bite', and I arrived at my destination unscathed.

I called during the week to see Hopkinson, and found him quiet and comfortable, as Irish had gone on board to sleep at nights, but was still drinking himself half wild. I visited, with Mr Phelps, some of the Popish churches. The day before our departure, he took a boat to go round to Porto Praya, a distance of 6 or 7 miles, to see Mr Blackburn's family, and we spent a pleasant evening with them. Next day, I took leave of him, not again to meet; Mr Henry Laird accompanied me to the beach, and I promised to write to him from Demerara.

On to Demerara

Again we put to sea. Of course the affair of the Theatre was brought up, but I met it, not by an attempt to justify or defend what I had done, but by at once admitting that I had been wrong. Of course my scruples were ridiculed, especially by Hopkinson, who felt that a residence in Demerara would soon cure me of that and other straight laced notions. I made no more protestations, and continued my Scripture readings, drawing occasional remarks. One from the Captain excited my interest: 'Ah, I remember when I used to read the Bible as you do, but I have been a wild chap and have given it up long ago.' This showed a feeling about the man I had not looked for, but he was a Scotchman, and therefore instructed in the Scriptures, and I saw that most of his crew, who were Scotch, had their Bibles out reading on the Sabbath.

Hopkinson was going out to Demerara full of the improvements which he intended to carry out, plans for the Eden he would make of his cotton plantations in three years and then leave to go: improved agriculture on scientific principles, improved cotton ginning and cleaning by machinery, and philanthropic notions for improved treatment and management of the Negroes. He found, however, before he had long tried the experiment, that slavery only works one way, if work is to be exacted, viz. by fear. He knew not what he had to encounter from the simple fact that such things had never been.

Mr Irish had left England with the intention of settling at Madeira, but in reality had no prospect of settling anywhere, as was quite clear from his conduct. He was going on to Demerara where he said he had a friend, which was all a pretence. There were two deck or fore cabin passengers: a decent Scotch lad Sandy McLaren who was going out to his brother with a view to become an overseer, a hard life of exposure to sun and weather; but from which young men, if steady, might eventually grow into managers, the great object of ambition, as the manager was the ruling power of the estate and negroes. The other was a Mr John Bancroft, who had been mate of a ship, but could not be so any longer at home, the reason being written on his groggified countenance. These two, Mr Irish and Mr Bancroft, were just going to add to the waifs and strays of a West India colony.

We had now (the beginning of August) got within the Northern tropic, and the temperature had become extremely hot, increasingly so as we drew nearer the latitude of Guiana (Demerara), 6 degrees North [Georgetown is 6°50' N, 58°12' W]. We lost 3 or 4 days, uncertain as to when we should get sufficiently to the westward to bear up for the Demerara river, not of course knowing how far we really were to the eastward; edging on during the day to get a sight of the treetops on the low swampy coast. At length our doubts and fears were set at rest by the appearance of a coasting craft, which proved to be a pilot boat, and a young mulatto man jumped on board. He was every wit as full of airs and impudence as a free man of colour, in those days, usually was, to shew unmistakably that he was not a slave. So he began to give the Captain his orders how to proceed, gave most laconic and contemptuous answers to the passengers, and went forward to gossip with the men ad libitum. At length the Captain sent the steward to tell him to come aft, who returned and delivered the message, nervously moving towards the companion stairs, 'He says Sir he's not a coming to be kicked overboard like the other pilot'. We all expected an explosion, but our noble Captain pocketed the affront, and the young mulatto lounged back and directed the steersman without any regard to the Captain. I was not a little surprised at this first specimen of free-coloured manners in a West India colony.

Being too late to enter the river that night, we anchored, and got under weigh at flood tide in the morning, as passing the bar (a large sandbank at the mouth) was difficult. Whilst standing for the river, we all began to 'titivate' preparatory to going ashore. Mr Hopkinson's hair style, from being dark and wavy, had all at once become black and frizzled! He said, 'I have been wearing a wig, as my own hair is not good, but I shall find it too hot for the West Indies.' We passed Fort William Frederick and the Lighthouse signal station on the eastern, or left hand, point: all along that side was Georgetown with its white wooden edifices, on the other, some 5 or 6 miles in width, the sugar plantations. The shore everywhere was dead flat, showing huge banks of mud at low tide. We anchored opposite Kingston Stelling (Dutch = wharf); I was surprised to see upriver, as far as the eye could reach, a large fleet of merchant ships, which gave me a much more important idea of the commerce of this colony than I had previously formed.

Georgetown: First Impressions
The Captain prepared to report ashore, but the pilot told the passengers they must wait on account of some sanitary regulation, which proved to be rubbish as the boat soon returned with a request that I would come on shore. To my surprise, Mr Hopkinson said he should wait and go ashore quietly by and bye. Directly up from the stelling was Mr Pattinson's house, of small dimensions, and built, as they all were, of wood frames shingled over on a basement of brick piers, which served for the warehouse or 'store' where the business was carried on. Outside at the back was a wooden staircase to the upper or dwelling apartments: three small sleeping apartments and a small pantry, and a dining hall across the width in front. Here I found the Captain and Mr William Pattinson, an epitome of his brother: like him in feature, but smaller, and conveying an impression not very favorable to his intellectual qualifications or strength of character. However, he received me with the deportment of a man expecting something superior and much written about! and I feared I should never come up to these expectations. So on August 18th 1821 [a Saturday] I found myself installed in my new situation, of Clerk to Messrs John & William Pattinson in Georgetown, Demerara.

I walked out with Mr Pattinson and the Captain to report at the Custom House, a very hot walk at that time of day, about noon. On each side of the street stood handsome dwelling houses in detached inclosures, some planted with shady trees, others gay with flowering shrubs. It seemed interminably long, and the glare from the white-painted houses and the white dusty road I thought intolerable; the only mitigation being a brisk NE wind off the sea, which I was told regularly blew the greatest part of the year. It was very wide, more like a public road; called a Dam, as all were, having been laid out by the original Dutch settlers, there was a canal down the centre with bridges at intervals, planted on each side with indigenous scrubby-looking leguminous Orinoque trees. The whole scene was gay and lively: throngs of pedestrians, horses and buggies; oleanders with large bunches of pink flowers, shewy scarlet hibiscus, the light feathery lemon and orange of the 'flower fence' or mimosa; orange and shaddock and lemon trees here and there, loaded with golden fruit; bright green cool plantains or bananas waving over the fence, feathery coconuts and towering stately palmettos over all. I was struck with the varied appearance of the Negro population: many of the men had scarcely a loincloth, but I was most shocked to see many of the Negro women with nothing on but a short petticoat, whilst the upper body and breasts were left exposed. On the other hand domestic servants were decently attired, the men in cotton jacket and trowsers, girls in white muslin or showy cotton prints, the head in the invariable gay striped kerchief put on turban fashion.

On our return, I found Mr Hopkinson had landed, and it was suggested that as he and I were to be fixtures in the colony, we should report to the Governor General Murray. His residence was near the sea, about as far the other way along the street as I had traversed already; we started on foot, as there were no public conveyances of any kind. Oh those long interminable streets! They seemed endless, and the bodily exertion called forth left me perfectly soaked in perspiration; this I found was common, and it was quite a regular practice to change the linen twice a day. The Governor was not in, or did not think it worthwhile to see us, but a youth, who we understood was his son John, told us to report to the Colonial Secretary; and so we came away much edified.

I found from Mr Pattinson that Hopkinson was a 'man of colour', which although he was somewhat dark, I had not suspected, supposing him of French extraction; I was not aware of the prejudices of the West India whites against the slightest taint of Negro blood, be it ever so imperceptible or remote, that consigned well-educated estimable men to ignominy and contempt. Pattinson told me that Mr Hopkinson, with all his accomplishments, could not be admitted into the society of white people! He had gone to live with 'Miss Johanna', his mother, a mulatto woman. This opened up to me the selection of so mean a ship as *Sir John Cameron*: to avoid collision with high and mighty white society in another of higher grade.

My New Position

I had never seen a West India store before, so all was new to me and I had everything to learn. A large apartment occupied the whole basement [= ground floor], opening on the street with large two-leaved doors and unglazed windows with outside shutters to close at night, and at the back a small counting-house raised on three or four steps. It had a medley of goods for sale, packed in tiers – butter, flour, soap, candles, glass and earthenware, nails, shoes, wearing apparel, cloth pieces, hams, cheese, wine, ale, porter, whisky, dried fruit, hoes, tools, 'cum multi aliis': as pretty a list of incongruities as could demand the attention of a young man willing to learn and turn his hand to anything. All were in most astounding confusion; packages were opened and their contents retailed out with very slight attention to readjustment. The only officials appeared to be a coloured man, Mr John Harris, in the counting-house; a raw uncouth Liverpool lout, Jack Sutton; and a couple of Negroes. Things were derangé, and the books in a terrible muddle. Harris – *he* said owing to misdirection, Mr Pattinson said owing to stupidity – had committed a fatal error on starting, and was now reversing all his entries in the books for 2 years past, which was consuming all his time and had put a stop to further progress, so the books were behind, thoroughly wrong and of no use; neither did Mr John Harris seem to possess the capability of putting them right. He was conceited and petulant, Pattinson irritable and impatient, so there was anything but order in the counting-house.

In the store, Mr Jack Sutton was conducting matters in a very loose offhand way. He was an idle prating ignorant fellow, the only son of a widow in Liverpool, whom Mr John Pattinson had sent out to help his brother in compassion to the poor old woman, who could do nothing with him at home. I found him doing pretty much as he liked, considering himself vastly superior in local intelligence, and very little disposed to pay deference to my authority, as I was only a newcome, and he accordingly placed matters on a footing of perfect equality. I saw this must be put an end to if I was to do any good; so I told him I intended to be master, and if he wished to stay, he must order himself. He was disposed to be high-handed, and absented himself morning after morning whilst Mr Pattinson was out; he told me he had been *dunning*, a very necessary operation, but I saw no fruits of it, and I saw too that I should make nothing of him.

Between him and the bookkeeper, matters were getting into a pretty mess. We had two vessels in harbour, the *Ann* requiring a cargo and *Sir John Cameron* discharging one, and were expecting *Ardent* with a cargo from North America: these took up all Mr Pattinson's attention out of doors, and he dropped the entire store department into my hands. Not a promising beginning, but I had now a Power and Grace to sustain and encourage me which I never had before.

Next day was the sabbath. I had understood that mercantile houses in the West Indies paid little regard to it, but Mr John Pattinson had told me his brother did not do business then, and it was an express stipulation that I should not be required to. I found it was the custom to rise at gunfire, or 5 in the morning, and to retire at gunfire, or 8 in the evening. Being so near the Equator, days and nights were nearly equal, with very little twilight. At gunfire, all were roused up, and a few minutes sufficed to make the house alive with our domestics: two Negro boys, Loveless aged about 14 and Sam, 11 or 12; a cook Peter, incorrigibly drunken and worthless, with a wooden leg, having lost the other by disease; an old man 'Cornwallis', said to have been born a King's son in Africa, now reduced to a cowherd and horse tender, and hardly fit for that, as he was very old and like all old Negroes, ill cared for; and a mulatto woman to wash cloathes and make beds. By 6 o'clock the boys brought a cup of coffee, an essential on first rising.

The custom was then to serve out the weekly allowance of salt fish for the Negroes who belonged to the house, and whose cottages were built round a quadrangle in the yard; as they had not a farthing of wages, the master had to provide food, a few pounds of salt fish, and a bunch of green plantains to roast with it or to make into a sort of paste, foo-foo, of which they are particularly fond. Hired Negroes were paid in money which they took home to their proprietors. I thought it best to make no protest against this Sunday morning occupation, as it did not last long, provided it did not proceed any further. We went upstairs to breakfast at 9 o'clock, served by the two boys, whose half-clad unwashed appearance was not conducive to appetite for the fish and plantain they pawed onto the table, particularly after a sight of Peter and the abomination of his kitchen.

Mr Pattinson and I prepared for church, where he said he always went for morning service. There was afternoon service, but nobody went then but Negroes, no white people; coloured people did, but *they* mostly went in the morning. This was disheartening: what was I to do all the rest of the day! So we put on our best coats, in Demerara indispensible on Sundays however hot it might be; and walked the way we had before, by that interminable road, till we came to a bend, and then saw a continuation just as immensely long. However, it was a great relief to me, already in a sop, to find the church [St George's] very near: an unpretending building, constructed like the houses entirely of wood, a small bell turret or steeple, with the invariable canal and avenue of Orinoque trees. Smart white folks were approaching; the Governor drove up in his buggy with his aid-de-camp. Gaily-attired coloured ladies, with two or three Negro girls walking behind them carrying their prayer-book, umbrella or reticule in great state, clattered upstairs into the gallery, the place for all coloured people, who were not permitted to sit in the same part of the building as the whites, who occupied the lower part exclusively.

It was curious to watch the formality of these old ladies, black or mulatto: a large prayer-book, finely bound with gilt edges, was indispensible, although they could not read a word. Mr Pattinson greeted many of them as old acquaintances, with whom he appeared to be an especial favorite; one, Miss Molly Lemon, who asked how Mrs Pattinson and all the others were at Liverpool, I discovered was Mrs Pattinson's aunt, her mother's sister. She had three coloured daughters for whom she would be very glad to find husbands, all these old ladies being constantly on the lookout to form good *white* connections for their daughters. Then there were younger ladies of a lighter hue, well attired and ladylike. I was shocked to find that the greater part were living with white settlers as their wives without the slightest idea of immorality, thinking it more creditable than to be *married* to one of their own colour; whilst the whites, who would not allow them to sit at their table nor in the same part of the church, did not think it beneath them to live in habitual and barefaced sin. This was a new and painful discovery of the social state of the West India colonies.

The clergyman was the Rev Wilshire [or Wiltshire] Stanton Austin, who conducted the service with plainness and propriety, and preached a thoroughly Scriptural practical sermon; an organ and choir led the Psalmody and a few chants such as are usually heard in Evangelical churches. Altogether I was pleased and thankful at this first attendance, and expressed my feeling to Mr Pattinson, who said 'Yas, yas, but he's rather severe, and people don't like it'.

After dinner, Mr Pattinson took me to the soldiers' barrack ground! where the 21st Fusiliers were going through their afternoon's parade. I found it a regular lounge for idle and profligate people, so I determined not to spend the sabbath afternoon that way in future. In truth I felt very miserable; we had had an idle godless man to dine with us, and several companions of Pattinson's now lounged in to drink brandy and smoke cigars. I had no room but my bedroom to retire to, which was very small and very hot, having no Venetian blind; and besides it soon grew dark, so that I could no longer see to read my Bible, and I was compelled to sit and listen to the folly and ribaldry of those around me. So ended this sabbath.

Mr Pattinson proposed I go next day to present my introductory letters before breakfast, ere the sun became too fierce. I had to go the whole way to the church, then a considerable way to the corner of Robb Street, in the thick of the business part of the town. It led into Water Street, parallel with the other long one: straggling and narrow, thickly built on each side with stores great and small, those on the water side set on wooden platforms built on the invariable brick piers which rested on the muddy river bank, so the greater part of the warehouses at the back projected over the water. At the end of each cross street, such as Robb Street, was a public wharf or stelling, crammed with rickety-rackety wooden houses and inhabited by dealers, a few white but mostly black and coloured. The waterside premises were too valuable to be left to small dealers, and the principal merchants connected with shipping were here. Near Robb Stelling but not on it, I found the large house of McDonald Edmonston & Co, and presented Mr Gladstone's letter to Mr Robert Edmonston, a gentlemanly Scotchman; his brother Archy had succeeded their uncle, old Mr Archibald, who had been an upriver timber merchant for many years. He received me courteously and 'hoped to see me occasionally', a hope I did not share, knowing the fate of introductory letters in general.

I took my leave, and went a long long way further, to an open space where there was a large market and a Scotch church, and a great inclosure which might be called the Whitehall of Georgetown, where stood a large old wooden building, the 'Count' or 'Committee House', the Government offices. I crossed a canal by a wooden bridge, to reach the tall gaunt-looking store of Messrs McInroy Sandbach & Co, looked up to as the Rothschilds of Demerara, rich and influential. Many estates were heavily mortgaged to them, their whole business connected with the arrangements to which the mortgagers were strictly tied down. All the sugar must be shipped home in *their* ships, under *their* agency both here and at home, and so much every year; all plantation stores to be bought of *them*; and other pickings. All highly profitable to the mortgagee, who got full rates and commissions: considerably more so than planting was to the unfortunate mortgagers, who got about as much as would just keep them on their legs. Other produce such as coffee and cotton was subject to like conditions. Here I found the Executive of this formidable establishment, Mr George Rainey, whom Mr Pattinson had told me I would find 'very keen': slow-spoken, he had a sharp visage, high thin nose, and a cold quiet calculating grey eye. He and his coadjutor Mr George Buchanan brought enormous gains to the Liverpool house and to McInroy Parker & Co in Glasgow, though they dealt fairly: their business was money lending. Lastly I called on Mr Edward Dawson. He was very young, and had been sent out to act as attorney or qq (cue cue) as all agents were called in Demerara, Dutch fashion. He received me kindly, but I found he was acted on by the influence of the accursed slave system, pronouncing his brother Ambrose's mind 'dreadfully warped' and Mr Wilberforce a d----d fellow.

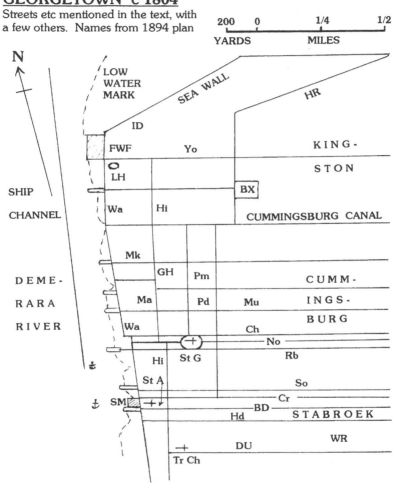

GEORGETOWN c 1804
Streets etc mentioned in the text, with
a few others. Names from 1894 plan

200   0   1/4   1/2

YARDS   MILES

N

LOW
WATER
MARK

SEA WALL

HR

ID

FWF   Yo   KING-

LH   STON

BX

SHIP

Wa   Hi

CHANNEL   CUMMINGSBURG CANAL

Mk

GH Pm

DEME-

RARA   Ma   Pd   Mu   INGS-

RIVER   Wa   Ch   BURG

No

Hi St G   Rb

St A   So

Cr

SM   BD STABROEK

Hd

WR

DU

Tr Ch

CUMM-

Plan of Georgetown

69

Sources: Three printed 19th C town plans of Georgetown (only a few exist) have been located:
(1) Stabroek 1804, inset on ref 1 in Map of Demerara.
(2) Similar inset on a map by W L Loth, published Amsterdam 1888.
(3) City of Georgetown and Environs, compiled from various sources 1894, no author given; much larger, highly detailed, all streets named and buildings numbered.

The present diagram is based on (1), being the closest to JCC's time. It does not include any street names, and these, plus some buildings etc, have been added from (2) and (3); correlation proved somewhat tricky, due largely to the somewhat featureless gridiron layout of much of the town.

Plan (2) is scaled metrically, (3) in Rhynland Roods and English Feet, and measured distances agree very closely. (1) is in Verges, and distances come out greater by a factor of 1.6, a considerable discrepancy; presumably the scale-bar, or my interpretation of it, is wrong. (2) and (3), being later, are more likely to be accurate, so their scaling has been adopted here (also two against one!).

Notes: Kingston extends south to Cummingsburg Canal, which on (1) (spelt Comingsburg) stops within the built-up area, a parallel 'Grand Canal' continuing eastwards. The other two show the Demerara Railway along this line – on the filled-in canal? Plan (3) has 'Station' one block east of Main Street and 'Terminus' (for passengers and freight respectively?) at Water Street. Also, 5/8 mile due south of Stabroek Market, near the shore, is a 'Car Barn' (the American term for tram shed or depot), suggesting that a tramway was planned or operating in at least part of the town; it would probably have been worked by mules, being better suited to a hot climate than horses. Cummingsburg extends to Church St; the area between North and South Sts is called Lacytown. Routes out of the town are called 'public' roads – a difference from the other streets?

Adjacent to St Andrews Church (the 'Scotch Church', the oldest church extant in Georgetown, completed in 1818), Plan (3) shows 'Public Buildings' – the 'Count' or 'Committee House'? St George's is now a Cathedral and reputedly the world's tallest wooden building,

143 feet. Trinity Chapel is possibly the one that the two 'John C's' (Cheveley and Chapman) went to? (see 'Staff Changes'). The sea-wall (Dutch-built) extends 280 miles along the coast, as a protection against flooding.

In his first impressions of Georgetown, does JCC exaggerate distances? – though no doubt walking in a strange town, and likely over-clad for the enervating damp heat, made it seem a lot farther than it actually was. His route to the 'Custom House' (Government House?) was probably along Main Street; then going to church, the bend would be where it kinks to become High Street again. Going to present his introductory letters would surely have been quicker directly along the waterfront!

Streets

BD	Brick Dam	Hi	High	No	North
Ch	Church	HR	High Road to Mahaica and Berbice	Rb	Robb
Cr	Croal	Ma	Main	So	South
DU	D'Urban	Mk	Market	Wa	Water
Hd	Hadfield	Mu	Murray	Yo	Young

Murray west of Main is called Holmes; now renamed Quamina (not difficult to appreciate why – see 'Slavery's Martyr'). Does Hadfield have anything to do with Isaac of that ilk?

Buildings etc.

BX	Barracks	Pm	Promenade
FWF	Fort William Frederick	SM	Stabroek Market
GH	Government House	St A	St Andrew's Church
ID	Immigration Dept	St G	St George's Church
LH	Lighthouse	Tr Ch	Trinity Chapel
Pd	Parade Ground	WR	Werk en Rust

To Work

There was plenty for me to do: the more I looked into matters, the more it became apparent that I had not come a day too soon. I had no benefit of regular business training but what I had picked up on my two voyages, yet I found I must do all in my power to set matters right and keep them so. Goods had been squandered on credit in all directions, and I had little or no help from the books or the bookkeeper Harris. Indolent Creole as he was, he tired of the task of putting the books right; Pattinson refused to pay him any more till he produced a balance sheet, although he had never had proper direction – which Pattinson, a somewhat weak and ignorant man, did not know how to give. He was extremely irritable, and drove Harris faster than he chose to be driven, who, finding neither money nor good words, gave up and left us. Mr Jack Sutton was too ignorant for rebuke to reach, all I could say went in at one ear and out at the other, lodging nowhere. In the store he was such an idle impertinent lout that I was glad when he was out. He was sent to get in money from the black and coloured ladies who kept hucksters' stores, the small retailers all over town who were our principal customers, though he seldom brought back much except gossip; indeed he was a great favorite with all the old ladies, who esteemed him highly for his conversational powers.

Another week passed. I had become anxious about the books and accounts, and I saw there was nothing for it but a few hours work in the evening. It was usual to close all stores at 5, the dinner hour, and I went down into the counting house to work afterwards, usually till after gunfire. I found the heat excessive, and the mosquitoes beyond anything I had ever experienced, day and night all the same to them. Good nets scarcely kept them out at night, and by day they riddled me with punctuations, so that I was obliged to adopt underclothing and boots in pure self-defence, which greatly increased the suffering from heat. Then came the well-known 'prickly heat' rash, and heat lumps or soft boils for many months, so painful that I could not rest on my bed with any comfort. Altogether I was in pitiable case, but I worked away and took courage, being told that these boils had saved me from a dangerous fever common to newcomers, and I thanked my Heavenly Father I was no worse.

After the second week I was getting pretty well au fait at the business, which was as varied as the articles for sale. As Pattinson sold cheap, the goods being on commission, there was a considerable run on him, and plenty of debts owing by various seedy people, to which I was very much averse, for I soon saw that if this went on, shippers at home would never get their money. As we retailed out a great many articles in order to get sales, the labour of keeping accounts, with the books at a stand, was almost impossible, and I contrived temporary books to know how things stood, as well as to dun those who owed money.

Sunday came again. Pattinson and I went to church in the morning, but alas! in the afternoon he proposed a drive in his new gig, and I again gave in. We drove to a plantation on the east coast, Bel Air, two or three miles from the town, where lived the 'Honorable'(?) Andrew Cochrane Johnstone, who had been involved in the Stock Exchange hoax and found England too hot to hold him. We found him revelling with a large party; God was not in their thoughts, but the Devil. Mr Pattinson saw I was uneasy, and took his leave. He professed to respect my views, for he read me a letter from a young lady at home who said 'I understand Mr Cheveley is a very religious good young man, and I hope you will be benefitted by his company and example'. This made me determined to have a plan for myself on the Lord's day.

I felt the impossibility of pursuing any improvement at home, where there was no privacy, and determined to go to church in the afternoon, which I was told was only for black people, but I found one pew reserved for such whites as thought fit to come; of whom there were 6 or 8, one a nice lady, Mrs Richard Jones, wife of the manager of the Houston sugar estate just outside the town. It was truly a refuge to be there, and I resolved to go regularly. I also attended the monthly communion, but from which many whites absented themselves, as well they might considering the lives they led. Even at the Lord's table the shameful distinction was kept up, as everywhere else, and no person with a tinge of colour might kneel side by side with a white!

Interpolation: Notes about British Guiana
[Largely from his supplementary book]

– Factual

A portion of South America, bounded on the east by Dutch and French Guiana, i.e. Surinam and Cayenne. The colony of Berbice is on that river (famous for the discovery of the huge aquatic flower Victoria Regina); the Abary river or creek divides Berbice from Demerara, near which was our cotton estate Dundee and Airy Hall, then Mahaicony Creek. After that, Mahaica creek and village: all these creeks had to be crossed by ferry. Thirty or forty miles brought you to Georgetown and the river Demerara. On the other side, the west coast running down to the great river Essequibo, which divided the colony of that name; at its mouth the cultivated islands Leguan and Waakenaam. Beyond, the Spanish American settlements [now Venezuela] of the great river Orinoque. The three colonies, taken from the Dutch in the last war and made over to England at the peace in 1814, are united now under one governor. Population: Demerara and Issequibo, Whites about 3,000, Free black and coloured 6-7,000, Slaves 70,000; Berbice 600, 1,700, 20,000. The computed value of slaves from actual sales: about 4½ millions sterling, awarded by Parliamentary commissioners as compensation at the emancipation.

The negroes work from 6 in the morning till sunset, 6 at night, roused before sunrise by blowing the conch shell, ringing a bell, or the crack of the drivers' whips. The Negro houses have a neat appearance; little Creols, or black children, run about stark naked like little pigs. Jupiter, the head Negro on our estate, made a contrivance to kill a tiger, or rather panther, which carried away the negroes' pigs, 'so nigger man fix Massa tiger' [a form of pidgin English, widely-used]: A dead pig hung to a tree, a loaded gun aimed at it, a cord from the pig round a pulley to the trigger; the tiger shoots himself, this was not murder it was suicide. These animals prowled about the plantations, and sometimes into Georgetown; one even got under the floor of a drinking house.

The Native Indians are a wandering race who live by hunting and fishing. They roam over the vast interior, and seldom stay long in a place, but sling their hammocks amongst the trees where they sojourn for a time. When they come to the town, they inhabit a logie or large shed built for them in the outskirts. A family walks along the roadside in a long string, one after the other: first come the men, oldest down to youngest, with their bows and arrows at their backs, little broad-shouldered flat-nosed copper-colored fellows with long straight black hair cropped round the neck, their only article of dress a skirt, nothing else, sometimes not that; followed by the women likewise, with only a very short petticoat perhaps. They were idle, harmless, not warlike. They were also called 'Bucks'. The Government appointed 'Protectors of Indians', not so much for their own sakes as in the interests of the slave owners, who encouraged these wandering tribes to attack and root out runaway Negroes who deserted the plantations and took refuge in encampments in the 'bush'. (The great naturalist Waterton affirmed that an inferior race of beings, or man-monkeys, inhabited those lonely forests – In fact they were baboons: a sorry jest for a scientific man to play, and did him no credit.)

Crops are sugar, coffee, cotton; sugar mills powered by windmills or principally steam engines [probably fired with bagasse, the sugar-cane waste]. Cultivation is in strips along the coast, running up from the sea to the interior and backed by the jungle or Bush (Bosch as the Dutch called it). Between the sea and the cultivation a good road runs the entire extent. On each side of the Demerara, especially near Georgetown, were some of the best sugar estates. On the east of the river, 3 or 4 canals ran into the interior, two cutting through the town and communicating with the back of the estates. Coffee cultivation was principally here and higher upriver, but no cultivation extended beyond 15 or 20 miles up from Georgetown. This river district was the most unhealthy part of the colony, the coast estates getting the clear sea breeze.

The country being dead flat, estates were subject to inundations from the sea in front and, in rainy seasons, from the bush behind; both had to be provided against by dykes, dams, and sluices, back and front, as in Holland. Another danger was the forests taking fire in dry seasons from accumulated vegetable matter, looser and drier than peat, to the depth of 6 or 8 feet, called pegasse [likely JCC's mis-hearing of bagasse]. A light from a stray negro's pipe or a fire kindled by roving native Indians [or lightning?] was quite sufficient to set it burning; once alight, it burned on and on for miles, clearing even the largest timbers as it advanced. This would frequently continue during the entire dry season until the rains extinguished it. Although many miles from the town, in 1824 it could be seen lighting up the horizon for miles as long as the dry weather lasted. Fine season July to November, February and March, rain April to June, December and January.

– Distinguished Ladies

Quite the head of the coloured class was Mrs Dorothy Thomas, usually styled Miss Doll: a dark mestizo (or mustee as we English will call it) with the deportment of an empress, and reputed to be wealthy. She lived alternately in a splendidly furnished handsome house in Georgetown, and on her cotton estate up the coast, called Kensington, on which she employed some of her negroes; others whom she kept in town were employed as usual in selling as huckstresses articles which she bought and for which they had to give strict account, the goods or the money. Like most of her contemporaries, she had in her establishment a white gentleman who was not rich, but submitted to the degradation of being domineered by this imperious old Dame. Her balls and entertainments – yes, balls!: many of the coloured ladies who had daughters to dispose of gave balls, as do ladies at home – were not for black or coloured, but for white young gentlemen, who were not ashamed to dance with coloured young ladies. But had Hopkinson appeared there, he would have been told that it was no place for *him*.

I called on Miss Doll to ask about some cotton she had promised Pattinson as freight, which had not arrived. She received me with the air of a superior, 'Oh, that must be great mistake of Pattison, I know better'. She called up her white gentleman, who had a meek chastened aspect: 'Pray why that cotton not been sent for Pattison ship?' He humbly gave some reason; 'Eugh, you go 'long' (i.e. get away with you, or none of your nonsense), 'when Mr Thomas was 'live things were different, you see about it.' Another similar lady, of darker hue and unmitigated ugliness, Miss Queen Breda, who had a fine house and retail store in Robb Street, and was a good customer to us, told me 'Eugh, what for Pattison send you? I not owe him one stiver, you tell he so – hearie?', although she owed a large bill and knew it. Another lady told me, 'Eugh, you go long tell Pattison come heself'.

The trading operations of these distinguished ladies were something of this kind [evidently they ordered directly from England as well as going through local stores]: I say Massa Captain when you go home you country you bring me out one trunk ob shoe and one trunk ob needle and tread and here de money for buy um twenty dollar - - one crate earthenware he must hab plenty jug and bason and bowl and cup and saucer, fifteen dollar - - one trunk calico dem must be berry nice print for gown piece - - Yes Miss [name] I heerie I shall bring um. Away goes the Captain, back again he comes in a few months. Tank you good Massa me berry much obleege. - - But: Where me trunk ob print, why you 'ain't bring um and me been gib you de peaper all about im, how you come to forget? – Well, you see, when I got out to sea, I sat with the cabin window open and laid the orders out with the dollars on them to keep them down, and some of them had got no dollars, so there came a puff of wind and blew them into the sea, and I forgot what it was all about, but take my advice and send the money with the paper next time.

Their negro girls go round huckstering things during the week, carried about in trays on their heads. Sunday morning is settling day. Miss Norah Leeds, an immensely fat woman of colour who lived next door to me [this was after a move up town, see 'Change of House'], was particularly famous for how she conducted these settlements. Seated in her shop in great state, with her girls drawn up before her, she begins: You [name], how much you been sell dis week? Six dollar Missy. Berry well gib me de money, you good nigger. – – Tree dollar and half Ma'am. Ough! go bout you business you lazy toad, pose you go on so Uncle Jim sall lay de licks upon you, you heary?

Then a defaulter: What you tan dere for, come here you! Yes ma'am (without moving an inch). Come here you good for nutting ting why you not move youself? What become ob you tray? (No answer). Where de dollar? Where me ting, where you been put um? Please Missy dem arl gone. Oh you hussy, you tief, you rascal, you villain, you make way arl me ting! Lay um down and flog um, bring de whip, you Jim. Oh missy! please Missy! Me walk arl about, me not sell one bit (the smallest coin in use, about fivepence), and one black man come and take away, ebery ting been go way wid de black man. Oh you bad nigger, you tell me such big lie! You Jim gib um de licks. Jim, in no great hurry, at length proceeds to execution, and amidst an uproar to set Babel at defiance and in which Miss Norah's tongue is heard above all, punishment is administered, tranquility restored, and Miss Norah prepares to go to Church!

– The Negroes and Slavery

So far we have seen the brighter side of West India life. Alas, it had a very dark one: that accursed plague spot, that devilish invention of man to enrich himself by the miseries of others; that enemy of all improvement, that determined foe of all progress in moral social intellectual or industrial improvement – that hideous thing called Slavery casts its blighting influence on our West India possessions and disfigures all that was attractive and beautiful in nature whether moral or physical. It is in its very nature to debase both the enslaver and the slave; the latter works by compulsion, with no hope of bettering himself, the former feels that without compulsion he cannot get what he requires. It was so common to beat a Negro who neglected his work that the very best-intentioned men were obliged to give in to it to get the work done. Where there were large gangs, as on the plantations, there was a head Negro or Driver over every separate gang, who carried a large cart whip to inflict punishment, to both men and women, when ordered by the manager or overseer. After my arrival, the flogging of females was forbidden by an Order in Council at home, but it met with violent opposition and produced the Negro insurrection of August 1823. The moral effects of this wicked system appeared in my eyes even more deplorable.

Under the slave system, the Negroes were very aggravating, and few except the really well disposed felt the slightest interest in what they did; their whole object was to do as little as possible. Peter our cook: dinner time came and not ready, no Peter, gone to the grog shop. A girl Betsy succeeded him: day after day no Betsy, I went to the gaol where stray Negroes were pounded like cattle, and home comes Betsy with a bill of 6 dollars. Damon, the son of Jupiter, was made houseboy, to sweep and get breakfast: but no breakfast, no Damon; finds his way to the jail, and another bill. And this is repeated over and over again. These are some of the domestic trials of the slave system, that peculiar institution which Brother Jonathan so much admires, which he says we don't understand and don't know the blessings of – May he long live in happy ignorance, I know too much of them. [He uses 'gaol' and 'jail' indiscriminately.]

Yet there are good features of the Negro character: Where they had inducements to be industrious, no people could work harder; but who amongst us would be willing to work from years end to years end without a farthing for his trouble? The Negro is light-hearted, merry, fond of dancing and drinking when he can get it, enterprising and persevering, but slavery renders him careless, obstinate, intractable and idle. All is for the benefit of others who tyrannize over him, and deny him not only the rights of a man, but if they could, the hopes and privileges of an immortal being.

By the laws of the Slave colonies at this time, no man or woman born a slave was his own master or mistress in any respect whatever. Mrs. Stowe's admirable and touching narrative 'Uncle Tom's Cabin' is a good exposé of the principles and detestable effects and practical wickedness of this Devilish device. The registration act compelled every owner of Negroes to have them all registered at the Government office, and every addition whether by purchase or birth, or every diminution whether by sale or death, must be duly registered. To insure this, no one could sell a Negro without a certificate from the Registrar shewing his legal title to him; and no slave could be removed from one Colony to another without special permission of the Government. Any infraction of these laws was a felony, and the death of a Negro by violence was murder by law, punished with death as severely as in the case of a white man.

Humane laws, wrung at various times from the British Government, afforded in some instances a protection to the West India Negroes which is unknown in the United States. But flogging for every offence great or small was too often resorted to. Sunday work was quite common, if not for the masters, to pick up a penny for themselves. The flogging of females was to a late period common. Marriage was forbidden amongst the slaves, and almost unknown amongst the whites and coloured people, the men and women living together as man and wife without any bond of wedlock. It followed that a man and the woman whom he called his wife might be separated at any time; the children must in all cases go with the mother, and the father has no hold upon them whatever. I must do the British slave system the justice to say that it had regard to the entire prevention of the importation of fresh slaves [abolished since 1807].

Slave Sales, the sale of human beings like goods and chattels, took place in the Vendue Office or place of public sale. On a platform stands a man with a black skin, nearly naked, a cloth about his loins; half a dozen white men are examining his limbs as you see buyers at home look at a horse. The auctioneer stands by, hammer in hand. 'Capital nigger gentlemen, name Joe, good carpenter, age 28, hasn't had the whip often' (Most Negroes bear these marks on their loins, many are scored with them). 'Now who bids? Walk about you and show yourself.' He is knocked down at last at 600 dollars. A woman and three children are next. 'Here's a good lot, capital washer – Stand up Polly girl and shew your legs – Three handy boys, must be sold with the mother, six, eight and ten, grow bigger and better every day, make capital fellows by and bye. Look smart you young rascals, you Sam 'pose you look sulky you catch licks you hearie? Come, gentlemen, what do you say?' The lot goes for 1,000 dollars. This odious scene was as every day an affair as a sale at a horse bazaar.

Mr Pattinson's Affairs

Our house was most inconveniently situated, and Pattinson was very much out 'up-town'. He divided much of his time between two worthies, Tom Johnson and Pat McClure. The former managed a large store in Robb Street; his pretentious qualifications commended him to Pattinson's flimsy ideas and led him into mischief and embarrassment, which I became aware of by degrees. This fellow persuaded him that it would be a fine thing to purchase a vessel to run between Demerara and the French West Indian islands Martinique and Guadeloupe with English commodities, to bring back

French wines and liqueurs that would command enormous profit if they could only evade the duties, which were almost prohibitively high on both sides. A schooner *Friendship* had been purchased and sent to Martinique. A plain sober quiet Scotchman, Mr I.D. Paterson, a timber cutter, lived about a hundred miles up river; wealthy and influential amongst the Indian tribes, he had been made a 'Protector'. He was to be the cats-paw, to smuggle in the French commodities; his domicile was considered a desirable point to run up to and discharge all the good things, which could then be brought down from time to time. The difficulty was to know how to get the articles sold; after some time, another unexpected one developed, for it came out that Mr Paterson and Tom Johnson had an old debt to settle; the canny old Scotch woodman thought the goods would be safest in his hands, so he 'keepit' them. *Friendship* was to start another trip soon after my arrival; as our passenger Mr John Bancroft had found me and wanted a birth, Pattinson sent him as mate.

Pat McClure – whether Scotch or Irish I never knew – formerly had a flourishing business in the American trade in pine boards (lumber), but being a very loose man, had sunk, and had little to show except a house and store with an extensive wharf. People said he was not to be trusted, and 'shied' him. He picked advantage from whatever he might chance on – just now it was Pattinson, who was a good deal puzzled how to dispose of the ships his brother was beginning to crowd on him, rather faster than his wits or his means would serve to find cargoes for. Constant talk about Pat McClure and his schemes to find freights: needless to add that he proved a humbug, and the only thing I heard was that he persuaded Pattinson to let him have the gig (brought out for his use in Sir John Cameron), and to take his in exchange as much superior, which afterwards turned out defective in the axle-tree, and one day came down with me.

Freights were so low that cargoes for *Ann* and *Sir John Cameron* would leave Mr Pattinson's brother at home little or no profit. At length he had to act; it was determined to dispatch the latter to Bermuda for a cargo of fish and lumber, and to take the best freights he could get for *Ann*. So we got rid of a plague, these lower ship captains, who did little but stroll from one store to another, always tippling and always thirsty, for the more they drank in that hot climate, especially spirits, the more they thirsted; yet few could resist the invariable 'What will you have to drink? Go upstairs and help yourself' – only too promptly obeyed, so they were frequently fuddled before the morning was half over. Captain Harrison of *Ann*, who often dined with us, was one day so overcome that he fell forward with his head in his plate, to my alarm, as I thought he had a fit of apoplexy; but Pattinson, more accustomed, had him conveyed to bed, and he appeared in the evening none the worse.

Mr Irish appeared in the store, and as he professed to be a first-rate bookkeeper, Pattinson set him on, but he made bad worse, and soon relinquished the attempt. Then we got a professed accountant, who worked slowly; the accounts accumulating daily, I was obliged to pick what I needed out of the day-to-day rough entries in the blotter or waste book. Then another ship arrived, *Ardent* from St Johns New Brunswick with a large cargo of lumber. The object was to make an immediate sale of the whole, as we had no platform whereon to stow it. The quiet canny Scot Mr Rainey told Mr Pattinson that as I had brought an introductory letter, he wished to give 'a turn' where he could to our house. Eager to sell, and somewhat flattered by the patronage to his young house by the old and influential one, Pattinson gave in to the terms, not by any means prejudicial to Scotch interests. The ship had brought an Irish lad, Mr Brady, who seemed in want of something to do, and as he came with a good character, Pattinson took him into the store as a temporary hand, and not before he was wanted. He was a thorough Pat, but steady and willing, and I was very glad of his help, which gave me more time to look to the accounts and correspondence with home.

In good truth I soon found that Pattinson was not a working man, talk being his primary gift, and brag at the close of the day when brandy-and-watered. I found out too by degrees that the notable adventure of the schooner *Friendship* was producing, not its expected crop of magnificent profits, but its very natural one of distrust, chicanery, bad feeling, and threatened litigation. Of the first three, Pattinson's post-prandial ravings were a specimen; of the last, the appearance of two or three lawyers like birds of prey was an alarming indication. The colony still retained the old Dutch legal

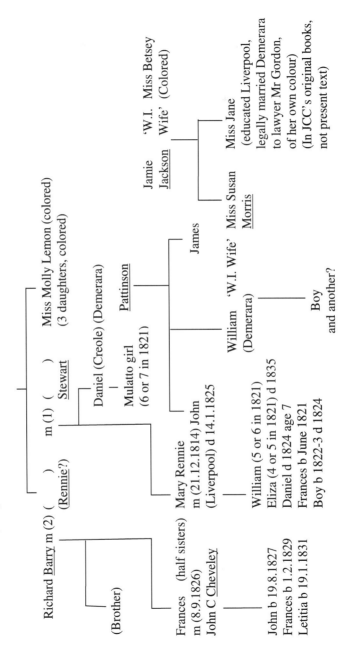

Pattinson Relationships

– So far as can be told, since parts of JCC's original text, possibly with some relevant material, have been excised. (Mary Pattinson would be JCC's half-sister-in-law, if there is such a relationship.)

Richard Barry m (2) ( ) (Rennie?)   m (1) ( ) Stewart   Miss Molly Lemon (colored) (3 daughters, colored)

(Brother)

Frances (half sisters) m (8.9.1826) John C Cheveley

John b 19.8.1827
Frances b 1.2.1829
Letitia b 19.1.1831

Mary Rennie m (21.12.1814) John (Liverpool) d 14.1.1825

Daniel (Creole) (Demerara) — Mulatto girl (6 or 7 in 1821)

William (5 or 6 in 1821)
Eliza (4 or 5 in 1821) d 1835
Daniel d 1824 age 7
Frances b June 1821
Boy b 1822-3 d 1824

Pattinson

William 'W.I. Wife' (Demerara)

Boy and another?

James

Miss Susan Morris

Jamie Jackson   'W.I. Miss Betsey Wife' (Colored)

Miss Jane (educated Liverpool, legally married Demerara to lawyer Mr Gordon, of her own colour) (In JCC's original books, not present text) systems, a puzzle to me as to poor Pattinson himself, rushing in headlong and headstrong to be victimised. [Several sheets cut out here in the original.]

Miss Susan Morris [she was clearly Pattinson's 'West India wife'] was still very young, of very fair complexion, unlike her mother Miss Betsey, who was almost a mulatto. She had been early sacrificed to this debasing and abominable system. Thus Pattinson fell into the mode of life which was so ensnaring to hundreds of young men who came to Demerara, and so detrimental to their moral character, while it encumbered them with large families, whom if they did not disregard, they found a heavy tax on their means of subsistence and a heavy burden on their consciences.

More about Georgetown

I kept up my acquaintance with Hopkinson; he was kind and amiable, and I felt much drawn to him. He lived upstairs at his mother's, who was, like most of the old ladies, unable to read or write, and she had her own apartments below. She viewed with regret the difference which education had produced between her and her son: 'Eugh! Ben 'shame' of his mother, better he bin bring up a carpenter as I tell he father, but Missa Hopkinson say no, Ben must be gentleman, so he 'spise he poor ole mother, but Ben be good son for arl that' – and so he was, for he could not be unkind to anyone. She was a very worthy and respectable old lady of her class, far more so than many I had to visit; for most of them required constant dunning to shake the money out, and I began now to go around to try to do what Jack Sutton had not.

[Sheet cut out here, possibly ending with: Going round dunning gave me a better knowledge] of the town than I had hitherto been able to acquire. It was not very difficult, being laid out by the Dutch in parallel streets with others crossing at right angles, not English fashion as if cows and sheep had been the first instigators. Georgetown was divided into three districts. The north end, where we were, was Kingston, the middle Cummingsburg, and the southern Starbroeck. The principal business street ran along the waterside; parallel to it the widest and best residence street, the whole length of the three districts, which were each separated by a navigable canal and wooden bridge (everything was of wood). Eventually it led to Werk-en-rust [Dutch = work and rest], the front of an old plantation now run to wrack, and used as the general cemetery of the town. Other parallel streets were laid out with good dwelling houses and gardens. Being dead flat, not the slightest rise anywhere, the only good view was from the top of the lighthouse at the river entrance; going there to see what ships were around was a Sunday recreation for half an hour between church and dinner.

One of these streets took in the Parade Ground, appropriated for military drilling every Saturday at 3 o'clock, an exhausting task in the hot sun, but a 'blessing' that had to be borne by those who benefitted under the slave system. Pattinson was in a rifle corps, a select company of merchants and clerks, into which the members were ballotted, and I was told I should have to go in. Every white or colored man not a slave was required to join a Militia regiment within three months of arrival, no volunteering as at home and no choice, under penalty of fine for the first and second default and imprisonment thereafter: so that all were soldiers and were obliged every Saturday afternoon to turn out to drill on the parade ground and on other special occasions. These Militia regiments were raised for the internal protection of the Colonies against the Negroes; besides them there were generally one or two regiments of regular troops. Having no military taste, I was determined to keep out until ordered and fight it off as long as I could, and as I was not molested, I evaded it all the first year.

A Ride East
The East Coast had hitherto been unknown, except for the short drive to Bel Air, yet it was one of the most important parts of the colony. I therefore felt much interest when Pattinson wished me to visit one or two estates where he hoped to get some freight for his ships. I set off on his horse long before daybreak to keep out of the heat, enjoying the coolness, and musing, for it was the first quiet time I had had since I arrived. It was still starlight: all was perfectly still save for the sustained chorus of croakings and pipings from the legions of all varieties and sizes of the frog species, a concert of every conceivable note from the shrill whistle of the little lively ditch frog down to the

deep bass of the great giant 'Johnny Crapeau', accompanied by myriads of crickets whose continuous chirpings nightly fill the ear, and the incessant flashing of thousands of fireflies that fill and confuse the eye. On the sea side, patches of scrub, here and there a tall graceful Coridda tree, something like a willow [possibly a mangrove? Spelt 'courida' on the 1894 map]; on the other side marshy pasture forming the front land of the estates, worked out and left uncultivated or to cattle. Cotton cultivation was nearer the road, not being so dependent on soil as sugar, which could not be grown on salty water. The road ran parallel with the sea shore in front of the various estates, which are separated from the road, or Dam, by a deep dyke, cut to receive the drainage.

Near daybreak, the crickets and the fireflies were subsiding; the little hummingbirds were on the wing, hovering bee-like over the flowers, tiny fairy-like things more like insect than bird. This half-hour was quiet, soft and dewy, cool, calm and delicious; but then up rose the sun, within an hour shining in strength, and the sea breeze with it, totally changing the scene. I came to 'Bachelor's Adventure', a large cotton estate owned by the family of John Hopkinson, Ben's white father's brother, both having left a coloured race behind them. By this time, the Negroes were all off to work, roused before sunrise; the old grannies left at home to look after the pick'nies, and the old daddies (the usual familiar term for a Negro) to cut grass for the horses and superintend the manager's stock and fowls.

Mr Hugh Rogers, a gentleman of colour, was managing the property, one of the most respectable of his class. I chatted with him, and after the inevitable cup of coffee, I proceeded to Plantation Le Resouvenir, which afterwards became famous in connection with the Negro rising two years later. It was in the hands of a manager, Mr John Hamilton, a somewhat crude Scotchman. One of my errands being to ask for some money which he owed, I was not very cordially received; I expected he would ask me to stay for breakfast, but no sign, and after some chat about ships and freights, I look my leave, with the customary planters' promise to call when he came to town: a convenient way of getting rid of a troublesome customer, which I evidently was.

A double avenue of tall palmettos, as on many plantations, formed the drive up to the buildings, very majestic, but conveying the idea of the plumes of a hearse; vulgarly called by the Negroes 'cabbage trees', from the green pod, said to resemble cabbage when cooked. I have reason to remember them on this occasion. As I was mounting my sprightly nag, he darted forward just as I put my foot into the stirrup, and before I could throw my other leg over the saddle, broke from the Negro holding the bridle, and started off at full gallop. Between the danger of the saddle turning and my being dashed on the ground, or my head coming in contact with the palmettos, or being thrown and dragged in the stirrup, I felt in a perilous position. My efforts were divided trying to get into the saddle and either rein the horse in or keep him clear of the trees; providentially, I got my foot clear and righted myself. I felt that I was now master, and if he had gone this gait for his own pleasure, he should go it now for mine; accordingly I kept him up to it for some distance, and actually got back to Georgetown in time for a bit of breakfast.

Home Thoughts from Abroad

Having been some three or four months away, I was beginning to look anxiously for news. I had continued to write to Mr Driffield and my family with accounts of my progress; and I daily watched the signal staff on the lighthouse, which telegraphed the various ships arriving. We mostly depended on merchant ships for letters, and Liverpool was the great point of interest, both for commerce and private advices. At length I had the glad tidings that George was coming out as second mate in *Cornwall*, belonging to Gladstone & Co. No particular change had occurred at home. Charles was working with Richard at his underdrainage with the mole plough. Henry had got from Hedingham to a grocer's at Bocking on Mr Brathwaite's recommendation, who found him getting rather too strong for him and not over-courteous to the old lady, and Harry had neither inclination nor tact to accommodate himself to her ways; he required to be kept well employed at active work. Tom was still at Colchester with Swinborne & Walter; he was anxious to learn printing, and found to his grief that although a noble art in theory, like most it was very ignoble when reduced to its dirty practical mechanism at workman's weekly wages and in close contact with the noble working classes. My Prescot letters were a great comfort, though Mr Driffield said George had been restless and unsettled after I left. I had also one from Mr Henry Laird from Madeira.

From John Pattinson, or rather JP & Co, we had advice of coming consignments, and severe comments on WP's bad management of what he had already had; account sales were wanted, the money was wanted, and there was great grumbling by JP at home at the low rates of freight accepted by WP abroad, so altogether things were not very satisfactory. Amongst other consignments was a quantity of bottled Seltzer water, which WP called a 'Menial' water, to my surprise at his ignorance, which was that of a schoolboy. I felt ashamed to set him right, but his friends were not so nice. This 'Spa', as it was called in Germany, was well-known here in the time of the Dutch, and drunk as 'Hock and Spa', but had gone out of fashion with the English, who, though they occasionally cooled their brandy-heated stomachs by a morning dose of it, preferred stiff brandy and water. [Possibly what we call soda-water?]

Early in 1822, *Cornwall* arrived with George as second mate: a strong contrast to George as Acting 5th Mate of HCS [Honorable Company Ship] *Prince Regent*. In his working attire he did not differ from the first mate, a great rough hulking tar, hands in colour and consistency like seal flippers (for which reason we applied the name to these West India mates and captains); had George been different in dress, he would not have been looked on as good for much. I asked him to spend the day with me on Sunday, and waited somewhat impatiently after breakfast. I saw coming up the street a sailor in Sunday toggery: wide duck trowsers, jacket with many buttons, and a Scotch cap with a gay ribbon fluttering behind; to complete it, a large bundle of washing tied up in a bandanna. It was George indeed; I had not minded his dirty working attire on board, but this was rather more than I was prepared for. Pattinson seemed disposed to treat him a la Jack Tar, at which I felt hurt and annoyed, so I got a frock coat on him, and persuaded him to give up the ribbon, and was somewhat comforted. It was weak in me, perhaps, to be so affected by outward appearance, but I was a young man and somewhat sensitive, and did not feel my brother should appear before my employer or his friends in a degraded light, in the lowest form of sailors' attire. We went to church morning and afternoon, and I found that he was still looking in the right direction. Situated as we were, we could not see much of each other; he got on shore on Sundays, but they were not sabbaths at Pattinson's, although we made them so as far as we could; on the other hand, I was awkwardly placed on board *Cornwall*, where he had his duties to attend to. So I did not feel his absence as much as I should otherwise, when he departed.

Mr and Mrs Driffield wrote that they had nominated me as the Sponsor for their first little daughter, who had been born since my departure and baptised Letitia; I felt gratified by their confidence in me, although my own mind was even then in doubt as to the practicability of the undertaking. My brother Charles had gone to London in the county Fire Office. Richard was superintendent of Brookhall Farm near Tiptree Heath, belonging to Mr Cline, a surgeon in London, who came down himself occasionally to find fault with things he could not understand: between which, and his snarling letters, poor Dick got to have not the easiest time of it. At Hedingham, Letitia was getting on with her learning at last, under Margaret's tuition, and was beginning to show considerable musical talent. She was having a few lessons in dancing, as Mother said 'so essential to a ladylike deportment, well worth the little expense'.

George made a second voyage as 2nd mate of *Cornwall* in the middle of 1822. On this occasion plenty of produce offered, and time pressed to get the ship loaded and dispatched. To economize the time of their Negroes, the planters sent their boats with produce on Saturday night, to get alongside the ship Sunday morning, and they insisted on loading with no delay, so the boat might return the same day and no time be lost. All hands on the ship were at work the whole of Sunday (I will not call it sabbath); George was grieved and indignant at being thus Heathenized, as he termed it.

I was anxious to do something in my Lord's vineyard, but shrank from any overt act that would expose me to ill-will of the community with which in business I must be identified. In this strange state of society, minds appeared to be misdirected, and everything that savoured of real Godliness was treated with derision, contempt, or hatred, even among churchgoing people. However, had I known, there was a band, though but a little one, of faithful followers. One such was a black woman who made little purchases, Roseanna Paadevoort, a former slave who had received her freedom at the death of her master and whose name she had adopted according to the Negro custom, especially those who had been freed. She was one of the lowliest, very poor, and ignorant, for she could not read, but she had knowledge of salvation, and it was a treat to converse with her; she was the only Christian friend I had in the colony – so far. Yet she had a heavy trial to bear, in the disgraceful conduct of a son who was a constant trouble to her: she had in early life fallen in the way of a military officer, and this son was the offspring. He was now upwards of 30, as noisy and obtrusive as his mother was quiet and humble; he swaggered about, not infrequently drunk, and was generally looked on by the black and coloured people as a public nuisance. In my early days, when I was innocent, he asked the price of this and that, and selected some articles; I hesitated to let him have the goods without money, but he said his mother would pay, and if she did not, he would call tomorrow and pay himself. I was done, and Pattinson told me he was the greatest humbug in the colony, his mother would never pay nor he either.

O.L. Schultz

'Friends' in out-of-the-way places can be those looking out for people whom they can bring to do out-of-the-way things: such was Mynheer O.L. Schultz, who found our WP. He was one of the Dutch planters who still lingered. He had been manager on a sugar estate near the mouth of the Essequibo; when the previous owner died, he had managed himself into the elderly widow's good graces, took her to wife, and became the possessor of Plantation Le Destin. He came up to Georgetown occasionally in his sailing boat, to negociate the sale of his sugar products. He did not appear to be very well off, and farmed his estate on very old-fashioned principles, for example he ground by windmill instead of steam engine, now generally introduced. He produced a middling quantity of sugar of inferior quality, dull grey and moist, and as it did not command first-rate prices, he dealt with those who had not much experience of a good article, which had bright gold colour and strong dry well-detached grains.

On most estates, much of the front land had been worked out, manuring being impossible, and it was easier and cheaper to go back towards the bush and take up new ground as the old wore out, which then ran waste to coarse grassland and served for cattle [a source of manure!]. Mr Schultz was anxious to turn his cattle into money; he invited Pattinson to Le Destin, and persuaded him that it would be a very fine speculation to transfer some to the waste lands of the Abary cotton plantation, now running into wilderness and producing little but expense. There he could fat them for the butchers at Georgetown, and sell the milk or make butter for the market, thus turning Abary to some account, pending his endeavors to obtain another of his desires, a coffee estate. This appeared to have tickled Pattinson immensely and to have been acted on instanter, for while he was still absent, an immense herd of cattle appeared in the street before our store, putting the neighborhood into commotion. While I was wondering what it could mean, a strange Negro appeared: 'Missa Schultz send um cattle for Missa Pattison and say must stop till he come'. 'What!!??' Ditto repeated. So here was a fix – fix *literally* it was not, for these wild young beasts, over 100 in number, having come off a land journey of some 40 or 50 miles up the west coast, and been ferried over the river to Georgetown, had not arrived in the most amicable mood, and were running about in search of food and drink and at each other, to the terror of the women and children and to my great distraction. I really felt at my wits' end at this unlooked-for invasion, my only hope being that Messrs Pattinson and Schultz would soon appear and set matters right. I called a counsel of our establishment, and the easiest solution was that 'Massa send um cattle to bush dere back ob Miss Sue, and Cornwallis go with de other men for watch um' – turn them onto waste land behind Miss Sue Perkins' house opposite.

The day wore away. Jim, a trusty Negro we had taken on as a porter, came in the evening to say 'Massa, Missa Pattison not come, 'pose cattle get loose Dienar take um to barrack' (constables; place for stray cattle and negroes). As a preliminary I opened Jim's heart with a glass of whisky, the readiest way to do it, and told him he must take Yan and keep a sharp lookout all night. Jim was an honest old chap, on whom I knew I could depend, Yan a big rogue on whom I could not unless he was watched by the other; poor old King Cornwallis would be sure to go to sleep, and I had no faith in the two strange negroes: all my hopes were with Jim. A pretty night I had of it; the poor uneasy beasts kept up a bellowing, and I frequently got out of bed and bawled to Jim to know if all was right: whom I found faithful to his trust. There had been no sleeping, all had been kept awake by the efforts of the cattle to better their situation.

Pattinson came up with Schultz next day and took it very coolly, dispatching Schultz's Negroes with the cattle for Abary, another 40 miles. I found Schultz was to be paid for the cattle, which to my consternation Pattinson had bought by gradual supplies from the store, and considered it a capital speculation. He wrote home for a churn and milk pans to commence butter making; but then came the difficulty both of making the butter and keeping and selling it in that hot climate. The last I heard of the churn and pans was that the manager's wife, a great lazy lollopping mulatto, had taken them to catch rainwater. The cattle were bought by our butcher, who gave about as much for them as covered our meat bill, and thus by degrees dwindled to an end this clever speculation; while Schultz paid himself out of our store.

So things went on. Pattinson and I continued very good friends, although I often strove to check his excessive proneness to scatter his goods amongst people who I knew did not intend to pay. His favorite idea of the coffee estate was ever uppermost, leading him into all sorts of schemes and speculations for getting something advantageous to bring it about. It was exceedingly vexing to me to see things thus squandered, especially as the goods were not our own and we had to account for them to people at home. I supplied these kind of orders with ill grace, and once or twice I nearly got into a scrape for refusing during Pattinson's absence and implying I looked on them as swindles. However, I brought him somewhat in check, and he said he always knew when an order was not quite right by my countenance. Nothing could be looser than such people's ideas of business: broken-down merchants, needy planters, upriver men squatted on a worn-out coffee estate, idle spendthrifts loafing about town, were constantly trying it on. People who had no money gave a promise to pay on a slip of paper, an IOU, and as it said 'Good to Mr W. Pattinson for (whatever)' and signed by the party, it was called a 'Good'; frequently passed from hand to hand like a bill, till too often it was found to be good for nothing. 'Goods' had one advantage, that they enabled you to sue a man at once, without being put to proof of delivery of the goods [= articles] sold.

Staff Changes

Business increased, and we wanted more help. We sometimes met, on our way to church, a young man, John Chapman, who was serving the fag end of a firm in difficulties; anxious for another engagement, he came to us during my second year. He was cool, steady and dry, with a vein of humour, moral in conduct, and neither smoked nor drank brandy and water, rare in Colonial life. John was conversant with books and accounts, and had a natural turn for business; he fell in with my ways, and was a great acquisition. We became the best possible friends, and if we did not accord on one primary subject, we never disagreed. He was addicted to little speculations which Pattinson called 'John's Wild Schemes': he was one of those who see no interest if there are no difficulties, in fact the greater they are, the more the charm. John had a good education in Liverpool, and came out to Demerara as his father, a retired physician, lived with his [white] family on a cotton plantation 'The Grove' on the east coast at Mahaica. His elder brother Matthew James Chapman was a physician with an extensive and growing practice in Georgetown. There were two other brothers, one in England studying law, another with his father on the estate, and one sister.

Dr Chapman senior had, like too many colonists, two families: viz. two coloured daughters by his 'West India wife' Miss Mary Fletcher, previous to his white marriage. Of whom, one was living in England; the other, Miss Louisa Chapman, very ladylike and attractive in person and manners, married Mr Watson, a young Englishman in the law, and a friend of William Pattinson. She had hitherto kept a school (jointly with another lady of colour), which she then relinquished. Her husband died of consumption the first year of their marriage, leaving a little property to his young widow. William Pattinson was co-executor, and he left matters to Mr Gordon, a lawyer, who did not trouble or hurry himself for a coloured woman, so Mrs Watson was dependant on her mother, an uncongenial position. According to West India etiquette, the white family ignored the coloured one, except for John's elder brother, an honorable exception, who helped his coloured sister when she was widowed. Double families were one of the most painful circumstances of West India life, the coloured wife and children often giving the father no concern at all.

John Chapman knew all the coloured ladies who dealt with us, and I gave all the dunning into his hands, much more to his taste than mine as he was a regular old gossip. I mentioned one day the difficulty I felt in introducing my parcel of tracts, and he told me he knew a woman who would distribute them for me, a Wesleyan. This was news to me; I questioned him, and found the chapel was near Werk-en-Rust, and they had evening services Sunday and Wednesday. John proposed we go on a weeknight and see what it was like; he had really no religious feeling, but an insatiable curiosity and fondness for anything of novelty and adventure. We found the chapel was both large and spacious. It was crowded with a Negro and coloured congregation, who sung hymns with all their might, and the pastor gave a good scriptural sermon. John and I frequently went, though as the novelty wore off with him, I often went by myself.

We also found another chapel on the parade ground, established by some missionaries who were located on the west coast, but it did not go on long for want of funds. Eventually Mr Austin the Church [Anglican] clergyman took it for a school for free coloured people, whom he induced to come on large numbers on sabbath afternoons: a move in the right direction, but it laid the foundation of suspicion and deep-seated enmity in the minds of the colonists. I also occasionally went to the Scotch church, at the same end of town as the Wesleyan chapel; the sermons were dry and orthodox, cold and stiff, and did not reach the heart. It was well-attended, but I never could see an advance beyond formalism.

The two Irish lads whom Pattinson had engaged found eventually other employment; the one he had put in the distant warehouse was just good for nothing. [Presumably this was covered in the pages cut out above ('Mr Pattinson's Affairs'); later he says that ever since my arrival, we had supplemented our storage by hiring from a Mr Strange a large warehouse and yard to store heavy goods.] We started a cooperage there for rum and molasses under a white workman to lessen expenses, which were heavy for houses that shipped home much colonial produce. But the experiment produced much trouble, as Pattinson left it either to me or to itself, and I had to deal with a very ignorant workman; it was difficult to disentangle the incongruities of his daily account and to drive it into his mind that I was taking a correct view. After 12 or 18 months trial it ended with no benefit to him beyond his wages; of course he considered himself cheated and 'done', and I was accused of (in modern parlance) 'cooking the accounts'. They however had nearly cooked me, as I began to find that night work in such a climate was more than was good for me. I was subject from a boy to violent bleeding at the nose [Vol. 1 p. 45], and on one or two evenings I lost a good deal of blood in this way, which frightened Pattinson so much that he would not admit of my evening work any longer; and I generally took a stroll with John instead.

Towards the middle of 1822, Mr Jack Sutton absented himself. One day, Pattinson met him strolling about in his best blue coat, and told him to state his grievances: it appeared he did not consider himself in his right place drudging in a store, and wished to go on a sugar estate. A birth was procured for this hopeful youth as an overseer, I was relieved, and he was satisfied.

Problems

Sir John Cameron reappeared from Bermuda with a cargo of lumber and cask staves. It was red or pitch-pine, darker and closer-grained than white pine, used principally for floors. It is not so saleable, and Pattinson found that he could not sell the cargo in bulk from alongside, as he had done before, and it therefore had to be landed. This was awkward, as we did not possess a waterside platform, so here was a fix again, from pure want of foresight in ordering, and of course a place must be hired to stow it on, which added a considerable cost, besides the delay of sale while John Pattinson at home was looking for the proceeds to be reinvested in produce and returned by the ship. As it was, it took months to retail it off piecemeal; the ship had to be dispatched with what freight we could get, and the money came in dribblets instead of being available to meet bills. JP was excessively irate with his brother, and I felt puzzled to understand which had been to blame: in fact they were beginning to blame each other, J blamed W for not seconding his plans and efforts better, W blamed J for overdoing him with vessels for which it was difficult to find return cargoes. The pitch pine was stored on a platform belonging to a storekeeper Isaac Hadfield, who was about to visit Liverpool for a season; alas, on his return he discovered the weight had sunk one end of his platform deep in the mud, and thus arose a vexed question of who was to blame.

Richard had asked me to enquire on behalf of a friend about a Mr John Lungley, who had left Kelvedon some years before and was in Demerara as manager of a plantation. His father, an old man in bad circumstances, never heard from him, although he had been written to repeatedly. I found he was well known in the colony, and when I saw him, I stated the matter as delicately as I could. He said he would write to his friends; I ventured to hint at assisting his father, but he gave me to understand he had other claims on him, which I later found were a West India wife and family. So I wrote home, explaining how I did not think he would help his father. It afterwards appeared that Richard had shown my letter to his people at home, who had written an angry epistle giving him a proper lecture about his immoral conduct, 'no wonder he could not provide for his poor parents &c &c'. However wrong and sinful such a life was, it had become a matter of course in the West Indies, and to him, animadversions of friends at home were simply an impertinence; but my having written about him was an offensive interference, if not a positive libel. So having learned that he considered my conduct an atrocity, I called on him to explain that I had stated to my brother nothing more than a fact which was patent to all in the colony: which he grimly received. This was a lesson to me to write home no more of the doings of friends in Demerara.

I nearly got into another scrape without intending it (who does), but owing to the intemperance of others. A Negro came into the store with a good deal of noise, and walked about asking prices till I became suspicious he wanted to thieve. I told him at last to go away, which he refused to do. Pattinson, who was in the counting-house, said 'Turn him out', which I proceeded to do; he resisted, and in the struggle I was nearly thrown off the bridge which crossed the invariable dyke between the house and the road. 'Knock him down!' said one, 'Break the rascal's head!' another. No sooner said than done: Pattinson rushed out with the bar of the door, and bestowed such blows on the man's head, that had it been an ordinary head unprotected by the thick Negro wool, would have produced something more than scalp wounds. He soon had enough, and ran off roaring, blood streaming down his face; very much to my horror and dismay, as it was said he was a 'King's Negro' in the Black Regiment, and we should hear about it.

Sure enough we did. In about an hour, up rode grim old Colonel Leahey of the 21st Fusiliers, demanding what we had been doing to one of His Majesty's Negroes. I told him what had happened, and that it was really in self-defence. 'That's nothing to me Sir, I'll teach you that His Majesty's Negroes are not to be injured by you', and off rode this protector of His Majesty's property (who by the bye the following year had no scruple in shooting Negroes by dozens). Pattinson treated this with indifference.

However, next morning in walked a soldier demanding the names of the men who had assaulted HM Negro; I replied JCC turned him out, in whose defence WP broke his head. Next, in comes a Dienar; Mr Heylieger the Fiscal's (magistrate's) compliments, and he wished to see Mr Pattinson and Mr Cheveley. The former said he was not well, so I went up to the Fiscal's, at the other end of town on the Brick Dam, a boulevard of nobby houses at Starbroeck: not without some feelings of trepidation. He was a remnant of the Dutch judicial system (which was accepted by the British during the war), and a very fair specimen of old Dutch colonial functionaries. I told him the whole story, and added that I understood the man had laid himself open to punishment for raising his hand against a white man, but I did not wish to press that. 'Very true' he said, 'but you know he is a King's Negro and we cannot offend the military; give him a couple of dollars for his broken head and we will hear no more about it.' 'Nay Sir' I said, for I knew I had the law on my side, 'with all due deference, that would be offering a premium to repeat the same conduct; either the man has behaved ill and deserves punishment, or we have done wrong and deserve what the law decrees.' 'Well' he said, 'get it settled' – and so it was, for I heard no more, except that a white sergeant of the black company told me some time after, that their Commander took a very different view than the old Colonel, and was sorry we had had so much trouble about the man, who was the most worthless and troublesome in the regiment.

So we had a fair specimen of Negro ignorance aggravated by the tutelage he had been under, resenting interference by anyone other than his officers. Next we had the usual uncontrolled ferocity of the white man where the Negro race is concerned. Then a good specimen of military pertinacity, which would listen to no arguments in extenuation of the injury inflicted; and to wind up, a specimen of Dutch colonial law as expounded by Fiscal Heylieger.

In addition to these King's Negroes there were also many in jail for various offences, who went by the name of the Chain Gang, from being chained together by the legs in strings of 6 or 8. These poor wretches were often employed working on the roads. They were let out occasionally for a sort of frolic to clear the streets of stray animals, armed with pikes (of course under supervision) to spear any stray pigs, whose carcases they were allowed to take for their own use.

Mr Bueno (1)

Soon after my arrival, John Pattinson's letters had referred to one Mr Bueno, whom WP had sent from Demerara to St Andrews New Brunswick to negociate for cargo. William talked a great deal about this young Spaniard as a very clever fellow, so I wondered how he had ever parted with such transcendant abilities, and that as humble an individual as myself should be filling the gap. He appeared to have carried things pretty much his own way; his handwriting in the books was first-rate, the style indicating decision and promptitude. He had gone ahead too quickly, leaving WP behind, so he had sent him away to exercise his talents and cool his heels. John P at Liverpool did not encourage it, and as he held the purse strings, this was a damper; and WP did not hear from Mr Bueno, which was another. I confess I did not particularly want him back, as I never got on with *fast* men.

By the middle of 1822, Pattinson had begun to wonder what had become of his clever man of business, from whom he had received no intelligence, at which he marvelled. I held my peace, as I did not know him, although I had got his measure from John Chapman, who did, and who chuckled in anticipation of some fun from this adventure, which he told me would end in flourish and fiddlestick. At length, a letter from St Andrews: Mr Bueno had been unsuccessful in achieving his object of negociating cargo, although he hoped to get something through some friends, Messrs McMaster. But he had made the best use of his valuable time and services with their sister Miss Elizabeth, a fine young lady whom he had persuaded to accept him as her affiancé: and it was on this he wrote, very different than what the expectant and much astonished man, who had sent him on a very different errand, looked for. This was not all, the wherewithal was required; the McMaster brothers ('cute fellows as most North Americans are') wished to know Mr Bueno's capability to maintain their sister, and a partnership was hinted at as the solution. At the same time, Mr Bueno intended to lay this and other matters before Mr John Pattinson, and settle terms of further procedure. William, vexed and annoyed beyond measure, told Bueno to return to Demerara instanter, but he was already off on the wings of love to Liverpool. In due time, John wrote alluding to Bueno, whom he did not seem much to admire. He was purchasing a fine brig, *Eleanor*, to be sent out regularly and supersede in some measure the not very successful chartering system; Mr Bueno would return by this ship, which neither I nor John Chapman were much delighted to hear.

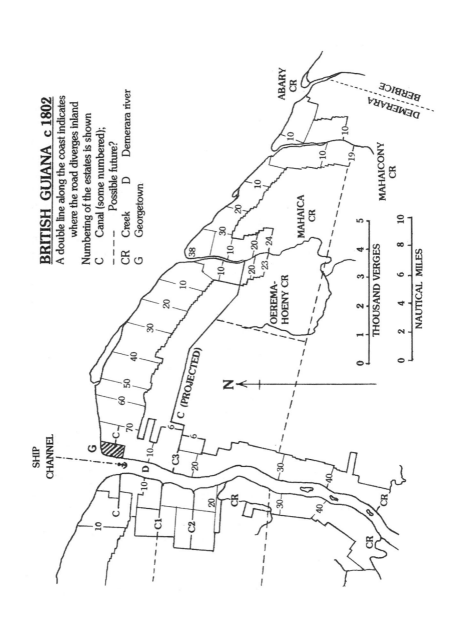

BRITISH GUIANA c 1802

A double line along the coast indicates
where the road diverges inland
Numbering of the estates is shown

C   Canal (some numbered);
        ----   Possible future?
CR   Creek   D   Demerara river
G   Georgetown

THOUSAND VERGES
0   1   2   3   4   5

NAUTICAL MILES
0   2   4   6   8   10

N

SHIP
CHANNEL

ABARY
CR

DEMERARA
BERBICE

MAHAICONY
CR

MAHAICA
CR

OEREMA-
HOENY CR

C (PROJECTED)

Map of British Guiana

Derived from two sources: (1) The whole colony, surveyed 1798 and 1802 by von Bouchenroeder, with additions and inset Plan of Stabroek dated 1804; published by Jas Wyld, Geographer to His Majesty, 5 Charing Cross Road, June 2nd 1828 (British Library Maps, 12.c.36). (2) Demerary from Essequibo to Berbice, by Robert Wilkinson, 1795. A copy of a Dutch map of a few years earlier, it lists the proprietors and, for many, the names of the plantations.

Both identify the estates in numbered blocks, the numbers running upstream along the waterways and from east to west along the coast, starting afresh at each creek or river. The estates are generally long thin rectangles, and within a block the long boundaries of one estate with another are parallel, hence at right-angles to the coast or river only by chance. There are, of course, occasional odd-shaped estates where one block meets another. Upstream along the Demerary river, the pattern is lost, and the estates become larger and squarer.

Along the east coast between Abary and Georgetown, the part of most interest to us, measurement from Wilkinson shows that the typical estate is a little less than ¼ mile wide and about 1⅞ deep, an area of some 2,100 acres – which may appear a somewhat odd size until it is remembered that the territory was originally Dutch! In fact, he copies the original scaling in Dutch roods, and the dimensions now emerge much more sensibly as 100 roods wide and 800 deep, area 80,000 square roods (1 rood = 4.12 yards, 3.77 metres). Some estates, mostly nearer Georgetown, are half-width, a few others 1½; those from Mahaika to Georgetown, also on the coast west of Georgetown (except at the ends of the block) are double-length.

Wyld is scaled in 'geographic miles, 60 to a degree', i.e. nautical miles, 6,080 feet, also in 'verges, each containing 12 Rhinland feet'; measurement of one against the other gives 1 verge as 12ft 5in (so a Rhinland foot is 0.3 inch longer than a British foot), and a verge is the same as a Dutch rood. 'Degree' is a mean degree of longitude; a 'statute' mile, 5,280 feet, is 33/38 (0.868) of a nautical mile.

Wyld has 'Remarks': 'The Sides of the Rivers or Creeks are almost every where covered with thick Forests; the immense plains or natural swamps, which lie between these Forests & the Sea Coast (commonly called Savannas) were also formerly covered with Forests, which have been destroyed by means of fire; much Brushwood however has since grown up, the branches & roots of which are so interlaced with each other, as to prevent penetrating through them, even in boats; the greatest part of these Savannas contain so much water which flows into them during the rainy Season, that the great heats of the dry Season are insufficient to drain them; the land therefore cannot be cultivated.'

His map shows the roadway along the coast, which it hugs, with occasional slight diversions inland, and no bridges across the creeks, all having to be crossed by ferry, as JCC says; it stops at the river Berbice. Roadways also run upstream along the rivers and creeks as far as the farthest estates (thus none are shown along Abary creek), though that along the Essequibo stops short.

He also shows a 'projected canal', linking Canal 3 to Mahaica creek, from which a set of parallel dotted lines runs up to the existing coastal estates; these areas were likely earmarked for backward extensions as the front land became worked out, rather than being intended as new properties fronting onto the canal. Further dashed lines farther inland could be less-advanced ideas for more canals – one such is clearly an extension of Canal 1. Some at least appear to have been built by JCC's time, as he mentions canals on the east of the river running into the interior. All the estates thus had a water frontage, which would be important both for drainage of the flat land – at which the Dutch are experts – especially in the rainy season, as well as for bringing out produce to Georgetown for shipping and taking empty barrels etc in. The steam engines in the sugar mills would not need fuel brought in as there would be plenty of wood for firing, besides bagasse, the cane waste. JCC mentions the planters' boats, and remarks 'the coast road had no heavy traffic to cut it up', which would hardly have been so had it been used for transportation of produce.

Spellings differ somewhat between the two sources and JCC's text: Wyld has Mahaica, Wilkinson Mahaika, and both have Demerary and Maicouny. Most of the estates that JCC mentions can be found on Wilkinson's map, though obviously some changes are to be expected in the intervening time. Details are as follows; the number indicates position on the map, and the spellings are Wilkinson's.

No.	Name	Proprietor
	East Demerary River	
4	Town of Stabroek	
5	Werk en Rust [Work and Rest]	Weber & Comp
	Coast Demerary-Mahaika	
72	Bel Air	John Haslen
57	Vryheids Lust [Desire for Freedom]	H van Cooten
51	Le Resouvenir [Remembrance]	H H Post
50	Success	C Hamilton & D Campbell
49	Chateau Margo	Wid van Baerle; 1823, Lachlan Cumming
48	La Bonne Intention	Weds Changuion
46	Beter Verwagting [Better Expectation]	I L C de Winter; 1823, Baron Von Grovestins
42	De Goede Hoop [Good Hope]	P van Helsdingen
32	Coldingen	Keith
28	Batchelors Adventure	B & I Hopkinson
26	Foulis	Dr Munro
25-24	Hope	Thos Porter
23	Haslenton	M Nihell
22	New Golden Grove	I Baillie
21	Noboclesh	Trotman
20	The John	M Nihell; 1821, Ben Hopkinson
19	Cove	Ben Hopkinson
11	Hope	J Baillie
8	Ann's Grove	Frislin
3	Grove	Wm Parkinson; 1822, Dr Chapman senior
1	Lancaster	J Philips
	West Mahaika	
15	----	L Rogers, M Chapman, each half

Other 'Hopkinsons' are:

Area	No.	Name	Proprietor
Coast West of Demerary river	4	Rotterdam	Ben Hopkinson
Coast Demerary-Mahaika	56	Sheet Anchor	R Skelton & B Hopkinson
"	30	Enterprize	B & I Hopkinson
Coast Mahaika-Maicouny	10	----	B Hopkinson
"	5	----	Ben Hopkinson
"	4	----	I Hopkinson
"	2-1	Taymouth Manor	Campbell, Baillie & Hopkinson
West Maicouny			
Coast Maicouny-Abary	10	----	B Hopkinson

Notes

(1) The Essequibo river, much larger than the Demerary, is about as far west of Georgetown as Mahaica creek is east. Leguwan and Wakenaam are large islands (with several smaller) in the estuary.

(2) Le Destin on the west coast and Dorenhaag on Leguwan Island are beyond the limits of the map, as is Dr Munro's estate on the Berbice side just over Abary, though his name appears as proprietor of 'Foulis' above.

(3) There are two 'Hope's on the coast: the one JCC mentions is possibly that nearer Georgetown.

(4) Estate 23 (Haslenton) is likely to be JCC's 'Haslingdon', though 42, from the name of the proprietor, might also be a possibility.

(5) Kingston (Miss Doll's), Houston (just outside the town), Plaisance, Sarah Johanna (20 miles upriver) and proprietor Chester or Chichester at Mahaica do not appear on Wilkinson's map. Nor does Enmore (between Hope and Beter Verwagting), though it could be estate 37 (proprietor Marchand) which is not named; other possibilities, 40 Nog Eens [Now One] (Rogier) or 43 De Eendragt [Concord] (I Hamer).

(6) The pairing of Airy Hall with Dundee (neither are named on the source map) suggests a mis-spelling of Airlie; there is an Airlie Estate in the city, and Airlie Hall is connected with the University.

Plantation Le Destin

John Pattinson was urging his brother to send remittances in produce, especially good sugar, a paying article. So William thought he could do something with Schultz, who had some to dispose of: as before said, not of the best. They negociated by samples, and Pattinson was to return with Schultz to see the bulk and complete the purchase. It was a Sunday, and I was preparing for church; Pattinson had been prating over brandy and water the night before, and was in bed with an intense headache. Somebody must go, it was quite clear he could not: would I, as it was urgent. I hesitated – and yielded. Willingly? No, I felt I was wrong, but it was difficult to keep clear of business on the sabbath, the planters generally were an ungodly set, and wholly disregarded the feelings of those who had some respect for the Lord's day. I tried to reconcile my deference for an earthly master with my duty to my heavenly one, and was troubled.

Late afternoon, we arrived at the Essequibo, larger than the Demerara river but not so cultivated and with no town. We entered a narrow creek, so overgrown it was difficult to force the boat through. The buildings were weird. The dwelling house was a large old Dutch wooden mansion, left to hang together as best it might. In the centre the invariable great porch, carried up from the bottom of the house to the roof: on either side, ranges of unglazed windows with external wooden shutters, which creaked dismally in the wind, some hanging helplessly by one hinge. The exterior had once been faced with clapboards, but they were now hanging about all ways, on one nail or gone altogether, exposing the inner lining of deal boards. All was blackened by age and weather, dismal and desolate. The windmill, boiling and curing houses were in keeping. The creek we had come up was the usual canal which every estate had, but so overgrown as to be almost hid from sight. Past the buildings, it ran straight up to the cultivation, bordered by trees, and reflecting in its dark waters the dismal mansion, a picture of a grim and ghostly lodge in the wilderness.

We went through the porch up a creaking stair, and whew! out flew an immense flock of pigeons: 'They are Mistress Schultz's, they fly in and out as they please'. We came to a room off the landing, the whole interior in naked woodwork, just as the carpenters originally left it, never a brush of paint and deeply coloured into sombre brown or blackened by age. In this gloomy apartment sat a tall thin pallid aged woman in ghostly white attire well-suited to this haunted-looking abode. She gave the impression she might have sat there ever since the plantation was founded, but the courtesy of her greeting, and the presence of two or three Negro girls and a young lady, living beings of flesh and blood, dispelled the feeling of ghostliness. The dining hall, which occupied the entire right wing on the other side of the gloomy landing, appeared to receive an occasional scrub, and looked pretty clean and cheerful compared with the rest, assuring the guest that at Le Destin he had not parted with all tokens of civilized life. Schultz and I did justice to our repast, and he entertained me with anecdotes both of Holland and of the neighborhood. He was an active lively fellow, tall and slender, very unlike the popular idea of a thick phlegmatic Dutchman. As evening neared, two or three gentlemen appeared; Schultz introduced one as 'Monsieur Garaud, the little France man'. They sat and talked, smoked cigars, and drank gin and schnapps.

At length Mr Garaud took his leave, and said 'Come, I will give you relish for your supper'. Schultz thought he said radish, and we sallied forth. He said it was only a little way, but it seemed two or three miles to a solitary logie, the homestead of a worn-out wilderness coffee plantation. In reply to repeated knocks, an angry female voice desired us to be gone and Mr Garaud to come in quiet. Schultz called out 'Miss Minna, you must give us our radish', to no effect; 'So ve vil go and help ourselves: come little France man, show us vere your radish grow'. 'Grow?' cried the latter, 'I never say they do grow – Miss Minna say de fowl all gone to bed and no egg lef in de house!' 'Eggs? You did not promise us eggs!' 'Yes, eggs and ham, dat is what I mean by relish!' I nodded assent, but radish or relish, we got nothing but a long walk and a scolding.

At bedtime the Negro boys brought up hammocks, the common method of providing for guests on the plantations. As there were no inns or havens of call, a very slight acquaintance with the manager or proprietor was sufficient to ensure bed and board for the wayfarer. These hammocks were of strong white cotton fabric, of ample dimensions, and hung loosely so that both head and heels were highest ['hung in a bight'? See Vol. 1 p. 96.]. They served for bed, covering, and pillow, and had the benefit of coolness. The ample size admitted folding over at the opening, so whilst there was sufficient air circulation within, it pretty effectually excluded those nocturnal pests the mosquitoes. What a luxury to fall asleep hearing their fruitless efforts and defying them!

At daybreak we turned out and took a stroll up the canal in front, where all was growing in wild neglected luxuriance; what a contrast to the dreary old mansion. It appeared that Schultz only wanted to get all he could off the property, but would not lay out a farthing on its preservation. After breakfast he took me to the boiling house and shewed me the sugar I came down to look at. I had only to see that Pattinson's samples did not differ, and my errand was done. I thought as I looked round at the old rickety windmill and the dirty ill-kept apparatus for making the sugar and distilling the rum, no wonder his sugars were bad quality. Then we drove along the coast road, a good one throughout the entire colony, made of shell and shingle from the beach, which bound down into a surface almost as hard as granite; with no heavy traffic to cut it up, it always continued as firm as a gravel walk in a garden. We came to the dwelling of a Mr De Groot, whom Schultz wished to consult on some matter. What a difference from Le Destin! A large productive sugar estate run on the best principles, and a modern English house.

In the evening, Schultz proposed we should dance; a negro man fiddled, and to it we went, old lady and all, the dead alive! She fell to me as a partner, and there was such a ghastly and yet comical character about her movements, I scarcely knew whether to be shocked or amused [Hans Holbein's Dance of Death: JCC II]. However, she danced away, to my terror and amazement, who could scarce believe she was really of this world, and I had a dreamy apprehension I should be clasped in her cold ghostly embrace and borne away to regions even more dismal than Le Destin. This eventful evening terminated my visit, and next day I returned with Schultz to Georgetown. The bargain was closed, the sugar shipped home; and Pattinson received a good dressing from his brother for sending such a worthless specimen.

Sundry Things

I had lost sight of Hopkinson, as he had gone to live on his cotton plantations on the east coast, the John and Cove, which he was trying to improve. His philanthropic notions excited derisive scepticism in his manager, who predicted he would soon tire of getting work by reward and no whip; and he gave the reins back to the manager, reserving to himself some checks on punishment, being kind and humane. He himself afterwards confessed that his plans became 'plenty good ting for nigger man' and little to show for it, and he became disappointed. But he began at the wrong end, with no account of moral condition. I had long tried to get him to give us some of his cotton as freight, but never could prevail, as both he and Rogers [of Bachelors Adventure] were loyally true to a ship commanded by a friend of theirs. Pattinson was much disappointed and vexed at this, but Ben was not to be moved, and I let him alone.

A Bristol ship, *Fairby*, was this year burnt in the river. She had just completed loading, ready to sail next day. The steward went into the hold to draw off some spirits for the men, his light caught the vapour from the cask, and the whole was in a blaze in a moment. She was towed out of the harbour, outside the other shipping, and deluged with water, but too late, she was soon past all hope. Thousands of people came pouring down to see the sight. The Negro girls lamented as if she had been a human, 'Aye me poor ting, me railly pity um for true, poor Buckra [white man's] ship.' But the poor ship was soon ablaze fore and aft; as it was growing dark, the effect was awfully grand, a vast furnace of glowing fire gradually burnt to the water's edge, till in two or three hours a few blackened timbers were all that were left.

Returning after it was over, I came up with a coloured man thumping a girl of his own class, who appeared very young, most unmercifully. I told him he ought to be ashamed of himself to treat a female in that way; 'You go way and mind you own bisness' was the reply. 'I shall make it my business', I said, 'to go to the Fiscal and report your conduct.' 'You may go to de Devil, she's me own, and Fiscal do noting to me for lick me own nigger.' Too true; but I told him I would remember him, as there was still light from the burning ship. Singularly enough, this very man came into the store a few days after. I said, 'I remember you, and you may go about your business, I shall have nothing to do with you'. Off he went; whether I did good or harm may be doubtful, but at any rate I gave vent to my feelings. No ill usage short of severe injury or death came under the law, and an instance of the latter took place about this time. A severe flogging resulted in death of the slave, for which the master, a Dutchman, was tried and hanged at Georgetown. The wretch on the scaffold, so far from acknowledging his guilt and sin, declared publicly 'It was a ------ shame a man could not do as he liked with his own nigger without being hanged for it!'

The Vendue office was in the hands of the home Government, let out to a sub-agent. All must avail themselves of it who desired to auction any property, estates, goods, Negroes, cattle, etc, no private auctions were allowed. We frequently required the auctioneer's services to knock off consignments of goods for us when they hung on hand too long and we required to wind them up and turn them at once into money. A Vendue at your store (or as the Negroes called it, a bandue) was troublesome to manage, as it was open to all comers, and we had to arrange that nothing but what was to be sold should be forthcoming, and not even that till the auctioneer took it in hand. Then all the coloured ladies of business came flocking in to make bargains, and it was the custom to have lots of ham sandwiches and 'Sangaree' (strong wine with brandy and nutmeg [Spanish sangria]) to put them in good humour and make them bid with spirit.

A ship arrived from Quebec with a cargo of horses, not unusual from Canada. Tom Johnson, Pattinson's fast friend, knew something of the man in charge of them, one Levy, and got him to consign himself to us for bed and board. Pattinson undertook to help him sell the horses, which I think went mostly through the Vendue office. I do not recollect what we got out of the transaction, but certainly a good deal of trouble and a good deal of empty prate. The best thing was a stout roan cob which Pattinson bought, which proved a very useful beast either for riding or driving, and to my relief he got rid of the skittish nag which ran away with me on the east coast.

Mr Bueno (2)

The time was drawing near for the arrival of *Eleanor* (which Pattinson invariably called *Allenor*). At last one Sunday morning, I had the news, 'She's come in, and Bueno is in her': not very welcome on the sabbath, as I knew all would be hubbub. Sure enough, he and many others were in our dining hall to get their letters. Before the mail steamers, every merchant ship of any note carried a letter bag, and the merchant consignees were expected to extract all letters for friends before the Captain sent the bag to the post office. Mr Bueno was, as I expected, an uncommon swell. Spanish-looking, black hair, of low stature, every inch was made the most of. He was sweltering in full European costume, such as a dandy would have had, ridiculously heavy for a tropical climate. He greeted us with a patronizing air of familiarity, and was very pretentious and knowing. I soon saw he would eventually 'snuff himself out', as he was so uncommonly fast, and I knew Pattinson was not in the best humour with him.

Captain Young of *Eleanor* was quite as pretentious in his way, hulking, broad-shouldered, unmistakably Scotch, boisterously and vulgarly defiant of all English opinions, and contemptuous of all south of the Tweed. During dinner and the rest of the day, he and Bueno kept up the talk, one about John Pattinson and their doings at Liverpool, the other about 'My Ship' and her doings under his charge. With the addition in the evening of Levy about his 'hosses, this here and that there', Tom Johnson, and another captain whom Young knew, there was anything but sabbath observance, so John and I got away to chapel.

We had Bueno's company in the counting-house, where he was a hindrance rather than a help. He cut a great swell amongst the customers, in his Liverpool toggery. How he had contrived to get so many things puzzled our simple minds, who thought one Sunday coat quite sufficient in addition to our ordinary nankeen or drill: who had paid, or was to pay, for them, was another problem. Pattinson was now lodging again up town with his Airey Hall friends, where a little boy had been presented to him as his son. Captain Young was asked to stand *Godfather*! for the little stranger, and *I* to be the other; which I refused, but was overpersuaded, as the christening was to be at the Scotch church, where no questions would be asked nor vows required, as they do not recognize such things. Capt. Young would have nothing to do with the English church, which he declared to be 'nothing but Puppery', and the compromise was fixed on; so having nothing to answer for, I did not object.

Bueno had Pattinson's bedroom, where he strewed his fine cloathes in all directions, very soon abandoning them to a cooler less imposing costume. He was full of John Pattinson, whom he had impressed with the feeling that William was mismanaging the business and required someone equal in authority to keep him right: that of course being Mr Bueno, who was to advise JP of all his brother's proceedings. He said that JP would soon order his brother home, when of course the business would be under his charge, and added 'Of course Cheveley won't object to that, and I have no doubt we shall get on very well together.' To this impertinence I merely replied that we must wait until the time came and we should see, while John looked at him with an expression 'What next?' We both said the Miss McMaster affair was behind it all. However, William was quite ignorant of all this, and it was evident that nothing had passed between him and his brother about Mr Bueno's position and prospects. He set him to hunt up freight for Eleanor; Mr Bueno became very busy and important, and found he must have a poney to carry him about. He was out all day, but with what result I could not discover. A month or two went on in this way.

I was not at all comfortable after Mr Bueno's arrival. He was assuming and noisy, and his vague and rash way of doing things was not what I liked. He treated the Negro boys cruelly, and we nearly got into collision when I interfered. He bragged about John Pattinson, whom he kept advised of his brother's proceedings with a vengeance, for he wrote a long letter setting forth all the peccadilloes he could rake together from every source: squandering the property; wild speculations, schooner *Friendship* amongst others; the cattle affair; and bad management in every department. He read it to John Chapman and me, and we told him that if he sent it, he might make up his mind to bid goodbye. 'Oh, you'll see something very different to that'; however, we felt pretty sure he had, both in matter and manner, quite overdone it, and waited the event.

Meanwhile Bueno had written to his lady love, and wondered why he had no answer; when lo! a lumber-laden brig appeared from St Andrews, with not only Captain Alan Mc Master, but his brother Angus – and Elizabeth herself! – come no doubt to see for themselves about him and his position. He dangled after them day after day, and helped the young men with their business, but beyond that clearly 'no go', the lady had changed her mind. Pattinson when appealed to gave no encouragement, the letter to John Pattinson had not had its effect at present; here was an end of his matrimonial adventure. The brig sailed and left Mr Bueno to mourn his hard fate. To get rid of him, Pattinson agreed to his idea to take a cargo of salt fish, which hung on our hands, to the Leeward Islands. He was away many weeks, but it did not pay.

At length, letters from Liverpool. Pattinson went upstairs to read his. Bueno was in a state of expectation, as no doubt an answer had come from John – so it had, but such as he had not dreamt of. He was summoned upstairs, loud angry voices were heard for some time, and at length down came Bueno, mortification and resentment mingled: 'John Pattinson has behaved like a traitor and I am dismissed!' Then bravado: 'The little humbug! What do I care for him?' It appeared that John had found Bueno's hash-up of high crimes and misdemeanors rather too strong for his digestion; he had sent the letter for his brother's perusal, which of course caused the explosion which blew Mr Bueno up, and instead of hoisting him into WP's birth, sent him to look for one for himself. After this, the sooner he was out the better, as WP was furious at his treason; John and I were already well aware of it, but of course did not betray it when he gave us the letter to read. Bueno left the colony soon after, and I never heard of him again.

Change of House, Change of Status

Our Kingston dwelling was inconveniently distant from the business part of the town, besides being too confined. So Pattinson let it and took some capital premises higher up town, where we had the advantage of a larger dwelling, extensive storage, a large platform and stelling, and the great convenience of being close to the right side. They were quite new, having been recently erected by one

Robert Arnott, a 'douce canny' Scot, who had long cast in his lot with Miss Norah Leeds, who carried on the invariable huckster's store in premises next door. However, our removal added considerably to our rent and expenses, and to my surprise and dislike to our family also, as I found Pattinson intended to transfer hither his Airey Hall establishment, consisting of Miss Susan Morris, the lately-arrived son, and a negress girl. It was understood, however, that they would keep entirely to one set of apartments and that I was not to be intruded on.

George came out again in *Cornwall* as second mate, but was dissatisfied at his third voyage with no promotion. He was moreover exceedingly disgusted with the conduct of one of Messrs Gladstone's other captains, a thorough ignorant Liverpool 'skipper'. He had applied to *Cornwall's* captain for some hands to assist him on some emergency; George was away with the boat, and on his way back, this man hailed him and told him to bring his hands on board. George said he must go to his own ship first, to report himself and get fresh orders, his proper course. Being then ordered to go to the other ship, he did so, when this captain abused him at such a rate, that George ordered the boat back to his own ship; whilst the captain went ashore to report to the agent, who came off with George's own captain. George defended himself, but was treated with contempt by these enlightened commanders. George replied that he was painfully aware he was no longer in the EICo service, but whether or not, he could not understand how it could be thought proper to obey orders from the Captain of another ship without referring to his own, or how he could be expected to submit to such gross insult and abuse as he had received. The agent took George aside, telling him he must not allow his feelings as a gentleman to make him forget his present position, &c, &c, a most unsatisfactory way of putting it. It left on George's mind a rankling feeling of gross injustice, which made him indifferent to remain in the employ, and soon after, a chance arose for him to quit.

Whether John Pattinson had really authorized Bueno to write about his brother I never knew; if he did, the letter was either so strong as to arouse suspicion, or he wished to give his brother a chance to vindicate himself. However, his eyes were directed to the necessity of a change on our side, and about the beginning of 1823, William expressed to me his own and John's wish that I become a partner. This required considerable deliberation. My first view was that it would not do, and I had better work out my three years as originally engaged. WP urged it on me, and said his brother would be disappointed; I could not very well explain my ground, viz. the embarrassment into which he had got the Demerara concern. He anticipated me, saying that though business in Demerara was not very satisfactory, the outturn at home was quite so, or his brother would not have made the proposal; and moreover, the new firm should not be involved in any way with the old one. However, we agreed to suspend it until his brother wrote to me.

This letter laid the proposal before me in very flattering terms, and informed me that having bought a small brig, *Anna* (an old concern of less than 200 tons which he had coopered up), he had out of regard for me offered the command to my brother George. He hoped the partnership would fall in with my ideas, as he was not satisfied with the conduct of the business in Demerara, hinting that his brother was overdone and wanted someone on an equal footing as his co-adjutor. He was pleased to say that from my ability and steady attention, I had quite borne out the character my friends had given me, and which his brother had fully corroborated.

A grandiloquent letter from George acquainted me of his appointment. He was evidently quite up in the clouds, deprecated the possibility of my refusing so advantageous a proposal, and seemed to think I should be as cock-a-doodleish about it as he was about *Anna*. Another surprise was that Henry was coming with him as mate! Mr and Mrs Driffield had proposed he join his brother, as being more suitable for a spirited active young man than serving in a grocer's shop (he had by this time left Bocking and got to Mildenhall, where he exceedingly disliked his position), and most gladly did he take this chance to escape like a bird from a cage.

How did I feel? Anything but pleasant. I had written to the Driffields expressing dislike of the place I was in and of its habits and society, and they feared that under this somewhat morbid state of my mind, I might be induced to refuse the partnership. I had still great misgivings about it; and as to George, I did not consider his command any compensation for leaving Gladstone's, where he was certain to have got on in time with steadiness and patience. Mr Driffield thought it all right, however. In truth I was in a dilemma! Prudence said keep out of it and stick to the three years. But the Pattinsons, George, and the Driffields, all working in different ways, decided me at length to give in. First, the hope that I might by care give a turn to the business and retrieve past errors; second, I had an obligation to shew the friends who had done so much for me that I was not unworthy. So I signed long and elaborate articles of copartnership, and the public were acquainted by advertisements and circulars that J. & W. Pattinson was now Pattinson Cheveley & Co. Thus began a new state of things, and with it new troubles and cares.

The Partnership Begins

John Chapman had been thinking of a change, to do something on his own account, and left us shortly after. He had told Pattinson that although we had been very good friends as clerks, he did not think we should now get on with our differing business views; as he had the spirit of scheming and speculating, and I none, I concurred in his departure with less reluctance than otherwise. We engaged as bookkeeper in his place Mr Gillis Brotherston, and a Scotch lad Alexander Tait, whose tact and shrewdness was exceedingly useful for our outdoor work. Also, John Pattinson sent us a youth William Collard, who had been giving some trouble at home, and to solve the problem was sent to *help us*! He proved most refractory, doing what he ought not, and doing nothing he was told, so we got him into a retail store, and after that he went on an estate as an overseer. Eventually he died of dysentery because he would eat everything the doctor forbid him, and actually lost his life through his own dogged obstinacy.

Eleanor returned with a young man Henry Fox, who became a hanger-on; he was active and industrious, and remained with us for a time. About this time, Charles wrote to beg that he might come out to me, as he was exceedingly uncomfortable at the County Fire Office. What could he be thinking of? Though I would gladly have changed places, I entreated him never to think of it, but stay where he was.

We were pretty busy, and at length *Anna* arrived, with Captain George, looking the commander, and Mate Harry. The pilot anchored just below our stelling, and George walked into the store with the air of a man who felt he had the dignity of his office to uphold, meeting Pattinson somewhat after that fashion, who received him somewhat differently. I was exceedingly anxious for George in his new position, that he should not by pretension draw on himself dislike or contempt by those ready enough to despise him, and I greatly dreaded anything which might call in question his professional ability. Judge my surprise and mortification next morning when not a vestige of *Anna* was to be seen! She had dragged her anchors and drifted with the tide in the night: there she lay about two miles below, at the river mouth in a very awkward position; fortunately the springs were rising, or she might have lain a month on the edge of a bank. George laid the blame on the pilot, but he said the Captain ought to have seen to it that the ship was properly moored.

To my intense chagrin, George got the blame [quite rightly so, really!]. It was mortifying for two or three days to hear observations about the bungling way that brig had been brought in, so I was relieved when she came up river. I soon heard Pattinson yelping 'You'll get her aground, &c &c', and George exhorting him in no gentle terms to mind his own business. In he came in sad perturbation, but I told him I was hurt that any difference should have arisen, and I exhorted him to follow my example and not interfere with George in his nautical duties, of which every a sailor was very jealous, and he must not conclude that George was careless or untrustworthy. So the brig was secure and peace restored, but this little fracas stuck in the mind for some time after.

Where we have expected an addition to our comfort, circumstances may make it the very reverse: such was George's arrival. Easily elated, he was quite disposed to play 'The Commander', Pattinson equally the big merchant, and I found an ill-feeling springing up which promised anything but harmony between them. Both he and Harry were highly excited by their indignities, so I left them to cool down, pointing out that the safety of the ship was a great pecuniary object to those on shore. Also, George was carrying

– and Business

Pattinson was beginning to feel the effects of his *Friendship* folly. Mr Paterson, being in possession of schooner, cargoes and all, had nine points of the law on his side; endless was Pattinson's litigation and the lawyer's long bills, besides the loss incurred and the liability of taking, as cargo for the adventure, goods entrusted to him. As soon as I got the reins more in my hands, I insisted that all this be confined to the old firm and not saddled on the new one, as expressly stipulated in our articles of copartnership. I had many battles and gave offence to many of his hangers-on, but I knew his brother now looked to me not to make ducks and drakes of people with whose goods we were entrusted. I began to fear that circumstances at home were not in an easy state, despite what William assured me. I began to feel new anxieties awakened by new responsibilities and new liabilities whose issue I could not see. I had inferred that when I became a partner, John Pattinson would extend his operations at once, but a somewhat dreary pause ensued. We heard that a ship was coming out, which looked like a beginning, but the same mail brought news that John had been ill and did not seem to be recovering strength.

We debated if one of us should go home to Liverpool for a time to assist him for an increase of business. William had got so involved in law matters that he could not absent himself, and I therefore seemed to be the right person. Meanwhile, a ship we had been expecting arrived, but to our annoyance was reported to have smallpox on board, and was ordered off into quarantine; this means in its full extent, forty days to purify before any communication with the shore, other than by the officer of the Board of Health, is allowed. This was a sad disappointment, as there were goods on board of which we might lose the sale. I therefore called on the Governor, General Murray, and represented to him all our hardships, as there was no actual case of smallpox then aboard, and the one man who had had it was getting well. But he would hear of no relaxation of the rules: in which he was quite right, and we had to wait.

It was determined I should go to Liverpool forthwith, and William partly engaged my passage on a ship soon to sail, when an event postponed my departure, and I feared would put an end to it, if it did not put an end to me. We come to a period which called forth such a demonstration of the horrors of slavery and of its sure and necessary attendant cruelty as will serve to show its odious character better than any other illustration which I can give: the Negro insurrection of August 1823.

PART 11

Interval, 1823

Insurrection

Public feeling on the slave question did not subside; every mail brought accounts of projected alterations by the home Government. Early in the year, the friends of the Negroes at home procured a resolution [proposed by Fowell Buxton, passed by the House of Commons May 15th, and given teeth by Home Secretary George Canning] for the amelioration of their condition in the West Indies and having in prospect their progressive moral improvement, and preparation thereby for participation in the rights and privileges of other classes of His Majesty's subjects. The Secretary of State for the Colonies, Lord Bathurst, was pronounced a traitor to his trust, or an imbecile, for he *of course* ought to have prevented certain measures. As to William Wilberforce, nothing could exceed his *wickedness* in attempting to ruin the Colonies.

An Order in Council arrived in Demerara July 7th 1823, laying down that the hours of daily labour would be reduced to 9, and that flogging of females was to be at once and for ever abolished. This put Governor Murray in a fright and the planters in a fury; they refused to obey, and he weakly yielded. They resolved to suppress the intelligence, and things were kept as usual for seven weeks, besides which, believing that religion put mischief into the slaves' heads, it was ordered that no Negro should go to a place of worship without leave of his master, which was often refused.

The Negroes got wind through a servant of the Governor's, who heard the talk going on at his table, until by and bye a report, that an order had come from the King of England for their freedom, spread like wildfire through the East Coast estates as far as Mahaica – 'Free paper come and Buckra man keep it away from we', and produced a universal determination to work no longer, to seize the managers, overseers and white people on the Estates, put them into the stocks (in which it was the custom to confine refractory Negroes), then to proceed to Georgetown and claim their freedom. They seized weapons, confined all the white people, and compelled a small body of troops to retire; in the skirmish, two white overseers were killed, and three wounded. This was the extent of the injury the white people suffered beyond excessive fright, supposing that the Negroes having got the upper hand and death was certain!

At length, on Monday August 18th 1823, the Governor went up the coast with some militia to tell the Negroes, what he ought to have done at first, the real nature of the home orders, but they were too full of ideas of freedom to hear a word. While he was parleying at Le Resouvenir, one of the Negroes, it was said, fired his musket at him, which sent the Governor off post-haste to despatch all the regular troops he could muster; and he issued a proclamation declaring the colony under martial law.

The Rifles Ordered Up
At about 10 o'clock that same night, I was roused by a bugle calling us to muster: we were ordered to march instanter against the Negroes, who were in rebellion. 'A pretty piece of business', I thought, 'to be called out for the chance of having my throat cut by these semi-savages'. Inclination said 'Keep where you are'; Prudence 'Mind, or you may be in trouble for skulking'; and Pride, 'What, play the coward's part, it is not to be thought of'. All this ran through my mind in less time than I can tell as I buckled on my armour.

I was soon jogging along with the second detachment of the troop to the East Coast. No-one seemed to know exactly what was the matter or the length of our march: the affair had been kept very snug for fear of exciting the Negroes in town and on the west coast, where all was tranquil. On we marched in gloomy silence, an occasional order in an undertone, keeping a sharp look out. The croaking of the frogs, the chirping of the crickets, and the flashing of the fireflies were scarcely noticed, so much were we all occupied with what was to come next.

We progressed about four miles, then a halt – a Negro recently shot dead, evidence of something serious. 'Keep a good look out and don't fire without orders', and on we went. Two or three miles further, at the entrance to the large sugar estate of Van Cootens, a Dutch planter, we saw on the bridge a Negro with a musket and bayonet who called to us to stop. Two of our men had him by the collar; he protested that he had been sent by 'Buckra massa at big house to tell us come up to all the rest of the soldier'. We intimated "pose he tell lie get bullet in he head'. The plantation, Vrijheids Lust, lay about half a mile off in the interior – and truly it was not the most pleasant walk, for having understood at Plaisance, a plantation a little below, that the Negroes were in great force, we had little faith in our guide and suspected he was employing a ruse. However, we found the main body of our Corps there, and the Negroes of the estate, though excited, quite peacefully disposed. Here we remained till break of day. At other plantations we found the Negroes had all ceased work and retired to the back of the estates without committing any excesses.

We hurried forward, being anxious to join the Regular troops, soon came up with them, and thus united (we were about 150), numbered altogether about 400 or 500. They were headed by Colonel Leahy, whom we found quite disposed to exercise the privileges conferred on him by martial law; the first thing he did was to blow up our Commander, Captain Croal, for not preserving better discipline, avowing with an oath his determination to hang the first offender on the nearest tree, which his whole aspect seemed to bespeak him quite capable of carrying into effect. We found him a terrible old tyrant, but (as Lancashire people say) we were *like* to submit, having no alternative but to follow him and his redcoats.

We understood that the Negroes of Chateau Margo and Beter Verwagting estates were off with whatever arms they could lay hold of, and were at Bachelors Adventure, a few miles farther on. The old Colonel went on to reconnoitre, and left us at Chateau Margo to await orders. The manager and the three overseers had been put in the stocks, to the infinite diversion of the Negro women, whom the manager had treated with great severity, and who now took it out of him by saluting him with a not very gentle slap on the face. A sly old negro who had been in the habit of very frequently going sick, for which the manager gave him a copious dose of Glauber's salts every morning, thought this no bad opportunity to pay him off in his own coin, so he presented the manager (who eyed it with anything but delight) with the dose that would have been his morning potation, 'Here Massa, something for do you good' – to which the manager dissented. 'Drink um arl up Massa, 'pose he good for me, he berry good for Massa Buckra, so drink um up 'rectly I say.' Non-compliance was out of the question, so down went the dose – The old 'daddy' was satisfied with his revenge on the manager, who was trembling in anticipation of much worse treatment.

The old proprietor, Lachlan Cumming (who was a regular old Turk), was in an awful temper, having got his nose broken in a scuffle. His newly-arrived friends, who penetrated his dining-room to shelter from the sun, he must have found rather more troublesome than his recently-departed foes, as being excessively thirsty we availed ourselves, without scruple, of his drinkables. Not until late afternoon did we resume our march, leaving matters at Chateau Margo not much more comfortable than we had found them. The proprietor of Beter Verwagting, my friend Baron Von Grovertins [or Grovestins] (who was also agent for La Bonne Intention), cautioned us to keep a sharp lookout, 'as the Negroes were doing all sorts of dreadful things', and urged me to take care of myself, though I did not see how I was to go about it.

We marched gloomily on till night overtook us. We came suddenly on a bivouack of Negroes, and were ordered to fire. Some were killed, the others scampered off, and we moved on in quick time, firing at intervals. We were getting into the thick of it, as through the darkness we could discern Negro heads over the cotton trees. Women and children begged for mercy: 'Oh massa, 'pare arl we, we no want for harm Buckra massa for true, 'pare we pick'ny!' 'Go and tell your men to go to work, then' was the reply.

The Battle of Bachelor's Adventure
We came to Bachelor's Adventure, where all was confusion and terror. The old Manager Mr John Grant and his co-partner Mr Hugh Rogers (who were not distinguished by particularly severe treatment of the Negroes) and the overseers had been in the stocks; the terror of his position had caused old Grant to lose his reason. A few of the

domestic Negroes had released them, and they were preparing to escape, but they knew not whither; our timely arrival however changed affairs. Here it appeared was the focus of the movement, where we must make a stand if we meant to crush it.

As day dawned, the real state of things became apparent: the scene was not pleasant. We were hemmed in between two large bodies of insurgents, continually reinforced by fresh arrivals until the road looked blackened either way; there could not have been fewer than 3 or 4,000, all armed in some way, many with muskets or cane knives fastened on poles. Everyone felt the crisis had arrived which was to decide who should be masters. The Negroes, shouting defiance, advanced as if about to attack, but halted, leaving about 100 yards clear. Our officers rode out with a flag of truce for a parley with the ringleaders. Asked what they wanted, they said 'Massa treat arl we too bad, make we work Sundays, no let we go Chapel, no give time for work in we garden, lick arl we too much. We hear for true Great Buckra (the King) give we free, and Massa no let we hab nothing.' To all this, the Colonel would make no reply unless they would lay down their arms and go to work: which they refused to do.

After an hour for deliberation, they still remained obstinate, and some of the fiercest called out 'Catch de big buckra, tie um!': when the officers galloped back and ordered the troops to attack instanter. Behold us then on the point of battle in right earnest! Whatever my abhorrence of slavery, I felt I was justified in defending my own life and those of others in peril. The Negroes had drawn up in closer order, shouting defiance. 'Right face, march!' and out we went, Regulars to the right, Rifles the left. 'Quick march! ... Halt! Ready, present! You Negroes, I ask you once more, will you lay down your arms and go to work?' 'No, no, we fight for we freedom!' 'Fire!' was the word, and a volley poured in from the front, repeated by the reserve; the Negroes returned fire with their muskets, but it was all they could do, they soon fell into confusion for want of method, and as the regulars poured in volley after volley, they began to run, leaping the ditches, where many tumbled lifeless, into the cotton fields, where the great body quickly vanished. As their heads appeared above the trees, the Rifles picked off considerable numbers, much to Leahy's satisfaction, who shouted 'Well done, Rifles!' However, there was surely no great cause for glory over a victory so easily obtained.

For my own part, I fired but one shot the whole time. I had been taken in by my rifle, which I had recently purchased it for its lightness, but it was good for nothing, as I found the night before that it missed fire. Our Captain Croal had ridden up to see what was the matter, and I thought I had satisfied him that the blame lay with my gun and not with myself, as feeling it a matter of life and death, I had no scruple about shooting in self-defence. I found afterwards that this circumstance was stored up against me.

We Move On

We retreated to the buildings, to go to the relief of plantations higher up the coast, taking with us all who feared to stay, amongst them, carried in a hammock, poor Mrs Rogers, who had just left her bed after being confined. No sooner had we departed than the defeated Negroes rushed in and set one building on fire; and finding the trumpeter of the Regulars, who had got hold of some rum and rendered himself incapable, and was accidentally left behind, they put him to death. The roadside presented a dismal sight of dead bodies strewed about; around 200 fell, whilst not a single soldier, except the trumpeter, was injured.

By this time, it was about noon, and we marched under a burning sun, half-dead with fatigue and thirst, having had little or no rest for two nights and days, to Mahaica village, five or six miles further, stopping on the way at Narbacle's, a large cotton estate. This was next to John and Cove, two united cotton plantations belonging to my friend Hopkinson: where we found him and his managers in the stocks, the climax of his schemes for the improvement of his estate and Negroes – singularly, almost on the very day we had landed two years before. In the afternoon we rested at Plantation Lancaster in a large logie, in one corner of which a swarm of marabuntas or colony wasps were constructing a nest, fortunately without molesting us. Here we found two wounded overseers, one with two balls in his wrist, which was dreadfully inflamed. Our surgeon Mr Miller said it must come off, but he had left his instruments behind, and ran about

ship seemed to be keeping on course by the cabin compass, but Buchanan would not be comforted. At last, down came Jones as merry as possible. 'What has been the matter, are we going ashore?' 'Yes, tomorrow I hope.' 'Is there no danger?' 'Danger? No, the stupid fellow at the helm yawed her about, that's all.' We felt that it was not quite all, and Jones had 'hugged the land' rather too close and did not choose to own it.

Glasgow to Liverpool

We had for some days been positively enjoying the feeling of cold, to which we had long been strangers, and seeing our breath. This morning it was blowing a keen north-wester, we felt the cold in right earnest and were glad to load on all the warm things we could muster. We dashed two or three miles through the Rachlin [Rathlin] Island channel off the Antrim coast, safe only with a fair wind, which brought the Giant's Causeway in view. Then the great bluff of the Mull of Cantire [Kintyre], little Pladda, Arran, and Bute; and we finally arrived at Port Glasgow about two in the afternoon. The passengers went up to Glasgow in a river steamer, the first I had ever been in

Next day, Sunday, Buchanan invited me to go with him to see his uncle. After church, we went to the house of Dr Rainey, a brother of the one in Demerara, and I had to give all the news I had about the insurrection. We rambled about on Monday to see the city, then in transition from Auld Toun to new, and on Tuesday, Buchanan accompanied me to Port Glasgow and left me with Captain Jones. The steamer left Greenock for Liverpool on Wednesday morning. The Duke of Athol and his family were going to his seat Mona Castle in the Isle of Man, and had taken the entire ladies' cabin for their own use, which drove the ladies into the general saloon, so the gentlemen consequently had to fare as best they might. The weather being fine, they were mostly on deck, and many of the ladies. Everybody was talking about the insurrection, interested to hear all particulars, and I found myself famous! I was taken to speak with 'The Duke', and returned cautious answers to his questions; at length he dismissed me, with the cheering observation 'It must be a wretched place to live if they all look as badly as you' – truly I was so thinned by exertion and thoroughly bronzed by the sun that I do not suppose I was a very good specimen.

During the day I met an invalid-looking man, no other than Mr I.D. Paterson of the *Friendship* affair, which had exploded friendships and all into litigation. I had felt so annoyed about it that I did not feel disposed to recognize him, but he accosted me, and I found him sober and sensible, not at all cantankerous. He convinced me that there was much on his side, and that Pattinson had been led into consummate folly by a man whose advice he should never have followed.

About 3 o'clock next day, we arrived in Liverpool. John Pattinson was waiting for me with a cab; he was in a thick greatcoat, and had an unhealthy hectic colour in his cheeks. He had removed to Anfield Lodge in the Breck Road beyond Everton, about 2 miles out, where I found Mrs Pattinson, her sister Miss Barry, and the five children, one added since I had been away. They had also an old lady, Mrs Pritchard, whom Mr Pattinson kept to look after the children; she was unlettered, and made sad havoc with the King's English [My old Nurse – JCC II]. There was also another friend of Miss Barry's, Miss Dora Dennison, a sweet good young creature in delicate health [I was a great favourite of hers as a little boy – JCC II]. I had again to go through Demerara affairs for their edification.

Mr Pattinson greatly blamed his brother for his proceedings, which had led people to suppose he had sent him out to Demerara to swindle people, and which had greatly affected his health. I said I had always thought his affairs at home were all right – 'Why, did he not tell you about my difficulties when he proposed the partnership?' 'Not one word, the contrary.' 'Then he deceived you, and now if you wish to withdraw you are at liberty to do so.' He said he had two vessels chartered, and if I could assure him that all future consignments would be sold in reasonable time and punctually remitted by shipments of produce, he could still supply us with plenty of business. But neither he nor anyone would rely on his brother. At once I told him I would continue to act, as I did not wish to desert the concern at this stage, although I felt I had not been candidly dealt with. I found my stay in England would be short, as he wished me to return on one of his ships, *William Wise*, to sail early in November.

The Sunday following, being anxious to pass the day at the Vicarage, John Pattinson lent me his horse, which proved such a slug that I was as long on the road as if I had walked, and I had ignominiously to enter Prescot Church sometime after the service had begun. I found the company generally, including Mr Driffield, believed that the missionaries were the authors of the mischief, inspired by the anti-slavery party at home. We had all yet to learn the truth, and to see how fearfully the pro-slavery feeling turned with savage unreason, irresistible in the West India colonies, on all who dared to think differently. I went with Miss Barry to a meeting about West African Missions, where the Rev Ambrose Dawson was speaking. I was very glad he desisted from asking me to give some account of the insurrection, for with all my care I had enough to answer for when I returned to the colony. Mrs Driffield was anxious about George, whose religious feeling had been severely tested by the thorough negative Sarah Rix had given his proposals, which had deeply affected him. He had now been sent with *Anna* to Jamaica, Harry again with him as mate. I had in Demerara noted his unsettled mind, and I left a letter for him with Miss Barry.

Last Exit from Essex
Towards the end of the week I started for London, outside the coach all night and nearly the whole day, rather a serious undertaking at the end of October for a man just come from the broiling sun. Charles, then at the County Fire Office in Regent Street, met me and took me to Birchin Lane, my old quarters [where I was for some years as accountant to Lloyds underwriters – JCC II]. It was almost deserted: the old folks away, Sophy married to Dr Fellowes, Harriet also married to Mr Leffler, but my old friend John there still. In the evening Charles and I went to Clapham, where we were to sleep at Ivy Cottage on the Common, the residence of Miss Rix and her grandmother Mrs Dowson.

Next day, I reached Castle Hedingham just before dark – a treat to hear the Essex whine! 'Wer, yaiou do look wuther beaten that yaiou do! That must be hot surelye where yaiou've bin!' Tom had come over from Colchester, grown into a man, Tish into a goodly young woman, Madge (aged 19) settled into a spinster; my father looking jolly, and happy to have me amongst them again, and my poor dear mother, given up to the delight of the moment. It was a pleasurable yet painful time, as my days there were numbered, for I had only five or six to spare, and I must soon change this scene of earliest associations for a far distant one, so different – almost more than I could bear. Yet I felt that my path was that of duty, and when Father asked me if I felt it necessary to return, my 'Yes' was unhesitating. Tom kept us up with his humour, and the girls played and sang. Monday and Tuesday went over; on Wednesday, Mrs Burleigh, recently become a widow, asked us for the evening, to take our thoughts off the following day; she sent for her little boy Laurence, about 7 years old, from school, as he had been a favourite of mine.

Next morning, black Thursday, was black indeed, pouring rain. Grave faces at breakfast, trying to assume an appearance decidedly not felt. My warm-hearted father said, 'I saw you in the night as I lay awake, just as you were when you were my right hand', and then described how I went about some of the domestic offices. This was too much, and we all burst simultaneously into tears. Departure time came, I tore myself away. I think I slept at Birchin Lane, starting next day at 2 o'clock by the Royal Umpire for Liverpool, outside as before. It was a rough day, raining and blowing fearfully. I weathered it wrapped up in a plaid cloak, and with an umbrella kept tolerably dry at other people's expense – generally, if you managed with adroit selfishness, your neighbors got all your drippings as well as their own. We reached Stony Stratford, about 50 miles, towards nightfall. There we found the river so swollen that the Mail had been overturned. We were detained many hours at the inn before we could resume, and then we had to plunge through flood, water up to the coach doors; sure enough, there was the mail coach floating about. This rough cold wet journey was a curious contrast to my march up the Demerara coast, and equally to the present convenient and comfortable system of railway travelling, not then projected. We did not get to Prescot till 1 o'clock Sunday morning.

Return to the Colony

William Wise was nearly ready for sea, but the wind did not permit; day after day went on, but I could not stir out of Liverpool. During the day I was engaged with Mr Pattinson, and returned with him to Anfield Lodge. The evenings were generally passed with Miss Barry at the piano, playing and singing some of the newest songs: 'Home Sweet Home', then just come out, 'The Banks of Allan Water', 'Those Evening Bells', and many others, which seemed to fix themselves extraordinarily in my memory. Probably more heart work was going on between singer and listener than either were aware of at the time.

Mrs Pattinson had very strong prejudices and passions. She execrated William, who she declared had ruined his brother in health and pocket, and equally unsparing in her commendation of me, who was to be the restorer; so she talked him down and me up, and took all my linen in hand to prepare for the voyage. It struck me that I might come in turn to be execrated if I did not meet her standard of duty or failed to save the sinking ship. She was always going on about or at her sister, harping on her idleness in not going out to earn her living; I had a hint that she considered herself wronged by her mother having left property to her sister which she ought to have had. They were half-sisters, with different fathers.

Sunday came. I deliberated about accompanying Miss Barry to church, but thought better of it, and it was well I did, as a message came to say that the ship was taking a steamer to tow her out of the river, after which the wind would suit. So we hurried down to the docks, and I took leave of Mr Pattinson.

William Wise was a regular North Country craft from Cumberland, where a successful tradesman invests his savings in building a ship, and shares responsibilities and profits, if there are any, with sundry minor adventurers in 64th parts. Many of these vessels might thus have a dozen or score of shareholders and part owners. When *William Wise* was built, the owner, who had given the ship his own name, wished that his wife should take a look at her. Mrs Wise had understood that her husband's likeness graced the stem as a 'figurehead', and she was on the lookout for it. Walking round, they came under the bows, from which a strong timber projects on each side, to which the anchor is hoisted; on the butt end is carved the grinning face of a cat or tiger, which has given them the name of the 'cat-heads'. The first thing which caught the lady's eye was one of these grinning faces – in amazement, and to Bill's indignation, she exclaimed 'Why that never can be our Bill, sure!'

Very soon I found myself off the Black Rock, watching the receding town of Liverpool and Everton church on the hill, which I could long discern over the low land at Hoylake. We cast off the steamer and pilot, and I was again expatriated. The Captain gave me his own state room for a sleeping cabin; the weather was rough and stormy, and I had to keep below the first few days, where the unsavoury smells and the other accompaniments of a small vessel knocked about in the Irish Sea added physical disorder to mental uneasiness. So, in November 1823, I was on my way to the colony from which I had had a short respite, with no very pleasurable anticipations. The passage occupied a month, and we made Demerara the beginning of December.

I found Captain Winder of *William Wise* difficult to deal with. As with his father-in-law, the owner, self-interest was his predominant principle, and he appeared to care for no-one but as to how he might turn him to some account. With such a man I could have no opinion in common, and on the voyage I had given myself up to the company of my religious books. At sea he had it all his own way, and we got on very well; on shore I wanted my way, in opposition to his. The first thing he proposed was that Messrs Murray Brothers & Co, to whom he had formerly been consigned, wanted him for the homeward voyage and we should give up the ship; which as she was chartered out and home by Mr Pattinson, I told him could not be thought of, especially as we had plenty of produce to fill her. He vented his disappointment by throwing all sorts of impediments in our way, and behaved in so sordid and unjust a way when we were making up our final dispatches and accounts that I told him I did not want any more transactions with him. I understood afterwards that he had given us anything but a flattering character, simply because he had found we were not to be *done*.

[From John's account, the likely schedule for the trip appears to be as follows:

Ride from Georgetown	Mon	August 25
About 7-10 days on duty to	Sat	September 6
Sail	Sun	September 7 (approx.)
Arrive Glasgow	Sat	October 4
To Liverpool	Thu	October 9
In Prescot	Sun	October 12
To London	Thu	October 16
and Essex	Sat	October 18
Return to London	Thu	October 23
Depart London	Fri	October 24
Arrive Prescot	Sun	October 26
Sailing – Scheduled	Mon	November 3 (approx.)
Sailing – Actual	Sun	November 9
Arrive Georgetown	Sat	December 6 (approx.)]

PART 12

Expatriate: Second Half, 1823-25

False Accusations and Bad Feeling

The tokens of the insurrection were but too plainly observable set round the Fort: 20 or 30 heads on poles interspersed with bodies on gibbets, appropriate garniture for a slave colony! After the first greetings with Pattinson and Brotherston, they said everyone had been speaking about me: 'That I would not fire at the niggers at Bachelors Adventure, I had let a prisoner escape, and I had thanked God I had shot no one; That I had run away from my duty and gone home without asking leave of the Commanding Officer; That at home I had abused the planters and taken the part of the niggers, had attended a missionary meeting and spoken against the colony. And some said that I should be brought to a court-martial.' A pretty catalogue of crimes! – some degree of truth mixed up with a large quantity of malicious falsehood. Pattinson said it was all foolish talk, but I said I would most certainly demand a court of enquiry before I joined the rifle corps again.

I called on Captain Croal. He said he did not believe half of these reports about me, and I asked if he believed *any* of them. I said I had not kept up my firing at Bachelors Adventure through the weak lock of my rifle, which I had shown him, and thought he was satisfied. The prisoner Prince was not in my immediate care, so that was no more my fault than anyone else's; and I was thankful I had taken no man's life, if this was a crime. My going home on urgent business had been settled before, but being ordered up the coast, I lost my passage and was the sufferer thereby, and after the danger I got away as soon as I could; although Captain Croal was the superior officer, he had been higher up the coast, and Lieutenant Rainey, under whose immediate command I was, had given leave for me to go home, and if he had exceeded his duty it was his fault not mine. Besides, he could never suppose it was my duty to stay up the coast on a point of military etiquette when personal duties were demanding my attention at home. I went home impressed as to the guilt of Smith and others from what I had heard ex parte, and though I abhorred the slaughter of the Negroes, I had thought it necessary. I had attended one Missionaries' Meeting, but it was about Africa and not a syllable was asked me about Demerara. I saw there was a prejudice hanging about his mind, and I therefore requested an enquiry to clear it up. While he was seeing about it, I enjoyed an immunity from drill for many weeks; at the end of which, he told me he was satisfied, and begged I drop it and join the Corps. I was not by any means sorry that Colonial tittle-tattle set me free for a time from military duty, but I began to see that a character for Colonial loyalty could only be preserved at the expense of a good conscience.

There remained after my return some more Negroes to be tried, martial law still being in force. Twenty-eight in all were publicly hanged at Georgetown; I was on the parade ground, where the gallows was erected, January 9th 1824, when the last four suffered – two or three deaths, for the ropes broke, and some sat on the grass staring wildly about them until new rope could be brought, and in half an hour they were hoisted up again. Besides these slaughterings, seventeen were sentenced to severe floggings and to be worked in chains. But these bloody proceedings had excited the horror of the British public, whose mind had by this time become fully alive to their nature. The debates in Parliament incensed the colonists beyond measure. It was declared there must be traitors in the Colony, although it was quite evident that their own local paper, the Guiana Chronicle in particular, had furnished sufficient for their own condemnation. And the dispatches of Governor Murray to the Colonial Secretary, Lord Bathurst, detailing all the proceedings, were quite sufficient to produce the Order from home arresting all further punishments and ending martial law.

[E. A. Wallbridge's memoirs of Rev John Smith, *Martyr of Demerara* (1848), say that on May 24th 1824, 50 remained under sentence of death, but the date does not square with what JCC has just said about the 'last four'. The part of the parade ground where the hangings took place is now the Promenade Gardens].

Slavery's Martyr

Poor Missionary Smith was still closely confined, and it was almost high treason to ask what he had done. I gathered that he was accused of concealing knowledge with guilty intention, preaching to put mischief into the Negroes' heads, and plotting the insurrection. But all that could be elicited as correct was that he had preached the Gospel faithfully, and that when some of the Negroes who attended his church had told him something was going on, he had counselled his people against having anything to do with it, when he ought to have communicated it to the Government: undoubtedly a mistake.

Mr Smith was tried by Court Martial, at which the main ground of accusation against him, that he and Quamina had conspired together and plotted to bring the rebellion on, was founded on a single circumstance: Mrs Smith, as soon as she had heard rumours of an intended rising of the Negroes, had sent for Quamina and had questioned him as to his knowledge of it – when Mr Smith had expressed his hope that he was not concerned in it, and his grief at the people being so wicked. Bristol, another deacon, and Romeo, a member, both gave direct evidence exonerating Mr Smith from ever having by his preachings urged anything to the Negroes other than obedience to their masters and all in authority over them. Mr Stewart, the manager of Plantation Success, who sometimes attended the chapel himself, commended Mr Smith's instruction to the Negroes, and testified to the obedient conduct of such as attended the chapel. With respect to Quamina, so far from his being active amongst the insurgents, Mr Stewart said that he did not see him taking part in the insurrection or doing any harm, but keeping the rest back from doing him any injury – vide Wallbridge's memoirs.

In spite of this evidence, and on the word of a few interested and infuriated white people and the most ridiculous evidence, principally that extorted from Negroes whom they frightened into the grossest allegations (and whose evidence normally would not have been taken, being slaves), Mr Smith was condemned to be hanged: a monstrous mockery of justice – which it was not, it was military tyranny. Execution was deferred to the King and Council at home, who at once sent orders to spare his life and send him home to

England; but in February 1824, before the decision arrived, his sufferings terminated, for God took him. Manager Hamilton was incarcerated all this time, and after a flimsy investigation, in which nothing whatever was proved, was discharged, but ordered to quit the colony; thus his prospects were blighted for no crime whatever, except that he was manager of the estate where Mr Smith preached.

After the insurrection, the Negroes on the whole were not worse treated, as public opinion in England and the eyes of Parliament were too fixed on the planters to admit of more stringent measures with the Negroes, whose condition benefitted thereby. Symptoms of a change were every day more apparent. The well-known proceedings of the Anti-Slavery Society succeeded at length in achieving the object of their protracted and arduous exertions. A Bill passed on August 1st 1834 emancipated all slaves in the British colonies, accompanied by a 7 years' preparation under the title of apprenticeship; but this worked so badly that it was abolished before its term. Full freedom was given on August 1st 1838, without the slightest commotion of any kind, the Gospel, widely diffused for some time previously, having well prepared the Negroes for the peaceful and happy enjoyment of their rights as free citizens which they now possess.

[A book *Slavery's Martyr* (Cecil Northcott: Epworth Press, 1976) recounts the history of John Smith and the slave rising. It states that the messenger of the 'freedom' rumour was Quamina, of 'Success' plantation, which was at the heart of the uprising and provided its ringleaders. The rebels were remarkably controlled in safeguarding lives and property, and no white man was deliberately murdered; it was tragically otherwise with the Colony's armed forces. The old chimney of 'Success', which was next door to Le Resouvenir, is now a historic Guyana landmark. John Smith was consumptive, his only hope of keeping healthy to remain in the country. After his arrest, held in the damp cramped conditions in Georgetown Jail, he had no chance, and gradually sank, dying on February 6th 1824, before King George's reprieve reached him. He has never been officially pardoned. He proved to be more influential dead than alive, as the book's title suggests. (The name of his estate seems – fortuitously – quite appropriate – CCT).

The book includes quotations from the 'manuscript Journal of E.C. Cheveley (sic), a young English merchant who arrived in Georgetown four years after Smith', referring to a typescript copy in the CWM Archives at the London School of African and Oriental Studies (sic). (The latter is near-identical to JCC's 'British Guiana' book: it corrects his spelling idiosyncrasies, but conversely mis-spells some proper names.). Northcote has a nicely readable literary style, but neither of his two maps show any detail, he uses the vague imprecise 'op cit' and 'ibid' style of referencing, and (worse) suffers from factual errors (all of this anathema to a professional scientist!). The last include: Lachlan Cumming as the proprietor of Bachelor's Adventure – not Chateau Margo. The battle is implied to be August 19th – JCC's account shows it was the 20th. Quamina 'was shot while struggling to keep the rebellion within bounds' – on August 21st, after it was over and he had fled in fear. 'No white man was murdered' – what about the trumpeter? The Rev W.S. Austin's initials are transposed, as are 'African' and 'Oriental' above, and JCC's first initial is incorrect throughout.]

The Fate of Mr Austin
I found the colony resembled a hive of bees which has been disturbed and cannot resettle: armed and ready to sting all comers who strive to cope with their determination to have their own way, and such ill-feelings and suspicions and quarrels among the white people that it was most odious. Minds were most virulently set against 'The Saints'. A great public meeting was held to consider the present state of the Colony and devise the best means of defeating the 'enemies'. A great many speeches dwelt on the wrongs of the Colonists, and denunciatory of the invaders of their rights at home and the supposed traitors within the Colony. Many moving pictures were drawn of the sufferings of the white people during the insurrection, denouncing the Saints who were the authors of it. A resolution that all missionaries be sent out of the colony and prohibited from entering in future, was proposed, and received with acclamation by a large number; but the more reasonable portion were

against it, as it 'would give a character of violence to their proceedings, which they wished to avoid'. Truly they had been so lamb-like hitherto! A majority was found to be against it, of whom, of course, I was one; my friend Hopkinson went on the other side (Since the insurrection he had quit his estate to live in Georgetown).

At length came an *explosive!* which fell like a boom [bomb?] shell and brought all these discordant parties into common agreement, at any rate on one subject. Mr Austin, though at first deceived by gross misrepresentation and impressed with the idea that poor Smith was a firebrand of sedition, had, like myself, changed his opinions entirely as to Mr Smith's part in the revolt, whose preaching he now believed had saved the lives of the very men who were now seeking his, by its effect on the Negro character. He thought the vengeance inflicted on the Negroes was cruel and unnecessary, and he had expressed this opinion to a friend at home. That friend had thoughtlessly read the letter (strictly private) at a public meeting; of course it went the round of the newspapers, and was quoted in Parliament. Back came the whole affair to Demerara with the effect above named. The Guiana Chronicle, rampantly pro-slavery, after a fierce invective of proceedings at home in general, took in hand poor Mr Austin in particular, commencing a furious article with: 'And now for that meek and gentle Christian minister, preacher of peace and goodwill, who vilifies his fellow colonists in the dark, that advocate of sedition and murder, the Evil Genius of Demerara', &c, &c, detailing his crime and giving a copy of his letter. This was left to work with promise of more; and work it did to some purpose, for it threw the whole colony into a frenzy, further stimulated by some excessively caustic letters accusing Mr Austin of immoralities and disgraceful conduct, which were too readily believed by his enemies.

The outcry against him was intense and universal, and I was shocked and dismayed at the feeling which this affair elicited: not only did the colonists assail him, but his own friends all turned their backs on him. I believe that Dr Chapman and I were at length the only persons who communicated with him; and I went by night, like Nicodemus fearing the Jews [John 3 1-2, 19 38-39], my mercantile position rendering caution necessary lest I expose myself to the fate of being mobbed out of the colony. A party was formed to go to church to pull him out of the pulpit if he stood up to officiate; but being warned, he refrained, and got a clergyman who happened to be in Georgetown to do the duty. I was confined to the house with a severe cold in the head, in that hot climate a peculiar thing and difficult to deal with. Dr Chapman was attending me, and he did not altogether acquit Mr Austin of blame; he thought the imputations which his letter conveyed were severe and unjust. Mr Smith he thought had acted with want of caution, like a man who fires a magazine or straw yard by using an unguarded light: the mischief was done though he did not intend it.

A memorial was soon got up and numerously signed, declaring Mr Austin unfit for his position and requesting the Governor to expel him from the colony. Pattinson signed because others did. I refused: the bearers, two principal merchants, wished to know why. I said I did not feel I was bound to give a reason; they thought I was. 'Well then,' I said, 'private friendship'. 'If it's not on public grounds, we have no right to ask any further', replied one – so I got off. The newspapers continued to rail and vilify Mr Austin's character; I called on him, and he said it was useless to attempt any defence of his character or conduct, which had been so wantonly assailed. He must yield so far as to abstain from resuming his duties in church, and he must be content to wait, hoping that matters would soften down and people come in time to a better state of feeling.

Weeks however past over, and the animosity continued as bitter as ever; there was a hatred of Mr Austin arising from the boldness with which he had preached the Gospel. The Governor was beset with applications for his removal, or pretended to be, for he had not been pleased with him for going up the coast during the insurrection, although why it was difficult to imagine. The Governor at length intimated that as public feeling was so strongly set against him, he had better withdraw. Strange to say, some of those who had been most clamourous to get rid of him, now began to taunt the captain of the ship taking him, for being his conveyor. As Mr and Mrs Austin knew no-one at Liverpool, he asked me the favor of a few introductory lines to Mr Driffield. I told him I had already sent an account of his ill treatment, and I would write at once to say they were on their way. I should send my letter by the same vessel; a course I preferred to giving it to him, which if it were to be known might subject me to be drummed out of the colony after him, and which, situated as I now was in business matters, I could not afford to risk. (I may add that Mr Austin occupied for a time the curacy of Clapham, and married my brother Charles to Miss Rix in 1829. He later moved to Stainton-cum-Johnston near Milford Haven, where I saw him on a visit to Haverfordwest in 1842.)

Mr Austin's successor, a Mr Miller, was a young careless man of the world, whose chief aim seemed to be to undo all that his predecessor had been doing for the poor people's improvement and comfort. The Sabbath schools for free black and coloured people, which were working well, were at once discontinued. It had long been the custom during the communion for as many as wished to remain in the gallery as spectators; the first Sacrament Sunday after Mr Austin's departure, Mr Miller requested all who were not communicants to retire, and the unseemly spectacle was presented of the clergyman, clerk and sexton walking round the church to see that all these intruders were sent out. Every arrangement made by Mr Austin was sedulously uprooted. Two new clergymen were sent out, both Essex men whose attainments did not beam forth with any remarkable lustre. They were intended to replace the missionaries, whose sin of enlightening the Negroes they were not likely to commit.

Meanwhile, poor Mr Smith and Mr Austin being disposed of, there remained another missionary on the west coast, Mr Elliott, so the Chronicle took him in hand; slander was in such a case accounted a virtue, and he eventually withdrew. Dark hints were given of 'an enemy to the colonists', which Dr Chapman understood to be intended for him, and to which he immediately gave a sharp and severe reply, that these insinuations were a gross slander and an 'unmeasured lie', stating that his opinions on all subjects were his own and he did not intend to be bullied out of them. So they let him alone, finding him an awkward hand to deal with.

Plantation Sarah Johanna

Letters from home the beginning of 1824 gave a somewhat better account of John Pattinson's health and prospects for business. He had made some arrangements for pecuniary assistance with Mr Rowland Roscow, a colonial broker, and he was preparing to send out several more vessels. This put us in spirits. I had also a letter from Miss Barry. But one which fixed my attention and excited my wonder most of all was from George, who after speaking of his Jamaica voyage, from which he had just

[Here a whole page has been removed, then the next sentence – referring to whom? – crossed out:] -ment that the lives and property of the colonists had been placed in jeopardy, and that far from being rewarded, he ought to be censured and sent home.

Pattinson had gone on litigating in the *Friendship* affair, and as the old Dutch law was admirably calculated to prolong proceedings, there seemed no probability of a speedy termination. Tom Johnson had disappeared; his principal Mr Lucas had come from England and discharged him for unsatisfactory management, and he had with his wife gone back to Canada, whence they had originally come. Pat McClure had been taken off suddenly by Colony Fever, as was all too common; you might hear a man was ill one day and buried next, and the first intimation an invitation card to his funeral.

Pattinson now turned again to his favorite project, a coffee plantation, in which brother John encouraged him, with a view to finding profitable employment for a score of Negroes on the neglected cotton estate (Dundee) at Abary, and his letters were urgent for something to be done with them. At length an estate about 20 miles upriver appeared to be the thing. A poor young Scotchman had tried and had enough, but died before he could get rid of it. It was one of a number worked by the Dutch, but fallen into decay under the English, with whom coffee was less in favor than sugar and cotton. They had either run to waste or were in the hands of needy adventurers who, with a few miserable Negroes, made a scanty living from a few old coffee trees, or plantains, or firewood. Many a hopeful fellow who had fallen into poverty from dissipation or misfortune, might be found wearing out health and life in one of these places.

Plantation Sarah Johanna was truly a lonely spot, but it was in better trim than its neighbors, as the Scotchman had expended on it his substance and some Negro labour; the coffee trees were young and thrifty [thriving?], well-protected with plantain trees, whose shade is essential to coffee cultivation in this climate. There were small but substantial buildings, so it looked promising, like an oasis in the wilderness. It was a narrow strip running far back from the river, divided from other human localities by strips of vegetation, probably never cleared. An awful stillness prevailed near the extremity, broken only by the screeching of flocks of parrots, and towards nightfall, the monotonous note of a bird uttering a mysterious low note like 'Who are you!', so distinct as to be quite startling to the stranger. The vegetation in the wilderness is most heterogeneous: the gigantic silk cotton tree, various acacias and palmettos, overgrown by creepers, many of them varieties of Passion flower with scarlet blossoms and yellow fruit.

The former proprietors had well stocked the sidewalks with fruit trees, oranges, lemons, limes, shaddocks, and many I had not known before, one with a strawberry flavour; breadfruit and breadnut, and the gigantic sowarro or Brazil nut, which grew in a husk about the size and shape of a melon, into which some half-dozen fitted edgewise. Guavas, pines [pineapples] and mangoes grew luxuriantly, everywhere and anywhere, but there was no cultivation of fruit, and no heed taken of them except by the Negro children, who ran about and picked whatever they could find; the pigs mostly had the benefit. The low creeping 'sensitive plant' frequently dispossessed the grass; the children amused themselves by passing their hands over it and as it drooped cried 'She-um!' (see him), from which it was called the Sheum plant.

Coffee is an extremely pretty cultivation. The trees, which resemble Portuguese laurel, are planted in rows beneath plantain avenues, whose abundant fruit supplies the Negroes with their daily food. The vista is a picture of beauty, Nature's own architecture suggesting and excelling the aisle of a Gothic cathedral. The berries form as the pretty white star-shaped blossoms drop; they are picked by the women as fast as they ripen, and consigned to the pulping and washing machine worked by the men. This is a grating process: a rough cylinder and much water clears off the pulp, reducing the berry to the hard inner skin or husk. This has to be broken off without breaking the coffee kernel within, so it is spread on a large platform of brick or stone in the hot sun, and stirred about until a rattling noise gives token it is dry enough. It is then pounded in large mortars of hard wood with a hard wood pestle, and when the husk is broken, it is winnowed off. The coffee is then picked over by the women, who sort it into good berry, pearl or small, and broken or inferior. No doubt there are better systems at work now by machinery.

This out-of-the-world spot being brought to the ken of the public, who were generally too wide-awake to fancy it, it appeared to William a capital project, so he went in for it. A Mr Ouckama, known as the 'wily Greek', with whom anyone needed his sharpest wits doubly sharpened, had the disposal of it. He was very *silky*, asked about £1,200, and agreed to take £1,000 payable by instalments with 'a small matter of interest to be settled hereafter'. So the Pattinsons became possessors of Sarah Johanna, the Negroes were removed from Dundee to this locality, and William persuaded himself of results in happy expectation.

Mr Mosquito Strange

After removal, we found we had as much room as we needed; our new landlord Arnott being a cooper by trade, we bargained for a supply of casks, our own cooperage being unmanageable and unprofitable. I proposed to give up Strange's place, as I saw no necessity to burthen ourselves with the additional one. Strange had retained for his own use half of the premises, house, offices, and store; he was a regular little schemer, and no sooner found we were likely to give up our portion, than he assailed Pattinson to buy the lot. I at once set my face against it, as the premises were old, out of repair, and far from the waterside. Besides I had great repugnance to incurring a large liability, especially in the precarious state of John Pattinson's health. So I said 'Let well alone'.

Strange, as indefatigable as a mosquito over a newcomer, and as exacting and thirsty, buzzed perpetually about Pattinson's ears till he had fully possessed him: against which I strongly protested. It was agreed to refer the matter home – fatal, as John seemed to be in favour though deferring to our judgment on the spot. But he consented that our former house in Kingston, which belonged to him, be given in payment of the first instalment, and this strengthened

William's purpose and weakened my opposition. So Mr Mosquito Strange buzzed away at Pattinson, and having finished him off, came to me. Such a situation, such comfort, such room, terms so cheap and easy, what better? Pattinson had given in, and at length, finding opposition useless, I gave in, with all the misgivings of an unconvinced judgment. I had done the same in consenting to the partnership; and this was the second false step. So the bill of sale was drawn up, to be paid in instalments of 3 years, and for the first a bill of sale of the Kingston house: which proved a fruitful source of disputation with Mrs Pattinson afterwards, who claimed the house was hers. William now began to run up an enormous carpenter's bill for repairs and alterations, which I soon put a stop to; I was much more concerned about business than either dwellinghouse or store.

A Difficult Season

1824 proved a remarkably dry season, which in Guiana is a terrible time to everyone, not only to the planter, especially of sugar, but all alike depend on the rains for every drop of fresh water. The soil being everywhere saturated from the sea, there is none from wells or rivers except at great distance in the interior, where the alluvial soil is succeeded by vegetable decomposition, which discolours the water and renders it scarcely fit to drink. Yet it is brought down by boats in very dry seasons as the best that can be provided, and sold by buckets full for high prices. The upcountry woodcutters used rather to prefer creek water to the clearer and purer water from the clouds.

The drought continued into April, and the cultivation was beginning to feel it. Produce was becoming scarce, and the vessels we had to load home, with the prospect of more coming out, gave me no small anxiety. Molasses was the chief article of barter, always a good freight, but we could not get enough. Day after day, week after week, very little progress; May, still no rain: the thirsty land and still more thirsty colonists longed for the precious drops, or rather buckets full, but in vain. The domestic vats were empty, and water was sold from the public tanks, large brick cisterns sunk in the ground, at a dear rate. The horizon was lighted up at night by fire, although at a safe distance, but its spread was rapid and certain. As it approached the back lands of some estates, the managers dug wide trenches for interception. It was only extinguished by copious showers in June or July, but too late then to benefit the cultivation [See 'Factual Notes about British Guiana'].

I hunted for produce at various estates without much success: amongst others Dorenhaag on Leguan, an island at the mouth of the Essequibo which with a neighboring island, Waakenam, contains some of the best sugar cultivation. I was let in for another sabbath, and a sad one it was, as always on a plantation, where all was revelry. In the midst of our perplexities, the *Britannia*, chartered by John to take lumber to Berbice, appeared 'off the river'! The trade wind was dead against him, and many weeks or months would elapse before he could beat up to Berbice; and then the cargo might be refused because the specified delivery time would have expired. This would entail terrible loss, and to keep cargo and ship in Demerara held no ameliorating prospect. Accordingly, as the lesser evil, the cargo was landed, and being unsuited for the market, we were many months disposing of it; *Britannia* was sent to North America under a new agreement to seek his fortune as best he might.

Letters from home announced that George had been sent with *Anna* to Brazil, and had left his wife at Hedingham with the family. 'Judge of my astonishment' said my mother, 'when we found she was black.' [And of ours when we learn that he has gotten married at all! Presumably JCC mentioned it on the sheet above (first paragraph of 'Plantation Sarah Johanna') which was later removed, whoever did so overlooking that George's marriage would disappear along with it.] As may be imagined, the West Indian proclivities did not fall in with Essex habits; the new daughter-in-law had a temper peculiar to many of her kind and their upbringing, and she led Hedingham a life while she sojourned there. John Pattinson's health was not improving, but he was still anxiously promoting business through Roscow and others; news of more vessels coming out in the present state of scarcity was rather more alarming than gratifying. Letters from Prescot were very comforting.

Towards the middle of 1824, our brig *Eleanor* returned; we had besides *Aimwell*, making a terrible hole in the 'laying-days' for reloading, agreed with all chartered ships, which if exceeded, a fixed daily extra rate of demurrage must be paid, a serious expense to the charterer. There had been a little rain, but produce was still very scarce and competition great, ships were detained week after week, and it required our greatest industry and perseverance to provide for them. The captain of *Aimwell*, a quizzical little fellow, visited every day with the same question, 'Anything for the ship this morning?'; truly he had me in his eye, and under his morning squint I felt like a schoolboy who does not know his task. A brig called *Ann* arrived, and another large new-built one, *William Salthouse*, on her [his??] first voyage. *Aimwell's* captain agreed to her despatch with what she had rather than run up heavy demurrage, and he sailed with two-thirds of a cargo, though satisfied that I had done the best I could.

All this time drilling went on. The Governor reviewed the Militia periodically, when we turned out in our best and presented arms. Promotions had taken place: Captain Croal to Major, Lieut Rainey to Captain, one Mr Davidson from Sergeant to Lieutenant, and a Mr Pearse to Adjutant. The end of it was we had too many officers and got into confusion and disorganization. Major Croal did not now think it necessary to attend our common drill. Mr Rainey was looked up to as the most astute businessman; but those whom he commanded had no flattering opinion of his ability on the parade ground, and amused themselves at his expense, though they dare not shew personal disrespect. When he gave the word to do one thing, a lot of young fellows, pretending to misunderstand, did another. Then marching in line, a number at the head of the column would suddenly surge to one side and throw the whole line into confusion. There was a determination to annoy Mr Rainey, who at length wisely refrained from command; and we fell in to Pearse's hands, who thoroughly understood what he was about and was much more successful.

Pattinson's Mixture

To add to my troubles, William had a severe attack of Colony fever. I was engaged one morning with a Vendue, to clear a great many articles and odds and ends into cash; old Bischoff, the Dutch auctioneer, was hammering them off, when a message came that William was much worse and the noise below was very disturbing. I was obliged to dismiss the vendue and go for Dr Chapman, who called in another physician considered the 'ne plus ultra' in fever cases. William's life was spared, but his constitution was so shaken that the doctors recommended an immediate trip to England, and it was settled he should go in *Eleanor*. William passed a general Power of Attorney to me, to act in all matters connected with him and his brother, a very agreeable complication for the edification of his locum tenens.

The prospect of being left to fight by myself was not cheering, for though in most aspects I could do better on my own, I did not view with satisfaction the liabilities of his various schemes. First, a conglomeration of law matters in the never-ending *Friendship* affair. Next, sundry claims on the late firm of J. & W. Pattinson, one from the astute Mr Rainey. Then there was Plantation Sarah Johanna to be supplied with what was wanted, through not yet yielding what was looked for. And the co-executorship with lawyer Mr Gordon. These were some of the components of Pattinson's Mixture, which I would be called on to analyse. I was left to my own resources: but I had one other that was not mine, abundant and greatly able to sustain me.

Sad news of John Pattinson's family: the death of his second son Daniel, aged 7, and another infant boy, and his own health worse. Miss Barry feared that business anxieties were too much for him, and I was therefore better reconciled to William's departure, hoping he might take some weight off his brother. He sailed together with Henry Fox, who had been assisting us as a clerk but had tired of it; he sought his fortune under his uncle Mr Roscow, and after many trials flourished as a successful shipping agent in Liverpool.

The Manager of Sarah Johanna had an offer from an estate up the coast, and as the river estate did not agree with his health, he was anxious to leave as soon as I could provide a successor. He had proved steady and trustworthy, and it seemed difficult to meet this character amongst the Colony waifs and strays, who alone would be willing to undertake the task with its risks of sickness and mortality for small pay. However, at length a big Hibernian, Mr Gardner, appeared, and I accompanied him to Sarah Johanna to be installed. I was glad to find the Negroes looked well cared for: there were 25 or 30 altogether, about equal numbers of men and women, and some children.

One grown-up girl Betsy had been transferred to replace our cook Peter, and two boys as house servants. Loveless and Sam had long been dismissed; they became so adept at avoiding the stripes laid on them that they inflicted as much pain on the flagellant as he inflicted on them, throwing up the elbow just as the whip descended, so its point caught the soft part of the master's arm. Their successors, Damon and Andries, were no better. Damon was wild as a young deer, and near as nimble, tall and slight, with restless eyes. He had an unaccountable taste for running away into the bush, whence it was difficult to extract him. Ask Old Jim 'You been see Damon?' 'Yes massa,' (with a grin) 'me she um go out ob de gate!' Picked up by the Dienars out after gunfire without a pass, he could be had out of gaol on payment of fees and expenses. Betsy likewise took to wandering and had to be punished; as I positively refused to allow her to be whipped, she had to stay in gaol for a week.

Ann and *William Salthouse* were soon reinforced by *Jess & Flora*, an old vessel come into Mr Pattinson's possession whose arrival increased my troubles. He sent out another horse for my use, or for sale, as I already had a useful stout roan cob. I had a suspicion I had seen the new one before. I mounted: suspicion confirmed, no mistaking the go of that beast if once ridden, the identical 'slug' Mr Pattinson had lent me to ride to Prescot on the Sunday while I was at Liverpool, when it would have been as quick to walk, and made me late for church; sent out like other waifs and strays to seek his fortune!

A Bad Sunday

I heard that something was offering about 25 miles up the coast: ought I to go after it on a Sunday? A still small voice within said '*You know* what to do'; a louder voice from without said 'It is your duty to seize every opportunity', and I yielded. I found out my mistake before I got home again. I found saddled for me not the cob, whose back had been rubbed sore, but The Slug; I might almost as well have ridden a donkey. I turned into Bachelors Adventure, still garnished with heads and dead bodies, and breakfasted there, but no cotton. The 'Hope' estate was my land of promise, but all my hopes were put to flight. I called at one or two other estates with like

160

success. Violation of all the remonstrances of conscience, all to no purpose; feeling self-condemned, I rode homewards.

While considering what to do, as The Slug would never take me to town that day, a horseman overtook me, Jones the skipper of *Glenbervie*. He said to come with him to Enmore, a nearby cotton estate, where he was going to dine, and the manager would give me a bed or a hammock. All was revelry; I sat by shocked, and sad that I should have brought myself into such a position. I left early, and as I felt unwell, I stopped at Baron Grovestin's 'Beter Verwagting', but could eat very little. Fearing I was going to be ill, I was anxious to get home, but found my beast's jog-jog-jog very exhausting. Within 2 or 3 miles of Georgetown, I felt so ill that I put in at a small wayside logie inhabited by one Dick Johnson, a loose man who had had a large business, but dwindled down through dissipation and an unaccountable taste for law, now 'living on his wits'. I called merely to ask for water, but seeing me so exhausted, he made me lie down, and I slept until the afternoon. I never was more humiliated than when he asked if I had got into riotous company yesterday. What a reproof from such a quarter! I returned home dispirited, I had sinned against God in my overweening desire to do my duty to Man.

Struggling On

William wrote that John's health was worse, and his books and accounts were in some confusion. A firm he had been much concerned with had suddenly given way, throwing him into the hands of Rowland Roscow, who was to receive all remittances and find money to carry on with. I was urged to send home all I could 'to keep the wheel revolving'. Produce now began to get more plentiful from abundant rain, and with it revival of trade. *Ann* sailed with a full cargo, leaving the other two large ships, *William Salthouse* getting on demurrage. I had hopes of getting through my difficulties, but I had a very hard fight, and I went wherever I thought I could get anything. It may be asked, why did you not write? Simply because there was no inland post, no means of conveying a letter except by sending a negro with it.

Some cotton was offering at a riverside estate; the manager called to enquire my terms for shipment, and as we differed, he invited me out to see the owner. His terms were so very much below mine that I hesitated, and said I would consider it. Alas! Returning to Georgetown, I met a ship's captain, who looked rather sly, and my mind misgave me; next day, I learned that he had secured all the cotton. My wish had been to avoid lowering the freight rates, which I had been accused of doing, to the general detriment and thus I was rewarded for my scrupulosity by one of my accusers.

I determined to make another trip up the East coast, as I had been applied to about freight for a considerable quantity of rum by Dr Munro, an old Scotch physician and planter on the Berbice side just over Abary creek. He had been a friend of Mr Richard Barry [my maternal grandfather – JCC II], an Irish Catholic cotton planter, who died comparatively young, leaving a son and daughter, then both children. His property was thought good, but his executors, to save trouble, and it was said with unworthy motives, sold off estate and Negroes at once; when all was wound up and debts paid, there was nothing left. Dr Munro appeared to have authorized this, and it so incensed Mrs Barry, the children's mother, that in her will she interdicted him ever having anything to do with her affairs.

A Mr George Anderson was going to stay with a planter whom he knew at Mahaica, Mr Chester or Chichester, out of whom I wanted to coax some produce; and as he had no conveyance, I offered to take him in my gig. Dr Chapman gave me a letter to his father's estate, the Grove, at Mahaica, for a spare horse for me. I called at several plantations on the way, breakfasting at Bachelors Adventure, dining at another, and finally arriving at Mr Chester's in the evening. Over cigars and brandy he spoke, rather evasively, about what he would do for me, joked away, and we were in great favor overnight; but alas next morning, when the brandy had evaporated, I found him quite cold about shipping, and could not get another joke out of him. I left Anderson there, to call for on my return. My intention was to proceed to Mahaicony and Abary, and to put up at Airy Hall with Jamie Jackson, another of Wm Pattinson's intimates, whose company was utterly abhorrent to me: yet I was necessitated to be his guest. His establishment consisted of his West India wife Miss Betsey, who knew well how to rule him, Miss Susan her daughter, and her two children, who when Wm Pattinson went home was consigned again to her mother's care. [Somewhat ambiguous; I assume the two children are William and Susan's, though elsewhere only the one boy is mentioned.] I staid there several days, as it gave me an opportunity to visit the plantations in the neighborhood, to which Jackson drove me in his gig. We crossed the Abary creek, a deep rivulet dividing Demerara from Berbice, where there was a ferry boat, and called on Dr Munro. He alluded to his former connection with Mrs Pattinson's family, but it was tender ground with which I had nothing to do, and I avoided it: my object being to secure the rum, which I engaged to take on *William Salthouse*.

I visited the Dundee cotton estate, where Pattinson's Negroes had formerly been: buildings now all tumbling to pieces and deserted to the mosquitoes who had apparently established their headquarters there. I was so assailed by a cloud of these little voracious bloodsuckers that I was obliged to take to my heels, beating the air to keep them off, much to Jackson's amusement; he said they would take good care of the property for us. Sunday overtook me again before I got home, but I preferred leaving Airy Hall to passing it there, and I returned to Mr Chester's to pick up Anderson on my way home, who told me at last he had promised all his produce elsewhere. I give these details to shew what a toil it was, at this time especially, to get ships loaded; and these are only a few specimens of what I had to encounter. I was left to myself to carry on a most arduous business, the difficulties of which appeared at times to be insurmountable. It was all in such contrast to India: there, servants ever at your beck and call, here in this slave colony you must run about in the hot sun to transact your daily business.

Captain Garniss of *William Salthouse*, a man of Christian principle, was kind and patient, seeing the unavoidable difficulty of the position and that I was doing all I could. He wished to see a little of Colonial life, and went with me to Sarah Johanna, where Mr Gardner received us with true Irish hospitality. We strolled towards the end of the cultivation; I felt pleased with his exertions, as the coffee gave promise of a good crop.

The quiet gloom of the bush is something awful towards evening, not a sound but the 'Who are you?' bird; then just about sundown, the shrill sharp 'Whirr' of the Razor grinder, a large beetle that sounds so like the knifegrinder's stone, the change from rough to smooth stone as perceptible as if the insect were imitating it. It is heard in towns where there are any trees, invariably as the sun sets, and in the East Indies also. It is rarely seen being very shy in its habits. The increasing gloom and quietude seemed too much for Garniss, and we returned to the house. He took a fancy that the Negroes should have a treat in honour of our visit, an allowance of whisky and dancing with singing, in those days their chief enjoyment. Next morning Garniss complained of feeling ill. Dr Chapman said he had a slight attack of fever, but nothing dangerous; however, it made him low and nervous, and I was doubly anxious to despatch him, which at length I did with a full ship.

Trouble Brewing

I soon had another perplexing case. I had advice of a cargo of lumber, to be sold and the value shipped home in produce. The ship's captain appeared, but to my surprise and indignation, instead of the bills of lading being transmitted to me in the regular way, they had been sent to a Mr Gilbert, with instructions to him to give them to me, on my paying to him the value of the cargo. First, I did not have the means to do this, next, I was not authorized to do so, and finally I knew that by giving in, I should subject myself to an exaction for what he would call transacting the business. I told Mr Gilbert, a greedy foxy-looking man, that I intended to take the cargo, but he could not expect money so unexpectedly called for, and he must take payment out of the sale as soon as I could dispose of the cargo. I already had an offer from a respectable house, whose guarantee he was content to take.

So the cargo was duly delivered, and paid for by shipping rum and molasses, for which the captain signed bills of lading. I attached these as security to a bill which I drew on John Pattinson for the value of the lumber, and gave it to Gilbert as payment. This being in accordance with usage, he could not object: if the bill were not paid, his agents at home could sell the produce. Evidently unprepared for it, he did not look benign as he enquired 'But who is to pay *me*?' 'Those who employed you, I did not.' He withdrew, leaving me thankful to have been brought through so well. This was my first

164

intimation of Mr Pattinson's impaired credit, which startled me; broader hints followed ere long.

Dr Munro had now heard some account of Mr Pattinson's difficulties, and wrote to say he should require some security for his rum that I had shipped. I replied I was not cognizant of anything being wrong, but this did not satisfy him. I told him I was not interested in home affairs, my business was to sell goods and remit the proceeds, and I could not be liable for the house at home, with which I had no concern. He said if I was so satisfied of its stability, I could not refuse to endorse his bill on it. I hesitated, but it was useless, the credit of the house was at stake. I felt I should not have my confidence betrayed, and yielded to the pressure. Alas! I found afterwards it *was* betrayed, and I was left to the consequences of my attempt to save credit, which was rapidly on the decline. This was false step No. 3.

Letters from home were not reassuring. William represented his brother as in a precarious state and growing weaker, but told me they could still send plenty of business through Rowland Roscow, if I could get funds round quickly. I had only *Jess & Flora* to dispose of, and as produce was easier, my difficulties in that respect had eased. *Eleanor* would come out on another voyage, but she had been brought to sale by her previous owners, as she was paid for only in part and they would wait no longer. In this affair, and others to do with the former J. & W. Pattinson, I had several interviews with Mr Rainey, of whose cold grey eye and impassible [impassive] countenance I always stood in awe. I considered he must measure people by one undeviating rule, the pecuniary-capability gauge, though I had no complaint with his conduct, which was straightforward and businesslike. I began to feel some humiliation about my position in the eyes of the mercantile community; under my power of attorney, I had many vexatious things to arrange.

I had constant application from Mrs Watson, John Chapman's coloured half-sister, regarding her husband's estate, as she could get no satisfactory account whatever from Mr Gordon, who treated her most insultingly. He told me he should please himself about it, and that she was a very troublesome woman. I was so indignant and disgusted at his behaviour that I was determined not to cease my endeavors until I obliged this hard-hearted man to do her justice, and I stuck to him for many months. Her affairs had got into such a state of entanglement that it seemed she might share the fate of many West Indian heirs and get nothing. Three other lawyers were involved, so the poor lady was like the wayfarer who fell among thieves, and I felt it my duty to do all I could to help her. It would scarcely be credited that, with no fault but colour and parentage, not one of her white family residing in the colony recognized her, far less interested themselves in her affairs. I must here do Dr Chapman justice, that when he later came under Divine grace, he acted a brother's part towards her.

I cannot detail now all the proceedings before I could worry Mrs Watson's affairs out of the hands of these lawyers. I alluded to my fear that this would never happen, in a note to her; one of them saw it, and considered it reflected on the honor of the profession. He rode up to the store, and told me I had better be cautious how I wrote, or I might get into trouble, then, holding up a handwhip rather conspicuously, demanded to know if I had intended to reflect on him personally. I saw he was getting up steam, and as I have ever held discretion the better part of valour, I told him I had spoken in general terms; and honor was satisfied. On another occasion, one Moliere, a Frenchman, thought I was serving my own ends, and abused me. Eventually matters were arranged and Mrs Watson got her own.

Another of William's matters had arrived at a stage which in Dutch law is called being in Guysling or Giesling. As far as I could comprehend, it meant the defendant had to shew himself to an official of the Court at stated periods. As Demerara was afflicted with a chronic disease of lawsuits, sufferers looked on the various processes with calm indifference, and going into Giesling was rather fashionable. I was, however, rather terror-stricken when the Marshal served notice for William Pattinson to appear in Giesling. I objected, as the day was Sunday, but fearing to involve William in evil consequences, I went, and soon found it a mere legal farce.

Hopkinson got wind of it; when I explained, he laughed at the idea of my acting by proxy, and said he knew enough of Dutch law to be sure I had given myself unnecessary trouble. Since the insurrection, he had taken a house in Georgetown, and I often dined with him. I attended a musical party at his house, when my savage legal antagonist Moliere was there, all harmony; I could not believe him the same man, but I kept aloof, knowing what there was beneath. My recollections of Hopkinson are kind and amiable, and I was much attached to him, although there was a great gulf between us on religious subjects.

A New Governor
Governor Murray had been recalled, succeeded by General Sir Benjamin D'Urban. No sooner had he taken possession than an order was given to take down all the heads and dead bodies which had been decorating the Fort and estates for the last twelve months, a standing disgrace which it was a relief to get rid of. I hoped it proceeded from improved feeling of the new Governor, but the pro-slavery party sneeringly said it was in deference to his wife, who could not ride about in comfort while such unsightly objects met her view. However, every vestige soon disappeared: not so the enmity, which was as furious as ever, and liberty of speech and of the Gospel were in danger of being seriously curtailed, if not abolished. There were two local papers: the Guiana Chronicle, always pro-slavery, and the Royal Gazette under the direct dictation of the Governor. One Mr Towert or Toward had been editor of the Chronicle, but left and started a new paper of his own, The Colonist. He took care to keep within the bounds of the law, but he fell into a pit which he did not see or look for.

The Governor's two sons had little else to do than ride about and amuse themselves. The younger one had taken it into his head, in passing up and down the town, which was very long and straggling from Government House at one end to the Government offices at the other, to gallop his horse at a furious rate, to the amusement, amazement, terror, or danger of the beholders. This senseless habit was repeated from day to day. At last the Colonist took it up, and in a facetious article gave the young gentleman some good advice, for which his father ought to have felt obliged. He however sent Mr Towert an uncomplimentary message demanding the handle of his printing press!, which the messenger, a Dienar, took away with him. Of course this created a sensation. As Mr Towert did not believe in the Governor's power to stop the press, he published the following week an article calling that power in question, and appealing to his right of law if he had done anything illegal. This was followed by an entire suppression of the paper, and prohibition of Mr Towert to print any more under pain of deportation. He protested against this tyranny, and threatened proceedings for damages, but he soon learnt that British Guiana, being a 'King's Colony' subject to Dutch law, was out of the pale of English jurisprudence, and in such matters the Governor could do just as he liked. So the Governor stopped the press, young D'Urban continued to gallop, and poor Towert packed his traps and departed for Barbados: being under English law, it protected his right to print the Colonist, which found its way into Demerara in spite of the Governor's efforts to keep it out.

Again it was said that Lady D'Urban moved the machinery which hoisted out Mr Towert, as it was her favorite son who had been told not to make himself ridiculous. There was a melancholy sequel. A few months afterwards, this youth was unfortunately drowned while bathing in one of the creeks in the back country. How it happened was never known; he went by himself, and was discovered as if he had plunged in head downwards and never recovered. Some thought that he had encountered an electric eel, of considerable size and power in some of those waters, by which he had become cramped or paralized for the moment. This would not be improbable, as I have myself experienced a shock from a large specimen of this fish, equal to a severe shock of frictional or galvanic electricity.

Problems, Problems

Letters from Liverpool did not cheer me much. John Pattinson continued to write, but Miss Barry's account of his health was not favorable. He said he had had to draw a bill on me for money lent him by a friend to assist him out of a difficulty, which vexed and alarmed me. When the holder of the bill presented it, I gave only a conditional acceptance and did not hold myself liable to pay, although in law I could be compelled. Not long after, another drag on me was tried by Mrs Pattinson, who expressed how sensible she was of my endeavours, but claiming my commiseration for herself, as Roscow was taking all I sent home to satisfy his claims, and she

basements a little cracked. All the superstructures of the buildings being entirely of wood, we owed our safety to their yielding character and the elasticity of the tough alluvial or muddy soil.

The Partnership Finishes

More letters from home: William giving particulars of the progress of the bankruptcy court, execrating all who were trying to work anything out of him, and urging me to work matters for our mutual advantage. Mrs Pattinson told me she had begun operations as John Pattinson's Widow & Co, requesting my cooperation and support, which I was in neither condition or humour to give. Indeed I was disgusted with what appeared to be a design of both parties to get hold of all they could and turn me to the best account. Miss Barry animadverted William, who had entirely separated himself from his brother's widow, and was paying attentions to a young lady friend of theirs, quite regardless of the poor woman and child he had left in Demerara; my opinion of him was not improved by recent expositions of his principles and conduct [Two children are mentioned in 'Struggling On']. She had no fear of her sister succeeding eventually, as she had shewn extraordinary aptitude for business, and the energies of her mind were uncommon. Eventually I found her *energies uncommonly troublesome*, directed as they were at my innocent head with a vigour and persistency which gave me no quarter, and a vindictiveness utterly unaccountable from one who had lavished on me the most extravagant praises as her husband's friend and preserver.

The assignees' accountant, Mr Bartholomew Prescot, solicited my good offices to speedily realize and remit any available assets; they had seen some of my letters to William, and passed a high eulogium on my conduct and character, expressing their confidence in my integrity, &c. Mr Driffield had been told by Roscow that he and the creditors entertained a good opinion of my business abilities and character; he inferred I should find new business in my favor, but I had not much faith in this, and felt I had too many difficulties.

William had given the interesting information that he had drawn on my firm for about £200 to pay his lawyers, and sure enough a gentleman appeared with the document, which I refused to recognize. But to my astonishment and annoyance, I found William had actually accepted the bill too, in the name of the Demerara firm. This I at once repudiated, as done out of the colony, and without my concurrence; the holder however said he could make me pay, and I found I was legally liable for the acts of my partner. But I felt determined I would not pay such a demand, and felt driven by this occurrence at once to advertise the dissolution of our copartnership in the Demerara newspapers, one of which I sent to William to shew him I did not intend to be thus put upon. So weighing all matters, and feeling I had done the utmost for all parties, without any advantage to myself, but on the contrary entangled in difficulties I did not see my way out of clearly: I resolved to keep clear of further complications, retire from the scene as soon as I could, and begin again at home. George supported me and offered me a passage home in *Anna*. Dr Chapman, with whom I sometimes talked over my state and prospects, observed 'How came such a matter-of-fact man as you into such a plight?' I found it was better for me to trust in God than in Man.

William Returns, I Depart

Matters thus dragged on through 1825. Of course no business from Liverpool, and all I had to do was realize what I had on hand, and get a freight home for *Anna*: a slow operation as nothing was offering but molasses, a dangerous cargo for an old vessel strained as she had been with heavy lumber. William had said that as soon as he got his discharge from the bankruptcy court, he should come to Demerara to realize for the creditors any assets he could from J. and W. Pattinson; I felt it was rather for his own benefit. So one morning he arrived at the store; he hesitated for a moment, but I greeted him kindly, and he became very cordial and confidential. His object was indeed to take care of himself, and carry on business in which he wished me to join him, but I declined. It appeared he was expecting some cargo or other, but the fact was, he had nothing he could in reality and honestly call his own, nor I either, and *that* settled it as far as I was concerned. In a few days, his domestic establishment was resumed, Miss Susan and his boy having come to town with her mother to greet him. He wondered why I had dissolved the firm in which I was a partner and sold the horse! I told him the one was to put an end to all further liabilities being entailed on me, and the other to help pay off such as were properly mine, which I had done to the best of my ability. With this he was obliged to appear satisfied, whatever he might think.

As I feared, I found Dr Munro's rum had been sold and his bill left unpaid, which was equivalent to fraud and robbery. Sure enough, in a few days he appeared in great wrath, and began on me as if I had been the culprit, saying I was avoiding a positive obligation to do all I could to get him paid. I said I felt my confidence had been grossly betrayed as well as his own, and as I did not possess any means, they must come from Mr Pattinson, whose duty it was to put the matter right. William set his wits to work to muster up something, notes of hand and other securities (probably *in*securities) which the Doctor took, and gave up the bill: greatly to my relief, but not much to his satisfaction, and he walked off making observations not complimentary to the honesty of those connected with the transaction, in which I felt he included me.

I saw that now or never was the time to get away with George in *Anna*. I had wound up, as far as I could, all in which I was immediately interested. Some I never could wind up, stay as long as I would: Mr Strange and his house, and the bills for which the people at home had rendered me in some way responsible, and I knew these claimants would prevent my leaving the colony. The legal process required for anyone wishing to leave was to advertise in the public papers at least a fortnight before, which gave opportunity for any creditor to enter a claim at the Government office; until this was withdrawn, he could not legally depart, and the vessel with him on board was subject to detention and fine. If I staid, I knew very well I could do no more than I had most conscientiously done, and would only drag out a useless idle existence, like many unfortunates before me; and I therefore gave in to the obvious alternative, the opportunity of my brother's vessel, as he would of course take me unmindful of consequences, which no other Captain would.

I laid the case before William, who agreed I was no use there and might do some good for the cause at home, although I did not see much hope in that direction. We also agreed my intention be kept quiet, and I should walk aboard *Anna* as if to accompany my brother over the Bar and return with the pilot, which was customary with those who had friends on board. And so, without taking leave of anyone but William, I left Demerara, where I had suffered so many anxieties and had worked so hard with no other result than another great disappointment: for I was going home in some respects worse than when I set out, not knowing what liabilities might be thrown on me from the Pattinsons' affairs, and with scarcely anything I could call my own. In fact I had so completely absorbed all my firm's available funds in paying liabilities, that I found, when I made up *Anna's* account, that the owners, whoever they might be, were in my debt. As security to press my claim against Roscow or the creditors at home, I thought it prudent to take a mortgage or bottomry on the vessel, which George as Captain could legally give, and armed with it, I could detain ship or freight until my claim was satisfied. William accompanied me on board, and looked rueful as he prepared to depart with the pilot. I felt some inward compunction: I was not satisfied at the way I was leaving the place, and him to battle through difficulties, but I have already stated my motives, and believed them to be correct, as I could do no good to myself or anyone else by remaining longer.

[In his supplementary book he says: 'I had not intended to bid a complete adieu to the Colony, but did not feel encouraged to return as I detested the whole system, and my affairs not looking prosperous, I gave up the idea and resolved to settle at Liverpool.' This does not exactly square with what he says above! – maybe because it was written for lecture purposes, whereas the main text is nearer the truth. But in any case, was there any need for his clandestine departure: could he not just have said simply 'I am visiting England for a while on business' (as he had done in 1823) – and then just never gone back? Or was it that the legal process applied without exception to all residents leaving, even temporarily, for whatever purpose?

Later on, at the point when he is in Barbados en route home, eight sheets are cut, then this paragraph is crossed out, from which it appears Mrs Pattinson went out to Demerara while JCC was coming the other way: … Daniel Stewart, an indolent Creole, being now the sole executor and trustee since the death of her husband. This brother had never attended to anything. And William Pattinson, deputed by his brother, had still possession of the property, which she went out determined, vi et armis, to wrest from his grasp. Of course she fell on him at once, which was just the way to provoke resistance, and when she found I was gone, whom she expected to assist her, she turned round on me and accused me of being in league with William as aforesaid.]

Addendum: Shaddock and Slaves

(1) The CWM/SOAS transcript of JCC's 'Journal' (*Slavery's Martyr* above) includes something interesting and totally unexpected: a serially-numbered printed form, for 'Return Of the Number of Slaves and Estimated Value thereof, in each Class, in possession of … on the 1st day of August 1834', with 'Name of Estate or Domicile of Slaves'. There are three divisions, Prædial (on the land) attached, ditto unattached, and Non-Prædial; plus Children under Six Years of Age on 1st August 1834, and Aged, Diseased, or otherwise Non-effective. In each of the first two divisions there are five classes, Head People, Tradesmen, Inferior Tradesmen, Field Labourers, and Inferior Field Labourers. The form is filled out for 'The Heirs of Chevely dec^d by Alice Bollers Att^y', address Murray Street, Demerara, and contains only Non-Prædial, comprising (sex not specified) as in the table below.

Interesting, but only serves to raise questions! It gives a clue as to where JCC and WP might have been staying latterly, though WP is not mentioned. The last name has clearly been altered from 'ley' to 'ly'; and why 'deceased'? JCC lived to 1870 (and by 1834 he did have an heir). Pattinson Cheveley & Co had been dissolved, so was it put about that he had died in order to cover his clandestine departure in 1825 when he severed all connection with Demerara? Do 10 adult slaves, rather more than the 5 that JCC gives as the domestic establishment in 1821, include the residue of Plantation Sarah Johanna? And which 'Chevel(e)y', as no initial is given – was there another apart from JCC of whose existence we are completely unaware?

Classes	Number	Value in Sterling
Tradesmen	1	180
Inferior do.	None	
Head people employed on Wharfs, Shipping or other Avocations	None	
Inferior People of the same description	3	300
Head Domestic Servants	4	640
Inferior Domestics	2	180
Children under Six Years of Age	4	200
Total	14	1500

(2) J.G. Stedman wrote a *History of Surinam* (Printed for J. Johnson, St. Paul's Church Yard and J. Edwards, Pall Mall, 1796). He was in the British Army, but was nevertheless sent out to Dutch Guiana (Surinam) to deal with a Negro insurrection there. The following are extracts:

(p. 21) I found the house entirely unfurnished, though not destitute of inhabitants, for, leaving my Captain's commission, which was of parchment, in the window the first night, I had the mortification to find in the morning that it was devoured by the rats. [So he too had rat trouble!]

(p. 22) The shaddock apple: A very agreeable flavour between sweet and acid; produced from a tree supposed to be transplanted from the coast of Guinea by a Captain Shaddock, whose name it still retains throughout the English West India islands, but called pompelmoose in Surinam [pompelmoes in modern Dutch; Grapefruit]. It appears to be of the orange species, as large as the head of a child of 8-10 years, the skin extremely thick, bitterish, and pale yellow or citron colour. There are two species, the pulp of one white, of the other a beautiful pale red.

(p. 295) Some slaves purchase freedom from their masters; others keep their money, preferring to be the slave of an indulgent master, being so long as they continue slaves, free from all duties and taxes, which in case of manumission they become liable to. Among the slaves, quaderoons are in general much respected for their affinity to Europeans, and are very numerous in this colony. Many

Quaderoon girls have European husbands, to no small mortification of the fair Creolians; yet should an European female be known to have had an intercourse with a slave of any denomination, she is forever detested and the slave loses his life without mercy – such are the despotic laws of men in Dutch Guiana over the weaker sex.

He gives a little couplet: 'The Samboe dark, the Mulatto brown; the Mæsti fair, the well-limb'd Quaderoon', but a 'family tree' best illustrates mixed-blood definitions. From what has been said, it will be appreciated that the coloured parent is normally female and the male is white.

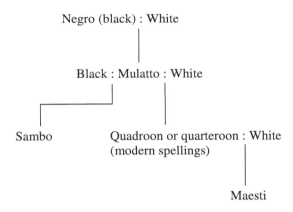

Negro (black) : White

Black : Mulatto : White

Sambo

Quadroon or quarteroon : White
(modern spellings)

Maesti

(All this calls to mind the old limerick:

> There was a young fellow named Starkie,
> Who had an affair with a darkie;
>   The result of his sins
>   Was quadruplets, not twins,
> One white, one black, and two khaki.

– Which might perhaps more likely be the offspring of two mulattos.)

Dictionary definitions: Creole: Strictly, a native of pure European blood, not aboriginal or indigenous, in contrast to immigrants born in

Europe or coloured natives; loosely, a native of mixed blood [By no means the same thing!]. In USA, a Negro born in America.

Mestizo [referred to by JCC]: Of mixed Spanish and American Indian parentage.

IV
Essex Man in Liverpool

PART 13

Escape to England, 1826

Making Water!

We got out to sea and lay on our course, and all seemed to be going comfortably. It was now the beginning of November 1825 [*Anna* must surely have stayed in Demerara a considerable time!], and although we might expect stiffish weather off England, dangers seemed hardly probable in these tropical seas. The vessel however seemed to labour, and I feared her load, mostly sugar and molasses, was too heavy. Next day I observed a good deal of pumping going on; George, seemingly inclined to treat me as an old woman, said 'Oh, we keep jogging her out, that's all.' Now I knew as well as he how often a ship needed to be pumped out in the ordinary way; but I saw clearly that something was wrong, and told him so: 'Now, no nonsense or concealment, the brig is taking in water considerably, and it behoves us to look at it while Barbados is under our lee, not run on into the danger of a winter's passage home, so get the well sounded and ascertain how much she is making.' We concluded she was making 6 feet of water in the hour, alarming enough to set us thinking what next to do, and moreover the pumping barely kept it under when the vessel worked. We concluded we could not proceed; to beat up again for Demerara was out of the question. As it was a case of distress, George told the crew the state of matters, and they agreed we bear up for Barbados, where George said the vessel could be repaired [approximately 450 miles from Georgetown, almost due North].

Accordingly we shaped our course thither, pumping pumping day and night, the leak gaining rather than diminishing: an anxious situation. We had one passenger on board, to whom George had given a passage gratis, a poor Irish widow of a soldier named Georgeghan [Geoghegan?]; he had been a free Mason, and as George was in that mystical and incomprehensible fraternity [then as now!]

he had undertaken, in the spirit of Masonic brotherhood, to restore her to kith and kin. She shut herself in her cabin, very seasick and dreadfully frightened, as she could hear all that passed, and was always asking when we should get to Barbados. Truly it seemed uncertain, as we were beat about by squalls, the weather dead against us; we had been expecting to run down in about two days, and four or five had already elapsed. I observed the ship laboured because she was too deep; George admitted it, and added 'If one of those butt ends at the bow were to give way, she'd go down like a stone.' He said afterwards that, considering the ship's age, this fear was constantly before him.

At length we sighted Barbados, but George must have run to leeward, as it took two whole days to beat into Carlisle Bay where Bridgetown is situated, where we found beautifully clear weather and smooth water. What a change! The leak ceased with the labouring, and our spirits rose with it. George knew the anchorage and the people, and determined to go in with eclat: so he stationed the men to take in all sail at once, man-of-war and East India Company fashion, and dashed in grand style. Just as he was going to give the word, he saw in the ship's path a hawser stretched from one ship to another; he bawled to them to drop it, but it was not in time, and he had to bring up his ship most ignominiously by letting all go flying, more discreditable than if he had taken in one sail at a time, in regular West India fashion.

Barbados: The End of *Anna*

We went to a friend of George's, an old Scotchman Henry Arnott, to arrange for a survey of the brig and effect repairs. A superficial examination would not meet the case, and the ship had to be brought into carinach or careenage, a sort of pier or dock where a portion of her cargo could be discharged and the place of the leak discovered. It was found that something was radically wrong: not only the planking, but some of the most important timbers of the framework were unsound. The surveyors finally resolved that she was unfit for sea without very extensive repairs, not recommended for an old vessel in a foreign port, where the expense would be more than the ship was worth. This was in fact a condemnation, and the brig *Anna* was adjudged to be discharged of her cargo, and the hull, rigging, and stores sold by auction.

To clear us of the charge of not having tried to save the ship from such a fate, I applied to the principal firms for an advance for the repairs, on the security of the ship and her freight, but they one and all refused; nor did I expect otherwise. We had therefore no alternative but to find another conveyance for the cargo; Mr Arnott negociated for it to be taken on the *Lancaster*, on which George, his mate, and myself would have passage home free of charge, and two boys from *Anna* would work their passages: these were Turnbull, an apprentice, and a little squalid-looking urchin, Stokes, whom George had in compassion taken off the streets of Liverpool to sweep decks, feed stock, and make himself generally useful. The men shipped on board other vessels to work home, and Mrs Geoghegan found another Masonic Captain to take her. So the unfortunate *Anna* was cleared, and everything belonging to her sold at auction, for an old song compared with her cost, but there was no help for it; on making up the accounts, I found the balance would not do much more than cover what she was indebted to me, after paying wages and other expenses. *Lancaster* would not be ready for some few weeks, so we had to take lodgings on shore.

George introduced me to a strange old Naval officer who held the Government appointment of Captain of the Port or Harbourmaster; like many other such, he did little else but lounge about, gossip and get half-tipsy. I did not at all like the affair, even less when George treacherously went off on some business and left me in this strange old man's possession, who rambled about and dragged me with him all morning. He said 'You must dine with me, what will you stand?' I stared at him – 'For drink – a dollar apiece? I can't give you any drinkables.' This was assumed rather than assented to. We encountered George on horseback, accompanied by an acquaintance with whom he was going into the country and could not therefore dine with us. So here I was betrayed into this old man's hands, who stuck to me like the 'old man of the sea'. Finally, having tricked me out of a dollar, he tricked a dinner out of someone for us both. I was welcomed very hospitably, but I felt the situation awkward, and apologized for my seeming intrusion; I was so ashamed of my companion, that I left as soon after dinner as I could. I was much vexed with George; it was too bad of him to play me such a trick, knowing as he did the man's character. I felt my society no longer pleased George or was sought by him. He was taken up with worldly amusements, and told me most warmly that he never would believe that religion was designed to cut us off from the 'innocent pleasures of life'. I was much grieved at all this, but found I could make no impression [Maybe George was tiring of his brother's sanctimonious attitude?]. Arnott once said 'Aye, Mester Chiefley, if you and your brother could jast mix up your deeferences, ye'd bring out a very fair average between ye! He'd have some of your releegion and you'd have a taste of his speerit!'

I felt a good deal out of my element in Barbados, an ungodly place like all slave colonies, though a more settled society than Demerara, being our oldest colony, dating [1642] from the first Stuart; many white families had been there for generations. There were also many poor whites, descendants of Irish settlers, known by their red sandy complexions, as the sun did not embrown their skins, who carried on petty huckstering trades, or squatted on small portions of land, and were generally at the head of all hubbubs.

I was foolishly induced one Saturday to go with a Mr Pearman to a distant coast town called Speightstown. I ought to have known from experience what I should meet with on the sabbath, but I thought it could not be worse than at Bridgetown, and I bargained that if I went, I should go to church. We met a dozen or so gentlemen at a sort of hotel, old stagers with a most inordinate love of little Barbados. I had a good opportunity of seeing all the peculiarities of their Barbadian character: eating and drinking appeared to be their entire purpose. Next day, Pearman and I went to breakfast at the plantation for which he was agent, bordering hilly country called Scotland [in the NE]. He assured me I should be back in time for church, but we rode about the whole morning, and it was past noon before we got back to Speightstown: when I was informed we were engaged to dine, and my reproaches were joked away. So the sabbath passed as it always did when I fell into the hands of Philistines.

George in a Scrape

On returning to Bridgetown, I found Arnott looking grave. My brother had got into a serious scrape, as he had had an altercation with a pugnacious Irishman and struck him. Arnott said he would assuredly get six months' imprisonment for the blow, as there were plenty of witnesses, unless his opponent would withdraw the charge. George could not be prevailed on to allow any such thing, he 'was ready to give him the satisfaction of a gentleman, and would not submit to compromise his honor.' I told him he would compromise it much more if the affair came to trial and he was imprisoned, and what would he do if his return to Liverpool were delayed six months, after our misadventure with *Anna*? I determined that come what might, I must get him out of it. Arnott saw it as I did, and through a friend of the Irishman whom he knew, negociations were set on foot, unknown to George who vowed 'No surrender'. At last the Irishman promised to withdraw the charge if a proper apology were made. Of course George said he never would, and rated me soundly for supposing such a thing. The magistrate's sessions were close at hand; George's obstinacy and perversity were unaccountable, and I could not help thinking he really wished to stay behind. Here he was facing 6 months imprisonment, his wife at home expecting his return, his ship sold from under him, I having to leave him, as I could not stay at such expense and nothing coming into defray it for either of us: how disgraceful would such a story seem in Liverpool as a finale to the loss of the ship, sure to tell to his discredit. Everyone saw the thing in its true light excepting George himself, who would be most affected by it.

At length he consented to write a confession, which virtually divided the blame. This, as I expected, was returned at once as perfectly unsatisfactory; and accompanied by one most uncompromisingly self criminating and apologetic, with an intimation that unless Captain Cheveley signed it, without any qualification, before the day was over, no further peace overtures would be listened to. Humiliation indeed! I felt indignant, George was furious. Arnott told him the writ was held over only in deference to his wishes, but once issued, the consequences must be met. The day wore on; at length George snatched up the odious paper, signed it, and walked out. It was accepted, and so ended this very ugly affair. At dinner, George charged me with sacrificing his honor &c. &c. to my feelings; I made an unguarded reply, which of course only added fuel to the fire. At once I felt I had done wrong, and I have often regretted it, but I was getting out of patience, feeling it hard to be blamed for doing my best to preserve him from trouble.

Poor dear George! I believe he was at this time greatly unhinged and unsettled, so that as we once saw eye to eye, we seemed now to be widely separated, and could no longer walk together. He had been grievously disappointed in the one true attachment he had formed for Sarah Rix, as strong on her part, which she had been induced to reject with a thorough negative. This had deeply affected him, and with his usual impulsive precipitency, he had at once renounced all hope, and rushed into an engagement which I believe, in his cooler moments, astonished no one more than himself. Too late he discovered that Sarah's rejection had not been her own free act.

Mr Arnott's Social Life
Christmas arrived, but Arnott, being a Scotchman, proposed a festive gathering on New Year's Day, a dancing party to please his mulatto daughter. George and I were invited, but I at once said it was not in my way, which Mr Arnott seemed to comprehend; he thought me 'far too releegious for a young man', and his daughter said she would expect me to open the Ball with her! [Here the eight sheets mentioned above (see 'William returns, I depart') are cut, so we do not know what happened at the Ball!].

A day or two before our departure, Arnott proposed a visit to a planter friend; knowing planters, I had misgivings about the entertainment this 'gude fellow' might have for us. Arnott's daughter, who was still in the dumps about the dancing affair and had not looked at me very benignly since [presumably JCC refused to oblige her?], told me that as I was so very steady and religious, she looked to me to take care of her father and bring him home safe, which I promised to do. Off we set, Arnott and I in one gig, George and a friend of Arnott's in another. I forget now anything but the immense drinking that went on; George and I manoeuvred as well as we could to avoid it, and found our way to the ladies, to the great offense of our host, but we stood our ground. Then we got again with the gentlemen; tea was brought in, which I looked on as a relief, but to my horror I found it was doctored with brandy! Was the drinking over now? Not by any means! And this was ordinary planters' fare in the West Indies: to get drunk and to make others so, seemed the height of felicity. Arnott could only just walk to his gig, and was so incapable, to the danger of getting my neck broken, that I called to his friend to go with him, while George and I drove on together. Arrived at Bridgetown I must assist him into his house and help him upstairs: to a pretty reception from his daughter, and I found that 'bringing him home safe' meant bringing him home sober! So she took her revenge for the dancing affair by rating me up as West India ladies know how, for suffering her father to get tipsy, which I cut short by getting out as fast as I could, greatly annoyed and vexed at having again been inveigled into such an affair and being blamed for failing to keep the party in sobriety. Thus I bid adieu to Barbados, of which I had had quite enough, as of West India life generally. Yet I had one deep source of consolation.

The Colonel and the Captain

Lancaster's Captain, Cannell, told us that some soldier officers were going home in her as passengers. He had got it into his head, and put the notion into theirs, that as we had free passage, we were only second-class sort of folk, not fit company for officers, and hinting we should be consigned to some secondary part of the ship. We could not understand it, supposing these officers considered us unfit associates, or that their kind of living was beyond our means. At last I got Mr Arnott to see the Colonel of the regiment, who was to be one of the passengers, to assure him of our respectability, and that we were quite ready to furnish our quota of the Mess requirements. He was satisfied with this, and said that any objections were of the Captain's own making: whose scruples were set at rest. Early in January 1826 George and I went on board, determined *we* would not make the first overtures to the soldier officers; so seeing two red coats seated on the larboard side of the skylight, we took the starboard. We had not long to wait: a middle-aged tall weathered-looking gentleman came round to us, said 'I am Colonel McAlister, I believe you are to be our companions', and introduced us to Lieutenant Moore, who was about 30, and his wife, unmistakably Irish, about 15 years his senior. We were soon relieved of all embarrassment, and talked over our mess and cabin arrangements; as Moore was disposed to take the lead, we agreed he be President and manager.

The Colonel had a hook nose and an obliquity of vision which when he was excited became a direct squint, otherwise adding a humourous cast to his countenance, which did not belie his kindly and genial disposition. He was a strict disciplinarian, and kept up his regimental state even with his reduced establishment. On Sunday morning, Mrs Moore brought up the 'Prayer Book', sufficiently large to show its official character, and he read the shorter part of the service, as he would on shore to the regiment at the drumhead. Yet he was by no means arbitrary or unpleasant, and his demeanor was gentlemanly and characterised by good-humoured drollery. He was accustomed to rule and routine, even on a small scale. He had a boy 'Dick' with him about 11 years old, the son of a serjeant, whom he was taking home to go to school, and to whom he was very kind. The boy waited on him in various matters, and was admonished with military exactness as to order and neatness. But Stokes was the object of his admiration. During the hot weather, he had reduced to a red woollen shirt as his sole garment, and the Colonel frequently met this specimen of street-arab life, broom in hand, on deck. He and George joked about the merits of their respective pages, and it ended in Stokes being stuck into a pair of canvas trowsers, in rivalry with 'Dick' to help wait at dinner; he became so expert as to extract commendations from the Colonel, all of which he received with imperturbable gravity, probably not understanding the Colonel's bombastic style.

Captain Cannell was every inch a Liverpool 'skipper', as unfit to command a ship as many skippers of that day often were: vulgar, ignorant and conceited, and did not understand the first principles of navigation. To the military officers he was servile, to us barely civil, as he considered us part of the freight we had put on board. He was a muddling fellow, tyrannical withal, and could never get on with his mate, always rating [ranting?] at him, frequently for the result of his own bad arrangements. He made a great noise about trifles, but had no regular system or real discipline. Our cabins were parted from the 'tween-decks by a deal partition or bulkhead, and George and I could see through the chinks what was going on there, where the mates and carpenter and some others had their mess. The ship was very full, and some cargo had been stowed in their birth. At night, I could see proceedings which excited some apprehension, as follows: 1st, a tier of puncheons of rum. 2nd, half a dozen fellows sprawling on top of them, smoking pipes and cigars over their grog. 3rd, a lighted tallow candle, unprotected and unsupported, stuck on the bilge of one of the said puncheons. 4th, other combustibles admirably disposed. Spontaneous enough would combustion have been if a fellow had kicked the bung out of one of those puncheons, which are always stored bung up: an immediate flare-up, from the candle to the vapour from the cask, would have been the result, and the ship on fire. I nightly saw preparations for catastrophe until I could bear it no longer, and told the Captain the ship would be on fire if those fellows went on smoking with a light on the rum casks. Stupidly, he went up on deck, and called down the main hatchway to 'douse that glim there', which was done in no time, and he retired to his birth quite unmoved by my representing it as a nightly occurrence. Thus I believe ships are jeopardized and not infrequently 'not again heard of'.

Lancaster was a large ship belonging, with many others, to Sir William Barton, Irlam & Higginson of Liverpool, a fine vessel, well-found and provided in every respect, even to a good chronometer which ticked away in the cabin – to no purpose, as the Captain was quite unable to determine longitude by its aid and might just as well have attempted to discover the position of the man in the moon. He said he could get on very well 'by dead reckoning without them sort of things, and he got his ship home as well as they did as made a great flourish about chronometers'. So he blundered on, and marked his course and daily distance on the chart with edifying precision.

George on the other hand had his own chronometer and sextant, and marked his own chart, which soon began to differ from the Captain's. The passengers asked him one day how it was that Captain Cannell never did anything with his chronometer except wind it up, and wished to know how the two charts tallied: which George could not tell, as Cannell kept his chart from him. The passengers were not to be done, for military officers are much given to wanting to know how things are going, so they had no scruples about looking over the Captain and his chart. It was soon obvious that George and he differed in longitude, and the passengers became so alarmed that they requested George to leave his chart about; and although Cannell affected to ignore it, they soon discovered that he made alterations and modified his longitude every now and then, to their comfort although not to their increased confidence in his abilities.

George Insulted!
We had been at sea a week or ten days when Captain Cannell took it into his head to have the hatches taken off and to hoist some of the cargo on deck: which he had no right to do, as stowed cargo should not be touched excepting on a great emergency, and if any part got wet or damaged, the insurers would consider themselves not liable to make good. I was therefore uneasy to see several bags of coffee, which I had shipped, thrown on the deck and very narrowly escaping a wetting, which would have been fatal. I pointed this out to the Captain, and George told him he should not move the cargo, and if anything happened he should hold him and the shipowners liable. He roughly told George not to interfere in *his* ship; George told him roundly it *was* his business to interfere for the protection of *his* cargo. At length Cannell, irritated and brutal [brutish?], told George if he interfered any more he would pull his nose for him. This was such an insult that we both felt it could not be passed by, but knew not how to treat it; we were talking it over unaware that Mrs Moore, who had been sitting on deck, had heard what had passed and related it to the Colonel and her husband.

In a short time the Steward summoned me to see the Colonel in the cabin. Squinting dreadfully, he said he understood a gross insult had been offered to my brother by the Captain, and wished to know what we intended to do to clear ourselves. I replied that I considered Captain Cannell a vulgar ignorant man, and we thought it best to take no further notice either of the matter or of him. 'That won't do for

PART 14

Restart, 1826-31

New Positions

I rambled about Prescot, and the five years in the West Indies seemed like a dream, so completely had things settled into their old state of stagnation. I felt I was again set down without prospect of retrieving my position in the business world. My family were anxious I come to them at Hedingham, but I knew that would be fatal, as I could hope for success only by remaining in Liverpool, which offered my only prospect. I endeavored to keep together my few mercantile acquaintances, and Miss Barry introduced me to Mr Edward Cearns, a rising man in the American trade; but none could help me in obtaining employment, the great object I had in view. Mr Driffield was most kind in recommending me wherever he thought possible; the influential Willis family of Halsmead in the neighborhood shewed an interest in me, and eventually his introduction to an elder son, Mr Daniel Willis, proved the way to a permanent and very long engagement.

I am surprised to remember how often I came over to Liverpool and fell in with Miss Barry, quite by accident of course, and what an interest I began to feel in the family, despite Mrs Pattinson's ill-feeling and unjust conduct. Seriously, things at Anfield Cottage looked precarious: nothing from Mrs Pattinson but promises, and how poor old Mrs Pritchard managed to provide for the family was next to a miracle. It now came out that Mr Pattinson had made over to Roscow, as security for money lent, the whole of his household furniture, and the assignees sent in their claim on it and served notice of sale. I met Miss Barry and Mr Ashe, and appealed to the creditors' representative not to turn the family out, but he seemed determined to stick to legal duty; till I thought of Miss Barry's friend Mr Cearns, to whom I ran and brought him to the conference. After much debate it was settled that the affair stand over to give time for

Mrs Pattinson to be communicated with, so *that* danger was for the present avoided.

By this time both I and Frances Barry had begun to arrive at the same sentiment, which had been longer gathering force in our minds than we were quite aware of, that our affections and interests were identified. She was supposed by Everton people to be well-connected, and she associated with many in works of benevolence or Christian charity; but when the exposure of Mr Pattinson's affairs came, these friends, with surprising prudence and self-respect, held off, and let her know that friendship was now at an end. She was naturally high-minded, and had a quick sense of what was mean and selfish, with a disposition to resent anything approaching insult, which did not improve matters; she was also thoroughly indifferent to the opinion of the world, but here made a mistake, for it does not suit to set the world at defiance any more than it does to comply with its maxims and practices.

I remained at Prescot till the end of April, when I was advised of a mercantile situation. I felt disposed to come to terms, but Mr Driffield had told me to do nothing, as he had something else in view. Mr Daniel Willis had told him that his firm, Willis Latham & Gair, would shortly be requiring a principal clerk; so next day we drove to their office in the Goree Piazzas, close to George's Dock. Mr Willis, a little, slight, invalidish-looking man, with a thin sharp voice and abrupt manner, asked me innumerable questions with an interrogatory stare; I felt more encouraged by the genial Mr Gair, a Bostonian, who attended to the American business. The third partner, Mr Arthur Latham, ran the home and shipping transactions. I would work mainly in Mr Willis' department, the East India, and it was arranged I should take my post at the end of a month, at a salary of £100 a year, not a brilliant success, but a considerable step forward.

I took the 'Royal Umpire' next day for London, feeling more light-hearted than for many months. A new era seemed before me, and I had again hope for the future, as well as the great incentive of the happiness of another being involved in mine. I was welcomed by Tom. He had come from Colchester a year or two previously to improve himself, finding the bookselling and stationery business too slow, and had engaged in a printing office, which he found rather too fast, as he could not keep pace as a compositor with the more practiced hands, nor could he fall in with their immoralities. He had found he was in the wrong place, and was now working with publishers Longman & Co at a small salary as a book collector, scudding about with a blue bag. He shared a bedroom at the corner of Bow Lane Cheapside, up four or five pair of stairs, with Charles, who had got from the tyranny of Barber Beaumont at the County Fire Office to the Bank of England. However, at this time Charles was ill with jaundice, and was being tenderly nursed by Miss Rix at Ivy Cottage, Clapham, a snug old-fashioned little place on the edge of the common, north of the church. Tom and Charles had found it a 'Goshen' [place of light or plenty] since they, as inexperienced young men, had been cast on the wilderness of London and its perils, and they fully appreciated such a refuge for their sabbath and vacant hours. What a change was working in us all at that time.

Next afternoon I was at Castle Hedingham. Richard was about to marry Miss Elizabeth Vallance, who lived with her widowed mother Mrs Mayhew at Warren Farm, St Osyth, near the mouth of the Blackwater. The engagement had the prospect of a comfortable settlement in life, but was for time, with no consideration for eternity. Father drove me over to Great Bardfield to see my old travelling patron Evans, and this was the last I saw of him. I was invited to join some reunions of old bachelor wine-bibbers of the Stammers and Brathwaite type, reinforced by Mr Laurence from Birchin Lane, but it was wearisome and anything but pleasing to see men deriving all their interest and pleasure from sensual gratification. I spent time with my sisters, sketching and taking black profile likenesses with the camera lucida. The allotted month passed as quickly as such months always do, so again I left, but with very different feelings from last time, as the sentence was not now banishment. I staid one night in London, where Charles was now well and at work again, and on June 1st I was back at Prescot Vicarage.

Willis Latham & Gair

On June 3rd [a Saturday!], my birthday, I commenced my new duties. I had to plunge in at once, but having never been in an

English counting-house, I found that with all my business experience acquired abroad, I had much to learn of the minutiae at home. The business of accounts was more intricate and laborious than I had ever dreamt of: the bill system, with days to run and days of grace, the credit system of sales of various articles with terms of payment almost as various as the articles themselves, and all accounts to be reduced to what is called Cash by minute interest calculations, which attended settlement of every account however insignificant. I had also to consider that I was now a subordinate, subject to the will and dictation of others, and it required some little self-control to fall into 'the ranks' again after having been so long a 'superior officer', but I had the advantage of no responsibility beyond obedience to orders. My business was to receive and pay all monies, advise the bank (Leylands), keep the cash and subsidising books, and assist the bookkeeper with the accounts. I soon discovered I had no sinecure. To my surprise and dismay, I learned that the hours of business began at 9 but were of unlimited duration, regulated by the press of business or caprice of the partners [Perhaps you should have asked before you took the job on?]. The post from London came at 8 in the evening and went at ½ past ten at night, as pretty a contrivance as could be imagined for keeping officials to their duty.

Mr Willis and his partners did not seem to be on very cordial terms. He was most thoroughly irregular, and never seemed to act with the others or have any fixed hours for doing anything. The Willis method was all by impulses and all in a hurry. Late in the afternoon or evening, when we thought we had got rid of the others and could be off, in he came with some troublesome bookkeeping job or letters to be written, without the slightest warning. Subsequently, it came on by degrees that he would keep me so I did not get home till past 12 at night. Yet I found he was a kind man, humane and charitable, and I learned to esteem and respect him, though my appreciation was sorely tried by his whims and irregularities, which made it difficult to bear with temper his excessive exactions on one's time and patience.

In fixing my place of abode, if under such circumstances I could be said to want one, I was led to seek lodgings near my work. I had first resorted to Anfield Cottage, a walk of more than two miles; the attraction there was considerable, but my stay was not contemplated as other than temporary. However a necessity was placed before me, that there was absolutely nothing for the family to keep house on. Mrs Pattinson sent nothing but ranting letters from Demerara, and not a sixpence was coming in. Under these circumstances, and setting aside all other consideration, I felt I must give the family the payment for my board and lodging, and the pound a week was valuable assistance in providing for them.

Now it may be thought very imprudent of me to take up my abode in the same house with Frances Barry, and a vast impropriety on both our parts, although we had Mrs Pritchard to matronize us. The first was set at nought, as is very common, by a power which sooner or later puts Prudence in the background. The proprieties had left Frances to take care of herself, and she did not much respect them; she was fully conscious of the truth and rectitude of her motives. Her former friends, however, were kind enough to consider how very improper it was to have me at the house in Mrs Pattinson's absence and how imprudent she had been. So after I had been comfortably domesticated a couple of months, I had a letter from Mr Driffield, and Mrs Cearns told Miss Barry the kind things her former friends had said of her. *She* was indignant, and I was puzzled how to act, as Mr Driffield told me I must seek lodgings elsewhere. This was out of the question, as my pound a week was too precious to be parted with, and we compromised by the lady going at night to a friend's house. Thus we dragged on and tormented ourselves for another month, till Fanny (as I may now call her) got out of all patience at thus trying to satisfy the Proprieties, who evidently would *not* be satisfied, as Mrs Cearns continued to tell her the pleasant things that were still being said.

So after talking the affair over and over with Mr and Mrs Cearns, they brought it to a crisis, and rather a startling one, by discussing a union of the twain. Well! This required consideration, as it brought me face to face with my old friend Prudence again. All I could look for at present was £100 a year. Fanny had a little from her small property in Demerara; by Mr Pattinson's death, her mother's will had passed into the hands of her indolent half-brother Daniel Stewart, from which she expected an addition when Mrs Pattinson had put

Portrait: JCC's brother George. (Courtesy Mrs J Cheveley)

everything to rights, though I had misgivings as to things going the right way if *she* got possession. However, we hoped for the best, and I wrote to Mr Driffield to say we had come to the final resolution. He candidly laid before me the prudential view: the small income, the possibility of liabilities from complications with the Pattinsons and Roscow, and the axiom that one and one did not always make but two: 'in my case', he said, 'they make 9'. He added that many men had been content, as he had been, to wait many years rather than view matrimony and poverty united; but he left me to be my own judge.

Marriage

Another conference, and the day was fixed; I called on Mr Buddicom, and requested his good offices, as Fanny's spiritual father and at her desire. I asked leave of absence for a week, and on the morning of September 8th 1826 [a Friday] at Everton church, I entered on the matrimonial life. We breakfasted at Mr and Mrs Cearns', and spent the allotted week at Chester. One of Fanny's many Irish cousins (Barrys and Heleys), John Barry, was there as editor of the 'Chester Courant'. He had been brought up Roman Catholic, but seeing its folly had abandoned it and gone, as often, from abject superstition to scepticism. Fanny had one brother, a Barry, who was for some years in St Domingo and later in New York.

Not long after we returned to Anfield Cottage, Mrs Pattinson reappeared. For a few days she affected to be complaisant, but it was all put on, a cloud on her countenance told the feeling within. She had always disliked her sister, and her ill-feeling towards me seemed intensified by our union. Nothing reconciled her, and her conduct at length became so positively hostile that we deemed it better to withdraw before matters became worse. She was thoroughly unreasonable, expostulation was out of the question. In fact it suited her to quarrel, as we found later she had a plot regarding their mother's property in Demerara, which she had got entirely into her own hands, so it was expedient to keep aloof from us.

We therefore left Anfield, and took apartments in Portland Place near Roscommon Street, Everton, after a month going to lodge in Moira Street, London Road with two old maiden sisters, with whom

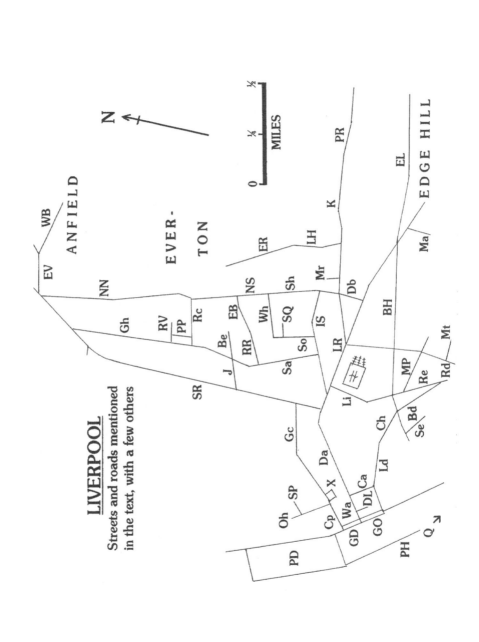

LIVERPOOL

Streets and roads mentioned
in the text, with a few others

N

0   ¼   ½
MILES

ANFIELD

EDGE HILL

EVER-
TON

WB
EV
NN
Gh
SR
RV
PP
Rc
Be
EB
RR
J
Sa
So
Wh
NS
SQ
Sh
Mr
IS
LR
Li
Db
BH
ER
LH
K
PR
EL
Ma
MP
Re
Rd
Mt
Se
Bd
Ch
Ld
Ca
DL
GO
Wa
X
Da
Gc
SP
Oh
Cp
GD
PD
PH
Q

Liverpool: Streets etc.

Everton Crescent: Between Richmond Row and Everton Brow; Richmond Fair nearby.
JCC's Clarence Street is at 55 Everton Road.
Pool Lane (where Mr Cheshire linen draper's shop was) not located – no longer exists?
Mount Street should not be confused with Mount Pleasant.
All names below are Streets if not otherwise defined; GO, IS, K, X are named as such with no qualifier.

Bd	Bold	J	Juvenal	Rc	Roscommon
Be	Beau	K	Kensington	Rd	Rodney
BH	Brownlow Hill	Ld	Lord	Re	Renshaw
Ca	Castle	LH	Low Hill	RR	Richmond Row
Ch	Church	Li	Lime	RV	Rose Vale
Cp	Chapel	LR	London Road	Sa	St Anne
Da	Dale	Ma	Mason	Se	Seel
Db	Daulby	Mr	Moira	Sh	Shaw
DL	Drury Lane	MP	Mount Pleasant	So	Soho
EB	Everton Brow	Mt	Mount	SP	St Paul's Square
EL	Edge Lane	NN	Netherfield Road North	SQ	Soho Square
ER	Everton Road	NS	Netherield Road South	SR	Scotland Road
EV	Everton Valley	Oh	Old Hall	Wa	Water
Gc	Great Crosshall	PD	Princes Dock	WB	Walton Breck Road
GD	George's Dock Gate	PH	Pier Head	Wh	William Henry
Gh	Great Homer	PP	Portland Place	X	The Exchange
GO	Goree Piazza	PR	Prescot Road		
IS	Islington	Q	Queens Dock		

we afterwards removed to 20 Daulby Street. We had a handsome drawing-room and good bedroom, with attendance, for 12/- [12 shillings] a week! Our weekly living expences did not exceed 20/-, and for two persons we managed well enough, but it soon became evident that Mr Driffield's axiom would be verified, and we began to bethink of increasing our means. So Fanny, who was a good musician, undertook to give lessons on the pianoforte. Of course, like most young beginners, we considered we had only to make our talents known to insure patronage, but alas, the public were deaf to our appeals. Mr Driffield distributed our cards at Prescot, from which Fanny at length had some engagements, visiting the Crosby neighborhood by the canal ferry, as there were no omnibuses in those days.

It was a wearisome winter, and well for me that I had not now to walk to Anfield. As the days shortened, the evenings at the office lengthened; I went home to dinner at five, and returned at 7, seldom to get home again before 9 or 10, sometimes later. Fanny began to tire of sitting night after night by herself, and frequently accompanied me when I went out, on her way to the house of one or other of her friends, from which I picked her up on my way home.

Ellen
The end of the year brought back George and his wife from the West India islands. He took a command to Pernambuco in the employ of Mr Hewson Dutchman, a thorough Yorkshireman; little dark Ellen was to be left at home, as Mr Dutchman did not approve of wives at sea, and George probably had had enough of the experiment. So she went to her old lodgings in St Paul's Square. The summer had been one of the hottest and driest ever experienced, followed by one of the coldest winters, which I found very trying after 5 years under a vertical sun, and my poor little sister-in-law still more so. She very soon began to shew symptoms of its effects, which as the spring advanced developed into rapid consumption. With her petulant and wilful mind, it became very difficult to deal with her; for some time she refused any treatment, and was excessively irritable with all who interfered with her. Her landlady had called in a low class medical man who was seldom quite sober and knew nothing of her complaint.

My wife was shocked at her altered appearance, and sent our medical man; he said nothing could save her, but prescribed some palliatives, which she rejected.

One day Fanny, to her surprise, found Ellen completely changed. Her mind had undergone a thorough revolution, and she opened up in the most candid and touching way. She confessed her heart had been hardened to the advice of those who had befriended her; she knew she had not long to live, and desired to tell what the Lord had done for her soul. On the morning of her death, a few weeks later, Mr Driffield and Mr Buddicom both saw her, and were much struck with her calm and simple dependence on Christ's salvation. Fanny and I were with her to the moment of her departure; she spoke of her prospects for eternity with calm and holy confidence, and died without a cloud on her spiritual vision. May my last end be like hers. George returned in Spring 1827, and so deeply was he affected by his wife's death that all his religious feelings seemed to revive. His impulsive nature was, as always, violently acted on; Ellen, with all her faults, had loved him sincerely, and he was not the man to underrate it.

I found, to my regret, that George had got into a dispute with Dutchman, who would not settle his wages. He put the matter into a lawyer's hands, a bad resourse [recourse?], as a Captain who goes to law with his owners becomes a marked man and has little prospect of getting forward. George had the worst of it, for although he brought his owner to a settlement, he did not stop his tongue, and was consequently a long while doing nothing. He was not anxious to go to sea again, and made some efforts to establish himself on shore. One was to teach navigation, so he took a room in Castle Street, and I was more surprised than edified to see a large blue board and gilt letters flaring away with 'Mr Cheveley's Navigation Academy', which speedily brought round me many enquiries, including Mr Latham and Mr Gair to know what it could possibly mean. A letter from Charles about this time, announcing the marriage of Sarah Rix, fell like a boom [bomb?] shell on George's hopes, which had shewn symptoms of revival, which took him much by surprise, and proved another unsettler.

Exit Latham & Gair, Enter Family

An event in preparation was the dissolution of the firm. Mr Willis and his partners did not pull well together, and as Mr Tom Willis, the younger brother, was entering mercantile life, they were to become Daniel & Thomas Willis, and the other partners Latham & Gair. Mr Willis expressed approval of my abilities and conduct, and made an offer to remain with him if I wished, which I considered my duty, as he had been the means, through Mr Driffield, of placing me where I was. He said he would be able to improve my salary, and I felt I should have no reason to regret my confidence in him; nor had I, for I ever found him (although fidgetty and exacting) a most kind and sympathizing friend. Mr Latham and Mr Gair kindly said they would have been quite prepared to make me an offer too, but I told them I considered Mr Willis had the first claim on me.

So at Michaelmas 1827, after 15 months, I became clerk-in-chief with Daniel & Thomas Willis. It was not a comfortable change, and I found it at first irksome. Mr Latham and Mr Gair were well-trained and regular, but the Willises were all uncertain and desultory, needlessly particular about trifles, weightier matters postponed, and the office kept open late at night to make up for time wasted during the day. This was discouraging, and made my work tedious and laborious, yet I worked for Mr Willis with pleasure, because I highly esteemed his character. [What price loyalty against better business practice? – though in view of what happened some 3 years later, perhaps as well!] My salary was raised to £120, not excessive but as much as I had expected, and I felt assured that more would not be withheld as business improved. From the old firm we had the custom-house clerk Aaron Appleton, with a young Spaniard of French extraction who was improving himself in English mercantile affairs, and two lads.

The event to which we had been looking forward approached, and on August 19th 1827 I had the strange never-to-be-forgotten sensation of an infant son added to our domestic cares and affections. I do not suppose any event in the life of two united people can ever equal the birth of the firstborn. I was thankful it was unattended by any trying circumstances. Another important change was the transfer of my parents and sisters to Liverpool, a formidable affair when railways were unborn. George had long set his heart on it; as he had settled with Mr Dutchman and found himself pretty well off, he broke the chief difficulty of paying the transit expences. It was a considerable undertaking for Mother, whose health was declining, but she was anxious for it; Father's active mind delighted in the idea of the bustle and business traffic; my sisters felt lost at Hedingham, and longed for change; and we all thought how delightful reunion would be, although those left behind in the south felt deserted. But we had to find out that parents, two sisters, brother, married brother with wife and child, and an old spoiled Essex servant [still Ann Livermore? – no name given], all together, was a compound of explosive materials, which would when shaken up blow hopes of domestic felicity to the winds.

Separations

It was quite apparent before we got through the first winter that we were out of harmony; and the discomfiture of all reached its climax next spring when we had Henry added to our party, bringing with him the rough and irregular habits of sea life, on his return from Jamaica in command of the brig *Gazelle*, his captain having died. By summer, Margaret had an engagement as a daily governess, and George and Henry were again at sea, which was a relief. Henry's owners, R & G Benn of Liverpool, confirmed his command, and he sailed to Buenos Ayres. But Mother's health was exciting our apprehensions. The removal had not been good for her, and after the novelty wore off, she never could be reconciled to it. After just a year, in autumn 1828, suffering from excessive weakness, she gradually sunk [and died August 30th 1828]. We all loved her, and she was worthy of it; Father mourned her loss most truly. She was interred in Prescot churchyard, close to the gate from the Vicarage garden, where Father was laid ten years later.

Henry wrote to me just after receiving news of his mother's death, from the Cape de Verde islands, where he had been sent for a cargo, returning to Buenos Ayres for the homeward voyage. Alas, poor Henry! We never heard from him again, and our next account was from his consignee at Buenos Ayres, to say he had been drowned in the River Plate. He had gone to a ship in the outer roads to enquire

Portrait: John's Mother, from a chalk drawing.
(Courtesy Mrs M. Timmington

for letters and news, a considerable distance; the captain was going on shore, and Henry offered to take two or three passengers in his boat. A heavy squall came on, very common in that river and very dangerous; the other boat was saved by running alongside a vessel at anchor, but Henry's was lost sight of. Next morning it drifted ashore, bottom up. The bodies of the passengers and others were recovered, but we never heard that Harry's was found. Poor Harry! He was very thoughtless, very venturesome; whether the disaster was owing to his want of prudence, we could not judge. His consignees gave him a high character for his social worth and kindly disposition, and indeed he had much about him that was attractive.

Our family incongruity fell to pieces very soon after, and we thought it best to separate our families. My father and sisters removed to a small house they hired and furnished in Upper Beau Street. Our new house was in Soho Square, a little nook out of Soho Street, then respectable, but now, in common with the once beautiful and aristocratic village of Everton and the entire north side of London Road, sunk in meanness. Father assisted me with £200, for which I was to pay him the interest he would have received; with it, we furnished two small sitting rooms, kitchen, and three bedrooms plainly but comfortably, and into this small Paradise we inserted ourselves, with one servant. Everything was new and handy, we seemed likely to want for nothing, Fanny was happy and frugal and industrious.

Our little square abutted on the right on meadows, nothing intervening but a new road cut through a rocky eminence to connect upper Islington with Everton at Netherfield Road South, on whose left side superior houses were being constructed, called Shaw Street. Then, Everton Crescent was the only row of houses between the top of Richmond Row and Everton brow and village. The steep ascent to the village had on the left a range of very old and picturesque cottages: the first, 'Molly Cooper's', of great celebrity as the Everton Toffee Shop; on the right, the thatched 'Rupert's Cottage' in which the Prince was said to have quartered when he invested Liverpool for Charles I. A row of large elm trees at the corner of Everton Road, which soon after my arrival made way for Clarence Terrace and Plumpton Terrace, gave character to the village, then a mixture of aristocratic residences and low-set centuries-old cottages, with here and there a milkhouse or 'shippon'. Rector Brooks' house and garden on the left were the only dwelling in Everton Road before Brunswick Road at the south end, where, on the right, was a large pretentious stuccoed mansion surrounded by shrubberies, known as 'Gregson's Well', from an excavation near its entrance into which he was supposed to have tumbled.

Now (1868) all is swept away, and the entire range of fields from Soho Square covered with small streets and houses. Everton's decline was begun and accelerated by Muspratt's chemical works and others which multiplied along the Leeds and Liverpool Canal, whose vapours destroyed all vegetation, killed the trees, and rendered gardening impossible, so that those who had property moved south beyond Toxteth Park to new mansions in Aigberth, Allerton, Wavertree, Childwall and Woolton. So the north end fell into squalidity and the southern end rose in dignity and beauty.

Small Income, Small Family

I now entered on a new and pretty long chapter in my existence, the most serious, although most prosaic, portion of my manhood. Hitherto my trials had been mingled with much variety and adventure. My position in life was settled, and family cares begun, two years since, but I was now to know the real difficulties of married life, as a small housekeeper on a very small income with a small family: all these indicated finality. My office work was very hard, and I was kept late, but I worked on, hoping that times would mend and my income, not yet beyond £120, increase. Both Willis brothers were desultory in business habits; they were bachelors, with no domestic establishment of their own, nor had they much thought for those who had. It was indeed a dreary affair when, at the close of a day's work, Mr DW would appear and I had to write some of his interminable letters, frequently exceeding ten or a dozen pages. Still there was much about him that was estimable and upright, and a benevolent disposition, so I regarded him with respect and felt that in him I had a kind friend.

Our household had started with a respectable servant girl, but she soon left us. The next followed the same course, left us in the lurch, and we were servant-galled after the approved method for young beginners. Nanny from Prescot invariably said 'Oi've been agate soidin' (siding), i.e. putting things to rights, while there was every demonstration they were all to wrongs. One Ellen was the dirtiest of the dirty, so a peaceful meal was impossible for the thought of what it might have gone through, which is saying a good deal for a man who had had years of seasoning on board ship and in the West Indies. With a succession of 'helps' like these, Fanny began to find the pleasures of a small household and small income, but she worked with indomitable perseverance and self-denying devotedness, especially after *little* Fanny came February 1st 1829.

Johnny was cutting teeth and fractious, and woke about one or two o'clock and roared to the full power of his infantine lungs, so I was constrained, out of compassion to his mother, to walk with him about the room: an act of parental weakness for whose continuance I had to pay the penalty, for vainly supposing I had lulled this bit of obstrepulosity to sleep, lo! looking over my shoulder I saw two eyes wide open, betokening unmitigated satisfaction with things as they were.

At 15 or 16 months old he was ready enough with his tongue, but did not shew any symptoms of going alone on his feet. To aid his locomotive powers, it was determined to have recourse to artificial supports, and a surgical instrument maker, Mr Dunsford, fitted him with a set of irons to support the legs, which enabled him to cruise about the room by the aid of the chairs. [This is the very first thing of which I have a distinct recollection – JCC II.] When Mr Dunsford came to see how they acted, he expressed his delight by looking up at him and uttering impromptu 'Thank you Dunsford for my pretty breeches.' [I think Ellen taught me to say that – JCC II.] Then our medical man, Dr Chalmer from Kirkdale, said Johnny must be plunged every morning in a cold bath to strengthen his limbs, but as we had no bath in the house (not so common then), we had him carried to a tub in the yard under the water tap, and brought in again wrapped in a warm blanket.

Ellen (whom it would have benefitted to go through the same process) had instructions for *one* plunge and out again, but to my consternation I found her sousing him *three* times over head and ears, and in future I superintended the operation myself. [One would hardly believe it, but I have a most vivid recollection of these sousings – JCC II].

His mother had early impressed on him not to meddle with anything without leave, and he observed 'not to touch' to the letter, though not quite in the spirit, as it was part of his amusement to put his finger close enough to give an idea of contact, look back at his Mama, and say, with a look half-incredulous, half-daring, 'Not to touch' [I remember this – my idea was to be loyal to the command although the temptation was strong – JCC II]. He was a great favorite with Grandpapa, and went frequently to Beau Street for the day, as soon as he could toddle so far with a helping hand, his irons and tongue going click-clack together all the way.

Dear little Fanny, a most affectionate and impulsive child, very early wound her tendrils round our hearts; she was long in getting on her feet, but she cruised about in the best way which Nature has as a substitute, and on several occasions was detected scuffling along the gravel walk in the little front garden, intending to see the world outside the garden gate [She was known as Little Miss Shufflebottom: there was a 'Job Shufflebottom', a cab proprietor – JCC II]. John at a very early age was attracted by the piano, and stood by his Mama by the half-hour while she played, and screwed up his tiny squeak to accompany her in singing, when not much more than two years old, while little Fan danced away with extraordinary agility before she could walk, Mama holding her under the arms on the table. I did not often come in for these frolics, except on Friday evenings, when the mail could not reach London for Saturday delivery unless there was a ship sailing for India or anything extraordinary. Mama had constructed a natural history picture book of small engravings pasted on muslin to stand the wear and tear, and it proved a great success; it is in existence to this day [1868], though probably deprived of some of its parts [I have it now, 1881 – JCC II]. We were not rich, but we made our means do; neither were we idle, for our children were naturally very excitable and required great good management and attention.

Catastrophe – and Good Luck

At the beginning of 1829, George was again home, and out of employ. When he left Gladstone's, he had got out of the groove of the higher class of Liverpool shipowners, and unless he began again as a subordinate (not to be thought of after so long as a Captain), he had little prospect except with low class owners, so sordid and penurious that a man of George's high spirit and somewhat expensive procedure was sure to fall out with them. I forget all the circumstances, but I spoke to Mr Willis, and to Mr Latham and Mr Gair, and at length the latter proposed he should undertake to solicit orders for copper sheathing; he remained with them for about a year, but they did not find it answered the additional expense, so the arrangement ended. His services were however called into requisition in a more befitting way.

Latham & Gair continued to occupy the offices in the Goree Piazza. Like most others, these were on the ground and lower floors, with three or four stories above them of large warerooms, always heavily loaded. At this time, they were stowed with barrels of American flour, whose weight proved too great for the floors to sustain. First the top floor yielded, and all its weight rested on the one below; then that followed, then the next, until the whole fell through to the bottom floor with a tremendous crash. This happened at about ½ past 6 in the evening; Mr Daniel Willis was at my elbow in our office, at the end of the building next to Water Street, when the shock made us start up. Looking down the Piazza, we saw what appeared to be dense smoke, through which we discerned an avalanche of flour barrels at Latham & Gair's door – Oh my brother! I cried, as we supposed the whole of the establishment was overwhelmed. We at first thought the place was on fire, but it was only an immense cloud of flour dust, which cleared in a few moments, when we saw more clearly the nature of the catastrophe. Someone who knew us said he had seen the bookkeeper and my brother lock up a short time before, so our apprehensions ceased.

The difficulty was now to ascertain who might be buried under the flour which had fallen onto the public footway. It could only be cleared by working from the top, and George, being well versed in matters of stowage, undertook to superintend a gang of labourers.

The process was slow; a report got about that a great many people were underneath, and a mob collected (mostly Irish of course) who began to talk of taking the matter in hand themselves. George told them he wished they would help and not talk about it; away went some to complain to the Mayor, that a lot of their people were buried and sure if his worship didn't look after it they'd jist do it themselves. His worship enquired of George why they did not get on faster, to which he replied by requesting his worship to come and judge for himself. The end of it was that after several days' hard labour, they came to the bottom of the Piazza, and found an Irish woman and her child lying crushed by the weight which had overwhelmed them.

[The Liverpool Chronicle of May 29th 1830 (Saturday) carries an account of the accident, which took place Tuesday evening (25th) about eight o'clock (a little later than JCC's time), stating that 500-600 barrels of flour were in the bonded room that gave way. The woman, named as Elizabeth O'Hare, and her child, not quite two years old, were not reported missing until Thursday; their bodies were discovered about half-past one Friday morning, she considerably bruised and crushed, the child uninjured, fallen materials having formed a complete cell around her, but her face eaten by rats. At the inquest, Mr Gair said that about 2 o'clock on Tuesday, he was told that one room had settled a little; he had informed the warehouse owner and called a joiner, who had wedged the supporters. The joiner opined that the beams were not securely fixed: they were not far enough into the side walls, and there were too few upright posts or supporters. The Chronicle agrees with the 'Mercury' in thinking a general survey of warehouses expedient and desirable, for many appear so slight and badly put together as to fill one with affright when crammed with the heaviest of goods.]

Eventually Mr Willis proposed that George come into our office to do what he could till something better might turn up, which it did most singularly. One evening, a young man, mate of a ship, came in to speak to Mr Willis; George overheard their conversation, which was about a vacancy in command of one of Messrs T H Murray's Demerara ships. It had happened that while George had been in Demerara in *Anna*, he had rendered an essential service in assisting to get one of the Murray's vessels to sea; so pleased was Mr Thomas Murray, the senior partner, with how George managed it that he told him, if ever he wanted a ship and he had one vacant, he should have it. (Murray Jones & Co. did the largest retail store business in dry goods – cottons and linen – of any in Demerara; the Murrays, Belfast men, later became Murray Brothers & Co, Thomas in Liverpool, Edward and Henry in Demerara.)

George quietly went out, returned in a few minutes, and whispered to me 'I've got it.' – 'Got what?' I said. 'Murray's ship, to be sure! Do you think I was going to let such a bit of information slip?' He had had an interview with Mr Thomas Murray, who at once recognized his promise. George acquainted Mr Willis with his good fortune, with as grave a face as he could assume, not wishing it to be known how he had acquired his information. So George was installed on *Pantaloon*, a small brig in respectable and regular employ in the Demerara trade, very much to his own satisfaction and that of his friends.

The years 1829 and 1830 went on so much alike that I can scarcely recollect any particular incident. In one of them [1829] we received news from Charles, unexpected although it had appeared probable, that his residence with Miss Rix [Elizabeth] and her grandmother Mrs Dowson, at their cottage on Clapham Common, was to become a permanency; and in due course he and Miss Rix were married, by my old Demerara friend Mr Austin. In 1830, Tom, after many ups and downs in printing and bookselling, succeeded in getting an appointment in the Bank of England in London. Thus we were all in our positions, and although our lot was not splendid, we had, after long struggle and uncertainty, the means of support by honest industry.

Friends and Acquaintances
Our friends included Mr and Mrs Edward Cearns, and Mrs John Ashe, Fanny's teacher at her school at Walton, who had married the brother of the school proprietress. He undertook (simple man) to conduct the affairs of 'John Pattinson's Widow & Co', but did not get very much out of that. His wife had started a school and proved the better man of the two, as a look at them might have surmised, she

being tall and large, he shrunk and pallid-looking. They were cousins of the well-known Liverpool Quaker family Rathbone, who were at the tip top of the tree, while the Ashes were at the bottom [unintentional pun?].

We had ceased to have any contact with Fanny's sister after we left Anfield Cottage. This unaccountable woman not only kept aloof herself, but railed at and vilified us wherever she went, and forbid her children even to speak to their aunt. She had taken a large house in Rodney Street, the most aristocratic in Liverpool, which she contrived to furnish and let out in apartments to mercantile gentlemen. When in Demerara, she had obtained possession (under her brother the executor) of her mother's property in which Fanny was interested, but refused of course to account to anybody but him. Fanny in her innocence sent her a statement of how the affair stood between them, as she imagined, charging Mrs P with what she considered her due from the property, and charged herself with her board at Anfield during the time Mrs P was in Demerara. This was enough to work on: she referred Fanny to her brother in Demerara for the one, and sent a demand for immediate payment of the other, about £25; and we had scarcely time to recover from this coup de finesse when we received a lawyer's letter threatening proceedings! Had not Mr Willis and Mr Cearns kindly interposed, this vindictive woman would have brought me to ruin. She had in fact no right to charge her sister with anything, for she had taken care of things during her absence.

Fanny and I settled down at St George's Everton under the ministry of the Rev R P Buddicom, where she had attended for years, and had been intimately connected with various of its operations. Mr Pattinson's failure and death had considerably altered her status there, but we always found a kind friend in our good pastor, who was ever ready to extend to us the hand and heart of Christian sympathy and counsel. We visited our friends at Prescot while Johnny was an infant, but after dear little Fan came, it would no longer do to take them visiting, and I kept strictly to home and office.

My circumstances were straitened, but I kept out of debt; I loved my home and family, and was only too happy to secure an entire evening with them. After many failures and considerable breakage, we had found a treasure, a large strong hard-washing hard-scrubbing two-fisted woman, one Betsey, a great acquisition who wrought wonders in our domestique. Her tongue wagged continually, but that kept the house alive and the children amused [She was very kind to me and I liked her – JCC II]. Thus our time passed on, the very greatest part of mine at office work from half past 9 in the morning till half past 10 at night, with the few exceptions above. The worst of it was that the junior clerks used to slink off one by one, and so absorbed was Mr Willis that he never noticed these breaches of discipline, nor seemed to have the slightest idea of correcting them [Could not you, as chief clerk, have said something?].

Towards the close of summer 1830, the Liverpool and Manchester Railway was completed, which had been in course of construction the past 3 or 4 years, an event which stirred up all the neighborhood. My father, who had been a constant observer of the works in progress, was there, with myself, wife, and sisters [Letitia says No – JCC II]; all was brilliancy and high expectancy, Liverpool poured out its thousands to see the carriages that ran without horses. The day [Wednesday September 15th] was bright, the people cheered, the Duke of Wellington and the great men acknowledged graciously, and off went the trains to Manchester, 6 or 8 in succession, to everyone's wonder, amazement, and satisfaction.

In the afternoon, the people again poured out to witness the return. Hours passed, but no trains came. It was rumoured that an accident had happened; and too surely it was that Mr Huskisson, President of the Board of Trade, had been killed by an engine passing over his legs, the company having incautiously alighted at Parkside while the trains stopped for some purpose. People had yet to learn that locomotives are not stage-coaches. Poor Mr Huskisson lingered for a few days at the house of Mr Blackburne, vicar of Eccles, where he died. He had a public funeral at Liverpool. Thus was inaugurated the Railway system, in a few years to spread all over England. [Parkside is near present-day Newton-le-Willows station. A pre-planned stop had been made for the eight locomotives to take water, and guests had been requested not to leave the trains, though some did. This was Britain's first recorded railway fatal accident, when the world's first 'ambulance train' was created to take Mr Huskisson to Eccles for treatment. A plaque commemorating the event is currently in the York Railway Museum].

Tragedy

The next year I was to begin a new experience of my Heavenly father's dealings with me [or perhaps cruel ill-fortune?]. January 19th 1831 added to our family little Letitia, our third child, but it cost her mother much suffering, and eventually her life. The circumstances were unfavorable. Suddenly, late at night, we had to send for assistance. We had hitherto employed a lady practitioner, but she was ill, and sent an assistant; whether this woman did not manage properly, or what might be the cause, I could not understand, but Fanny was greatly exhausted, and I had to run for Mr Parr, a good medical man nearby. Restoratives brought Fanny round after some time, and all seemed well. She never however got up her strength, and in April or May it was recommended she go from home for a time. A kind school-fellow in Manchester, Miss McGhie, sent her an invitation, where she went with the two youngest children and Betsey to take charge of them. Johnny and I meanwhile boarded at Grandpapa's, and the house in Soho Square was shut up. So here was the beginning of the break-up of our domestic comfort.

My brother Tom came to visit my father, and his company broke the loneliness I should otherwise have felt. He left soon after Fanny returned a month later, I feared not much impressed with my domestic happiness. I was grieved to see no improvement in Fanny's appearance, although she reported herself better. In fact it was becoming too evident that it was but a question of time. Mr Parr attended her regularly, but could only palliate symptoms, though he did his best as a good Christian friend to comfort us. Mr Willis sent his chaise almost daily to take her out for airings, which always seemed to give her new life. Fanny could not nurse Letitia, and we were casting about what to do, when God in his providence opened the way. Mrs Pattinson having gone out to Demerara, old Mrs Pritchard had been obliged to stay with friends, when to our surprise she one day appeared at our door, and we were only too glad to welcome her to take charge of Letitia. We could not pay her, but she was glad of an asylum, and we felt we were helped through a great difficulty.

Summer passed heavily away. It would be painful, even at this distance of nearly 40 years, to particularize the sad alternations of hope and fear, lighted up by the more recent sufferings and death of our two dear girls. Towards autumn, it was suggested our house, being on the ground, was prejudicial, and a week before Michaelmas, preparations were made to move to Great Homer Street near Everton. By this time, Fanny's strength was rapidly giving way, and I feared her ability to bear the removal, for which I had not much heart. Mr and Mrs Cearns, who had been most attentive, insisted she stay with them until all was ready at the new house. My father took little Fan, John went to a Prescot friend now living in Liverpool, and Mrs Pritchard had charge of Letitia. Fanny had an alarming attack one night, and the whole family was roused up, but a restorative brought her round, and to my surprise she rallied and begged to be taken home. Whilst in the air, enjoying the carriage exercise, she appeared to have new life, but flagged as soon as she was taken into the house.

The month which followed was one of intense suffering from exhaustion and occasional delirium. My sister Margaret was much with us, but I felt I could not leave Fanny, as she would suffer no-one to wait on her but me; my attendance at the office was most kindly dispensed with during the whole time. The Willises, though generally exacting, were most considerate in times of sickness or trouble.

In Great Homer Street we had two rooms on the ground floor, communicating by folding doors; one of these we made a bedroom, so that I could carry her with more convenience. On the night of October 20th I did this for the last time; I placed her in bed and she sat up for a few minutes to knit out a row in a little cotton sock which she had been engaged on for some time [I have it now – JCC II]. She put it up with great care, and lay down; I did the same and fell asleep, as the constant strain made me very tired. About two or three in the morning, she called me: 'I thought I saw Mrs Pritchard with that dear child in her arms.' Then she said 'I feel very faint'; I got some port wine, but she could not touch it, and in a few minutes more she ceased to breathe.

227

Mr Parr arrived before daylight; as a healer of the body his office was gone. As comfort to the soul, his visit was kind and salutary, and I felt comforted by his Christian sympathy, but the Great Physician can alone fill the dreary void when you feel that you are indeed alone in the world. Visits and letters poured in from all our friends, and my father put himself at my disposal to arrange that which I could not well attend to myself. As interment at Everton was found to be very expensive, it was arranged for Walton, the parish in which we were situated, giving right of free sepulture. There, at the west end of the church, near the wall bounding the road, a flat stone marks her grave and records her departure, October 21st 1831, aged 33 years. [The Burial Register for Walton-on-the-Hill confirms her abode as Great Homer St, Everton, the only entry on this page with an address, possibly being beyond the parish boundary? It states the ceremony was performed by R P Buddicom, but gives the date of burial clearly as October 19th: a slight puzzle! – Surely not a slip of the pen (for the 29th?) in a 'official' document, though it seems strange if John should have got his beloved wife's death date wrong.]

PART 15

Widower, 1831-37

On my Own

The process of reconstruction was slow and painful, as always in such circumstances. Johnny came home, but dear little Fan remained with Granpapa and aunts till the new arrangements for my household were completed. She came to see me once a week, and evidently looked for something she did not find. She was a sweet, impulsive and affectionate child, and did not ask for her Mama, but when going away, burst out crying. She was robust, florid and dark, a striking contrast to Johnny and Letitia (baptized Mary Letitia) who were both pale, delicate, and light-complexioned.

Another school-fellow of Fanny's, Miss Collard, appeared. When we first married, we had lodged with her and her sister, but after a drunken outrage by their sailor brother, we left, which so affronted her that she completely cut our acquaintance for five years; now, in an agony of grief and remorse, she could not do enough to make amends. She and her sister kept a preparatory school close by, and begged that I send Johnny in every day. I found it a great convenience to have him placed out of mischief while I was at the office, for although only 4, he was rather too much for Mrs Pritchard; she had enough to do with Letitia, who was already beginning to shew symptoms of an unhealthy character, caused by want of good nursing and more active handling than an old lady could give her.

Fanny had long arranged with her friend Mrs John Ashe to take charge of household and children after she was gone. Mrs Ashe had been left a widow some little time since, and had been keeping a small preparatory school; but as it barely maintained her, she willingly agreed to give it up, although I could not afford to pay her very handsomely. Two nephews living with her, George Harris and George Putt, of 11 or 12 years, I felt the greatest obstacle to comfort, as I soon saw to my dismay that the first was petted and under very little control, and the latter was snubbed and surly, though after a year he went home to his mother. However, it was too late for hesitation. Poor old Mrs Pritchard had to vacate, which I was very sorry for, as she had no resources of her own. I made up a little purse for her from my own pocket and that of friends, and she went for a time to some friends of her own. Eventually the Miss Collards, myself, and some others, made up a little weekly sum, on which she subsisted until her death.

Came January 1st 1832, and with it Mrs Ashe, her boys, goods and chattels. The new life was a great change. Mrs Ashe, though a thoroughly good teacher, was no trainer: impatient and impulsive, she scolded the servants, and was irascible with the children, which had an ill effect on them, and was so opposite to the course their mother and I had pursued that I was grieved and disheartened. Letitia she took to at once, for like most impulsive people, she was very feeling, but then Fan was snubbed, which almost broke her heart, and mine too. I ventured to remonstrate, but it led to nothing but wonderment what I could possibly mean by such an accusation. She was not a woman to be reasoned with. Yet she was estimable, well-principled and pious, cultivated and intellectual, and could be a pleasant evening companion, so I much regretted that an exceedingly sensitive and uncertain temper often marred the peace of our household. It was painful to come home and find that something I had, or had not, done or said, of which I was wholly unconscious, had been brooded on during the day, producing silent reserve and black looks, vulgarly called a fit of sulks, while I was left to divine as best I could what was the matter, as ladies in this state of mind have an act peculiar to themselves. There was nothing for it but to let it work off, which frequently took many days, when the succeeding sunshine was as unaccountable as the preceding gloom. But though I was not comfortable in some respects, I owed much to her care and good instruction of my children.

Business as Usual
I have but a confused recollection of this dreary time, and many months, nay years, had to pass before I could get over a loss which I then thought nothing earthly could replace. It is however a blessed

thing that tranquility of mind gradually is restored and the wounded spirit healed. My children were everything to me, and if I could get home on Fridays early enough to have them with me before bedtime, it was a treat for all of us. My brother George was in 1832 commissioned to superintend the rigging and outfit of *Isabella*, a new brig the Murrays were building at Belfast, of which he was to have the command. There, he had ample opportunity to indulge his proclivities for female society; and Harriet, one of seven sisters, became his new wife simultaneously with the completion of his ship. My father and sisters had by now removed into William Henry Street, newly cut from Soho Street across the meadows. [In Slater's Directory of Ireland for 1846, Nobility, Gentry, Clergy, Capt George Chevely (sic) is listed at 22 Eliza Place.]

Next who should get into matrimony, to my great surprise, but Mr Daniel Willis, well on the wrong side of forty. The newly-married pair passed several weeks on the Continent; at Bordeaux, his ardour was excited to speculate in wines and brandies, and French and Swiss produce, manufactures and dyestuffs, which he bought to a considerable extent. This mania for speculation alarmed his brother Tom, but he protested in vain. It however proved in the end disastrous, and laid the foundation for much loss and disquietude. I could not believe but that he saw his way through, and thought his brother somewhat unreasonable; I was sorry to see ill-feeling growing between them, which henceforth never subsided.

Mr DW had begun never to be satisfied with things as they were or to let well alone. His thorough knowledge of bookkeeping unfortunately led him to be constantly interfering, and he so elaborated things as to throw more work on the bookkeeper than one man could possibly get through. He insisted on putting Aaron Appleton, our first-rate custom house clerk, to the books, at which the poor fellow fagged till he lost his health, so the books went astern and at last came to a standstill. My hands were full of other work, and I urged that a regular bookkeeper be at once engaged. One Abraham Collard, brother of Miss Collard aforesaid, was at this time out of employ; I knew he had extravagant habits, and I did not like the family characteristics of self-will and obstinacy, but I knew nothing against him for honesty, and as he had a wife and young family, I desired to give him a lift, and to get a competent person at the books before Mr Daniel's return. Mr Tom did not apply to his former employer for his character, and he was engaged.

For a time things went well, but my mind misgave me when I saw he was too often out to keep the books going. Mr Daniel returned, and seemed to approve; he found out that Mr Collard was well up in the business of wines and spirits through his employment at Fletcher Yates & Co (where he had speculated in Jamaica rum, but had got into complications and either left or was dismissed), and set him to sell brandies and wines to publicans and dealers. This was unfortunate, because it took Mr Collard out of the office and off the books, which continued to go astern; I found, too late, I had taken a wrong step in recommending him. The worst of it was that he had gained Mr Willis' ear, whom I could not persuade that he was neglecting his work, and the only response I received was that I must keep him up to it. Collard was so emboldened by Mr DW's trust and his quiescence about the books, that my authority was nothing. Thus I had innocently laid the foundation for a vast deal of mischief, without being at all conscious of it.

A Trying Period

In summer 1834, Mr Willis kindly invited me and the two elder children to stay a week with him and Mrs Willis at Waterloo (Crosby), where they had taken a house. Mrs Willis, who had by this time an infant of her own, was exceedingly kind to both children, but took most to Fan. Our stay included one sabbath. It was no holiday for me, as I had gone to my office work every morning as usual, but it was great enjoyment that the children had such a nice treat.

In September or October, my father, who was remarkable for uniform good health and activity of mind and body (he was now nearly 73), was suddenly seized with a paralytic attack. It affected one side, and he required constant attention; unfortunately people in this state are generally unaware of what is the matter, and are very unwilling to be assisted. My sisters were worn out, so I was obliged to be with him at nights, and at the office as much as I could during the day. The doctor quieted him with small doses of morphia (which I subsequently knew too well in my own dear suffering child Letitia).

232

After many days we thought him worse and dying; a physician was called in, and Charles and Tom came down from London. This was a great relief, and indeed not at all too soon, for a day or two after, I felt very ill. My appearance so alarmed Mrs Ashe that she made me go to bed, and sent for Dr Parr. By the time he arrived, excessive diarrhoea had set in, and I was quite prostrate. He pronounced an attack of Asiatic cholera, and recommended that the children be sent out of the house. They could not go to their Grandpapa's, but Miss Collard came to the rescue and took John and Fanny; Letitia was too young to go anywhere, and must risk it. Charles came several nights to sit up with me; Mr Willis sent me something nutritive almost daily, generally game from his father's at Halsmead near Whiston, and I lived for many days on partridge soup. All that was passing was kept from me as much as possible, and I was surprisingly tranquil and trustful.

Reports of my father's state were unfavorable, and Richard from St Osyth, Harriet, and Mrs Charles were added to the party, so the house was overflowing. But all at once, a turn came, and one morning when I asked apprehensively how Father was, Charles said 'Well, I can only say I have just left him shaving himself.' From that time, amendment went on, and my brothers returned to London. After about three weeks, I was convalescent, getting downstairs to the dreary prospect of a disordered house. Johnny came home, but Mrs Ashe sent Fan to her relatives, as she fancied she could not manage with all at home; this was sad to me, as I had not seen the dear little thing for several weeks. Our Prescot friends said I must come to them to get thoroughly strong and well, where I staid about a month. Mr Willis would have me over to Halsmead for a few days, which I did not much fancy, as I did not feel quite at home in a large house with grandee people, particularly as I was still somewhat an invalid. I took walks in the grounds, my first to any distance, but it was a not very interesting visit.

Back at Liverpool, I found Mr Willis' head full of schemes and speculations; amongst others, he had taken a large share in a ship he was fitting out to go to China. Of course, Mr Collard had been much occupied during my absence, though I could not discover with what, his books were more than ever behind, and he was swaggering about after anything but his proper business. At home it was pretty much the same; the servant left, another come and gone, and Mrs Ashe all in mess and muddle. She could not get on long with them: there are some who have the unhappy faculty of driving them away by perpetual nagging. I really felt very grateful to her for her kind ministering to me, but the reaction was something unbearable. To mend things, Mr Willis would have me away again to stay at Crosby to finish convalescence; the children strongly protested, as they had looked forward to Papa being amongst them again, but I was obliged to comply, and was away another fortnight, going to and from town morning and evening. I ought to mention that Mr Willis paid my doctor's bills, which were considerable.

It was now near Christmas. We had an awkward servant, and as the washing was done at home weekly, we had to hire a woman to help. In Liverpool, you can scarcely avoid an Irish woman in this capacity, and as they are all Papists, they are difficult to manage in some matters. I always wished the washerwoman to come up to morning prayer, and I found that she kept the whole time muttering to herself; at first I thought she was following me, but was soon told she was reciting her own prayers, to neutralize my heretical proceedings.

On washing days, the servant was busy below, and did not go upstairs to prepare the beds till just before the children's bedtime. One day during this time, she made the astounding discovery that all the sheets were cleared off the beds, six gone at one fell swoop. She brought up Mrs Ashe, who found all in confusion, the closet ransacked, and her best cloak, some articles of dress, Johnny's best coat, and many minor things had disappeared. Consternation! The staircase window, looking on the back yard, had been left wide open, with a convenient low wall close below; I could not help suspecting the old woman below knew something about it, especially as the servant let out that she had a son who was a bad character. However, not a shred was to be found on her premises, and she knew nothing of her son's whereabouts. I gave Mrs Ashe a new cloak, and had to bear my own loss as best I might.

Emily Pellatt; Rose Vale

In 1835, George had been home from Demerara, and his wife had come over from Belfast to give him their firstborn, little Fanny, not then (I forget the exact time) more than 18 months old. George was sorely annoyed at Mr Murray making him answerable for a deficient hogshead of sugar. He considered that the mate (who had negligently miscounted them when George was on shore) was accountable, which Mr Murray overruled and deducted the value from his wages, in George's eyes a great injustice, and he could not get over it. He had subsequently been ordered to London instead of Liverpool, and with so short a stay there was no possibility of meeting his wife. This produced great dissatisfaction, which operated injuriously to his interests, for on being ordered to London a second time, in disappointment and anger he wrote to Mr Murray to provide himself with another captain for *Isabella*: which sure enough he did, and on arrival in the Thames, he came on board with George's successor. Thus George in a moment of haste knocked the boards from under himself and had to look for new employ, which he obtained with Newman Hunt & Christopher on a brig, *Fox*, which had once been a sloop of war, for a voyage to China.

In May, Charles wrote to me, that a lady was coming to Liverpool on her way to her brother Mr Frederic Pellatt in the manufacturing glass trade, and as she would have to remain Sunday and two nights waiting for the Glasgow steamer, he wished me to meet her and receive her into my house. He could put to rest any fears about Mrs Ashe's domestic arrangements, which I knew were none of the most superb, as Miss Emily Pellatt was a woman thoroughly independent of circumstances. I had heard something of her when Charles was at Liverpool during Father's illness: she was the sister of the wife of his valued friend Tom Phillips, a fellow clerk in the Bank of England; the Pellatts were also the family of the late Apsley Pellatt, head of the well-known glass firm of Pellatt & Green in Blackfriars and St Paul's Churchyard. So on the whole I had misgivings about entertaining a lady who, in spite of Charles' assurances, might be grand in her ideas. However, I got Mrs Ashe into the right humour, and went to the Angel in Dale Street to meet the Birmingham coach. I scrutinized the interior: no lady there. One outside passenger remained, a solitary and apparently unprotected female. There she sat, perfectly quiescent like Patience on a monument; grand she did not appear, as a weather-stained head-covering and camblet cloak [camlet] were all I could discern of the little person. Looking up, I asked diffidently 'Are you Miss Pellatt?', to which she gave assent. She was a Dissenter, but we did not clash in opinions.

A proposal from Mr Willis gave me a great deal of painful thought. Having sent his ship to China, he talked about establishing a firm there, connecting his own firm and Willis & Earle of Calcutta in the China trade. The question was, who was to be resident in China; to my surprise and some gratification, though still consternation, he pitched on me, promising my children should be well taken care of! The more I thought of it, the less I saw my duty in it, and after much prayer, and advice from Mr Buddicom, it was settled in my mind. I had afterwards abundant reason to rejoice I had not yielded.

In Autumn, a gentleman Mr Charles Spurden from London called on my father about the projected union of his daughter Matilda with my brother Tom, which took place soon after, and on which, as both subjects are still living in happy domestic and Christian union, I need say no more. Father had rallied most surprisingly from his attack, and was out and about almost as before, although his mind was occasionally a little confused, and he talked much and loudly without seemingly being aware of it.

Also at this time we changed our residence to Rose Vale, which was round the corner at the then termination of Great Homer Street, some ten or a dozen houses then pretty clear of any others; it had a small garden or forecourt, and opening behind on the meadows of Everton Valley. This was a decided improvement for the children, and I could exercise my floricultural taste. The house was much more roomy, so I did not grudge £28 a year, an extra £3, for the rent. We had several revolutions with servants, and at each Mrs Ashe seemed to get out of the frying pan into the fire, lamenting over the one who was gone. The children were becoming old enough to read their Bibles (Johnny began reading his between 3 and 4), so I instituted a little afternoon Bible class on the sabbath.

Another catastrophe was the loss of the greatest part of my silver plate, not very extensive in quantity, but it put me to great inconvenience. Though our house stood back from the road, we had constantly people from the neighborhood finding their way to the kitchen door. Little Fan was by herself at the front parlour window, when she saw a ragged urchin running down the garden path with the plate basket in his hands. Instinctively she scampered after him, crying Stop thief! which no-one thought to do, and pursued him till she lost him at the corner of the next street, into which she dared not venture. The urchin had thrown down the basket, but its contents, the greatest part of my stock of spoons, were gone. The servant had taken them down to the kitchen for cleaning, and had, most cleverly for the thief, set the basket on the table by the kitchen window, which was wide open.

Miss McGhie, my wife's school-fellow, a West Indian lady of colour, generally came to Seacombe, on the Cheshire side, for a few weeks sojourn every summer, and had the children over there, which was a treat for them. Indeed I owed many kind acts to her; she sent the children presents of clothing soon after their mother's death. She had Mrs Pattinson's two girls left on her hands by that unscrupulous woman: who, after getting into debt when her lodging house in Rodney Street failed, had gone out to Demerara, placing her girls at a boarding school where they could not have remained but for Miss McGhie and other friends. The eldest girl Eliza was to go in a sailing packet from Liverpool to a place as governess in Bordeaux. Her father's brother James, a little worthless man, entirely failed to make arrangements for her; hitherto she had obeyed her mother's injunction to have nothing to do with me, but now in her perplexity she came to consult with Mrs Ashe. I need not say that my house was her home until the vessel sailed. She arrived safely, but a few months after, died from an attack of fever.

William Mulvey

In 1836, George returned from China in *Fox* with abundant materials for contention with his owners, who at once began warfare by refusing to pass his accounts, which included his pay. This brought on litigation, and poor George was again in a fix. He put the matter in the hands of a young legal friend: who it was discovered months later had spent what he had been paid, utterly neglecting to carry on the suit, and George felt obliged to proceed against this friend (!), a relative too, for recovery of what he had received. He could not live on air, and with his wife and child visited Charles at Clapham, Richard at St Osyth, and subsequently Billy Brathwaite at Hedingham.

Mr Willis' China adventure did not end profitably, tea prices being low. Next, he was led to turn his thoughts to an export business that one Mr Penny carried on at Mazatlan, on the Pacific north-west coast of Mexico, at the mouth of the Gulf of California. He plunged in with his accustomed enthusiasm, and in connection with some other project was induced, much to my surprise, to purchase a brig called *William Mulvey*. As I viewed shipowners and brokers pretty much on a par with horse dealers, I felt assured that Mr Willis would be jockeyed unless he took great care, and I urged him to have someone competent survey the vessel, but he received my advice coldly, and completed the purchase. The project then appeared to fall through; so now here was a puzzler, as Mr Penny did not think the ship was large enough for the Mazatlan scheme, but at length it was decided she be sent there. This was a serious undertaking, as it involved passage round Cape Horn; a supercargo was to be landed at Istapa on the Guatemala coast, to go (on a donkey!) to City of Guatemala, 100 miles distant, and purchase indigo and cochineal to be shipped on the vessel's return. Then they wanted an experienced captain; I thought of George, who gladly accepted the proposal, as situated as he was with his last owners, he had little hope of getting a ship.

George soon brought Mr Willis an account of all *William Mulvey's* wants, which set him wondering, as the 'respectable broker' with whom he had dealt, had assured him she was well supplied. Again I suggested it would be better to have someone look over the vessel, as I did not like the idea of my brother incurring the responsibility, but no, he would leave it to George: and to it George went, determined to have everything complete. Carpenters, ropemakers and sailmakers were found needful; the vessel was had into the graving dock, to examine planking and copper; the cabins required to be refitted; and some pretty long bills were run up. Mr Willis and Mr Penny found the cargo between them; and I found Mr Penny's precious scheme at the Mexican port was to bribe the Customs officials and pay a 'composition' for the import duties, a very small portion of those legally due, and in this evasion lay a large part of the profit. At length George sailed, with Mr Willis' expectations of abundant success, and Mr Penny's of a flying passage out, which some vessel had lately made; but excessively bad weather round Cape Horn and head winds for many weeks greatly delayed the passage to Istapa, to Mr Penny's indignation: dispatch being everything with him, winds and waves no obstacles! George continued his voyage, to which for the present we leave him.

I heard from Charles that Miss Pellatt was again on her way to Glasgow, her brother having just lost his wife, leaving three little girls motherless, and Charles again commended her to my attention. This time she was coming to Liverpool by steamer from Haverfordwest, where she had been staying with her married sister Mrs John Phillips. I went to the steam dock, and found that she had already arrived: the captain said 'Miss Pellatt is gone to your house, and would have gone on to Glasgow if she had been in time; she is the most plucky little woman I ever saw, doesn't seem to care for weather or anything: why, she wanted to sit on deck all night, if I'd allowed it!' I went home and found my guest seated by the fire; and the following day I saw her on board the Glasgow steamer, although I had by this time begun to find out that my 'plucky little woman' wanted no looking after, as she had ways of her own of doing things.

My spare time was now greatly engrossed by the children. Do what I would, I was sure to be kept late at night, and my best plan was to go home to dinner in the middle of the day, whereby I screwed an hour for myself which I gave up to the children. Letitia was naturally indolent within doors, and being weak in constitution, we let her indulge her propensity to be out of doors; her favorite amusement was to hang through the garden gate, sucking two fingers, which she had done from infancy, observing all that was passing in the street. They generally took a morning walk with Mrs Ashe, and she interested them about wild flowers. She was an excellent instructress, but she neutralized her efforts by her irritability and want of self-control. I saw with dismay a system of favoritism and want of impartiality; and the worst of it was that expostulation made matters worse, which was exceedingly uncomfortable and excessively trying to a man whose patience had been well exercised during his daily official duties.

More Discomfort

With 1837 came fresh causes of discomfort. Our management did not improve: we had plenty of hands, too many, yet nothing was well done. Mr Willis took no notice of my constant complaints of idleness and neglect. He got acquainted with a young fellow, Mr John Clarke, who undertook to sell India dyestuffs; he commenced operations in Manchester, and went on very satisfactorily for some time, but a large stock of dye-woods and other articles was accumulating.

[A sheet cut out here in the original.]

Dear little Fan was delighted to be with aunties and Grandpapa, when her turn came. She was, as I have said, an impulsive child in everything, and full of affection, but this often led to troublesome consequences, as it required very little rebuke or disappointment to produce an exhibition of direst grief which was very difficult to suppress. It was found that the best method of bringing her round was to tell her to go into a closet in the sitting room [The little dog Jetty's cupboard – JCC II], and remain there till she was good; at length, when she knew she was naughty, or felt a demonstration coming on, she would go of her own accord until it had passed off, which under this voluntary system of solitary confinement, was short work. Then the coming home again was to be feared. Mrs Ashe was jealous for Letitia (who being delicate, did not go), and put it into her head to long for Fanny to come home: and when she did come there was always a hubbub, her affection was not warm enough, or she had been at Grandpapa's too long, and the snubbing that Fan got broke out the floodgates, and led to a scolding. This produced anything but pleasure, and in fact worked mischief, to my dismay and disgust. John had begun to play the piano, and could improvise little airs of his own, which he dotted down in a ruled book that Granpapa bought him.

Office work went on unsatisfactorily, and Collard's excessive idleness and extravagance grew worse; he absented himself whole days together, and came back with pitiable tales, to which Mr Willis gave ear and sent him money. The trouble of all this fell on me, for the books were useless, and yet this unaccountable fellow had the impudence to tell me that people had said they never could get an account from me: while he was the delinquent and I the sufferer. Mr Willis fidgetted and said 'Mr Collard must attend better and get on faster; really Mr Cheveley you must see that he does.' In vain I told him that Mr Collard set me at defiance, and there was no remedy but to get rid of him. So it went on, Mr Willis did not interpose his authority and Collard did as he liked. [Why did JCC put up with such a situation?].

Proposal – and Acceptance
I now had thoughts rising up, more distinct than the hazy distant views I had the year before. I had a problem as to what really was in the distance, and whether I could make it clearer. At length I wrote to Charles, and received an encouraging reply, but was advised to put off further consideration until I could come to London, when we could talk it over more fully. Summer was drawing on, and I asked for leave of absence for a month for my visit to London; but Mr Willis had not of late heard from Mr Clarke with his dyestuffs, and becoming a little uneasy, took me over with him to Manchester to investigate. We were told he was at home, not being very well, where we found him, not apparently very bad but looking somewhat confused. He stammered something apologetic, which roused Mr DW's suspicions a little, and we returned the following day, to find considerable defalcations; at length we discovered that a large quantity of dye wood had been taken from the Canal Company's warehouse, where it was to have lain subject to our orders. This and other matters caused my journey to be postponed until the end of June.

As the 'Grand Junction' or Liverpool and Birmingham Railway was not yet complete, and the London and Birmingham was in course of formation, the stage coach was still the only conveyance available for this journey of 210 miles; so I took the Royal Umpire, the favorite London coach (owned by the veteran and almost universal Liverpool coach proprietor Bartholomew Bretherton, formerly a stable keeper, now a millionaire), which started from the Saracen's Head in Dale Street.

This was my first real holiday since I entered the Willis' office 11 years ago. As the horses cantered off gaily on this fine summer's morning, I felt before me the prospect of a month's association with friends and localities endeared by early recollection, as my aspirations towards the south were undeminished, although I owed much to the north for time and especially for eternity. The short midsummer night passed in an uneasy doze; morning revealed the pastures of Leicestershire with a mist rolling over them, to which the beams of the rising sun gave the appearance of broad sheets of water, so deceptive I could scarcely persuade myself of its unreality. Then the day became exceedingly hot, and about 1 or 2 in the afternoon, covered with dust, hot and feverish, we dragged through Highgate and Islington to the Bell in Holborn.

I met Tom, and we adjourned to Clapham to find Mrs Charles in Lark Hall Lane, with its snug cottage and garden; but how to bestow my dusty self? Everything had just been cleaned up for the summer – skinned, Tom called it, so he rid me of my greatcoat and gave me a dusting in the garden. He was living with his new wife in Albany Road, Camberwell. Charles returned late; he was now in the Branch Banks Office where the work was irregular. I enjoyed exceedingly the following week; my kind sister [-in-law] did all in her power for my happiness and comfort. Her [half] brother Samuel's wife was staying at Hastings with her father Mr Amoore [Maiden name of Charles' second wife – she became Whitworth].

Now came the discussion of the matter which I had mainly in view in coming to London. I found them both still favorably inclined, but they seemed to have a great fancy that I be introduced to another lady; she declined all invitations, and as I had a glimpse sufficient to shew that she did not look like what I wanted, I would waste no further time, but called on Mrs Phillips [see *'William Mulvey'*] who quite entered into my views. And so, with the sanction and advice of all parties, I wrote to Miss Pellatt at Glasgow, making my proposals, setting forth candidly all the pros and cons: particularly income, which was considerably under £200. I have often wondered at my impudence, and confess I had some misgivings in unsettling a lady who was living with her brother, in charge of his children, and in comfortable circumstances, inducing her to come and take charge of me and mine, in very restricted circumstances. [I wish to Goodness he had let her alone – JCC II.] At first I thought it was not to be, for the reply, though very kindly expressed, was decidedly declining on the ground of insufficiency of income. Nothing daunted, I applied to Mr Willis, who at once screwed up my salary, so here was a main obstacle cleared. Eventually Miss Pellatt came to London, when all preliminaries were arranged, and her family recognized me as the *accepted*.

As the month was waning, I resolved to see my friends in Essex. I visited Richard at St Osyth; next morning a pacquet of letters arrived from Liverpool, one from Mr Willis requesting my immediate attention to some bills for East India produce. Dick at once had to drive me over to Colchester for the London coach; of course these country folk, and especially the wife, wondered what I could possibly be in such a hurry for, to come one day and run away the next morning. Country farmers are never in a hurry, except after the hounds in a fox chase, the most important event of their lives. The business proved a complicated affair; when it was satisfactory, I passed some days with Richard. His matrimonial felicity was marred by a somewhat cross-grained piece of stuff sharing his bed and presiding at his board, with whom he did not appear to live in unalloyed conjugal enjoyment, especially as there was an old lady mother, an auxilliary poker-up of grievances and a wonderful picker-up of trifles with which her daughter bombarded poor Dick's peace of mind. I left him with sad feelings, and he was loth to part with me.

I took the omnibus from Colchester to Halstead, where Mrs Dorothy Cheveley, my uncle's widow, now lived; in the evening, Brathwaite (who had come to the funeral of Mrs Edwards, the successor of the illustrious 'Aunt Edwards') drove me to his house at Castle Hedingham, presided over by cousin Mary Cheveley (Polly), his mother having been sometime dead, and the shop converted into a dining room. His uncle, old Bob Stammers, was still living, and very vigorous for considerably over 80. Like the Dodson family, the town was diminished by death or departure, everything seemed to have changed hands. I took the Bury coach for London the next week, and met Dr Chapman, my old medical friend from Demerara! We chatted all the way and then parted, au revoir at Liverpool, where he was now in practice.

Soon after my return to Clapham, Emily Pellatt arrived from Glasgow to stay with her sister Mrs Phillips, so we were now able to see and know more of each other. But I had a difficult part of the affair to dispose of, to inform Mrs Ashe of what must necessarily produce a great change in her position: all were unanimous I could not retain her after I married. I felt in duty bound to see her in some way provided with the means of living, and told her, which was also Emily's feeling, that I could not think of marrying until she was provided for, yet I did not at present see my way through. Her reply was, like her, impulsive, semi-reproachful, and pettish, and what would become of the dear children when she was gone, who were all distressed at the idea of losing her. [So we were, had quite a scene; never liked Emily Pellatt, and our forebodings were justified – JCC II.] I was however soon relieved by a letter from Margaret, informing me that at the termination of the midsummer holidays, she and Letitia were to start a preparatory day school in a small but respectable house at the corner of Clarence Street, Everton Road, to which Mrs Ashe would convey herself; she had the promise of several respectable pupils to begin with, and my three children should form the nucleus. [The beginning of *our* misery – JCC II.]

The India bills, more difficult than first imagined, brought Mr Willis to London, which I rather feared, as I knew he would absorb time I wished to devote elsewhere, and his needless particularity, caution and procrastination would greatly delay results; and so it proved. My month was long past, but I did not object, as Mr Willis wished it, and it favored my own personal wishes, but I paid for it in personal fatigue, as Mr W. never seemed to know what fatigue was, and dragged me about till I was nearly walked off my legs. At the end of August, he had to go back to Liverpool, to which I had no objection; although Emily soon had to return to Glasgow, which she did outside the mail to Liverpool, thence the steamer. The distant mails then left the Post Office in London at 8 in the evening, and it was quite a sight to see the fleet of coaches and four with the scarlet liveries, pouring out and branching off to their destinations: all very soon engulfed in railway improvement. Emily started in this style for the 'Land of Cakes'; all was arranged for our future, and we had settled we should wait till next April for the consummation. Again Mr Willis came to London, and we dragged about, till it was decided he should remain for a time, and I return home. This I was very glad to do, as I had been separated from my children upwards of three months.

Father's Homecoming

I started by the night mail coach to Birmingham, and after breakfast took the train for Liverpool: the Grand Junction then just finished, the beginning of October. I found my father very well, considering all he had gone through: of which there were some symptoms hanging about, occasional loss of memory, and going into the wrong house. My house was deserted except for a great clumsy servant woman who seemed fit to do nothing, lumped about, and made the house shake whenever she bestirred herself, which was seldom. [She was very kind to me – JCC II.] The children had not improved, having been left too much with a servant at Mrs Ashe's, and they had picked up expressions and rudeness in manners which vexed me. [Naturally, having been grievously neglected whilst my father was courting his new wife – JCC II.] I met them at church on Sundays, and they spent the day with me; John at length came home to sleep, as Mrs Ashe could not be troubled with him at night. [A boy of 10 amongst a parcel of girls, who were, however, kind to me – JCC II.] [Many people seem to have been kind to him! – CCT.]

Mr Willis returned from London, and we had to take up the matter of our Manchester factotum Mr John Clarke. We found a gentleman who called himself Mr Clarke's partner, but was not answerable for previous liabilities; Mr Clarke was not forthcoming, and we made the unpleasant discovery that he was insolvent. We eventually brought to terms the Canal Company, who had delivered property without our orders; Mr Willis wanted more, though eventually we got nothing but trouble and vexation.

Just before I left London, Lloyds had a report of the wreck of *William Mulvey*, but with no particulars; in November or December came confirmation that she had gone down at anchor at Mazatlan. Mr Penny's friend, the consignee, had had the vessel laid too close inshore, despite George's remonstrance; the 'rollers', or great ocean swell, which set in at certain seasons, had come earlier than expected, and so suddenly that George was taken by surprise. Never was destruction so unlooked-for or complete in one half hour, in a smooth and tranquil sea, with scarcely a breeze stirring, all seemed quiet and security. The swell came in like an avalanche, the rise and fall so tremendous that with every depression the vessel's bottom was banged violently against the rocks beneath, till she was hammered to pieces and sank. The crew were saved, but with the loss of nearly all they had; George, who was the last to leave the ship, had his legs severely injured by a carronade adrift on deck. Fortunately the outward cargo had been discharged, and only a small quantity shipped of the homeward, but of course all hope of homeward advantages was at an end. The supercargo was waiting in vain in Guatemala, but there was not much to deplore, as that somewhat wild republic was like most South American ones, anarchy reigned, and neither indigo nor cochineal were to be had. To my mortification, I found George was blamed, though it was difficult to see how he could have avoided what happened [As Captain and responsible for the ship, could he – and should he – not have insisted on lying farther out?]. However, in the end Mr Willis made, I think, a better thing than if the voyage had been completed; he had insured every possible risk, and recovered not only the ship's value, but a large amount for freight expected, with no expenses of a homeward voyage.

My father interested himself much in my new arrangements, but was not to see them completed. One day, he said to me 'I cannot expect my health to last long, but I hope I am in the right way for Heaven when it shall please God to call me.' A very few mornings after, he came downstairs as usual, to check his watch. Margaret observed him fumbling at the key, looking confused and helpless; it was a renewal of his paralytic attack, the doctor said most likely his last, as there was no doubt water on the brain. The trial of watching day and night was renewed, more fatiguing as he could not move himself. I was compelled to leave Johnny many nights with that clumsy servant, of whom I knew nothing, but he slept so soundly he was unaware of my absence [I was always a quiet sleeper, except when troubled with nightmares, which is hereditary in the family – JCC II]. Poor dear Father lay for a month helpless, speechless, and almost unconscious, except for an occasional gleam of recognition. After Christmas he gradually sunk into greater weakness. I sat with him on December 31st 1837; about 4 in the morning, aged 75, his breathing ceased, and his countenance assumed a calm and tranquil beauty, bringing before me my boyhood remembrances of him: a much-loved father, whose love I had shared. The link with bygone years was snapped; I felt his death left a void. Charles and Tom [no Richard?] came to his funeral at Prescot, where we laid him to rest by my mother, in sure and certain hope of finding grace and mercy through his Saviour. [Their gravestone was inscribed 'Richard Dodson Cheveley, late of Messing Lodge in the County of Essex: Died at Liverpool 31st December 1837, aged 75 years. Also Mary Lettice Cheveley his wife, daughter of the Rev Gideon and Mary Lettice Castelfranc of Jamaica, who died at the same 30th August 1828, aged 66 years.' When the churchyard was levelled in 1969, it was moved from between the church and vicarage garden, regrettably becoming broken in the process, and the surviving piece was laid in the paving near the north-east corner of the church. It was lost in the redevelopment of the area around the Millennium.]

[John makes no mention of his father's will, which turns out to be interesting. He bequeaths to Rev C Driffield of Prescot and to John Lawrence of Birchin Lane London, who are named as his executors, the trust money already vested in their names, a portion thereof to be transferred to each of his four sons Richard Dodson, George, Charles, and Thomas (no mention of John!), and to his two daughters Mary Letitia and Margaret; however, if both of his daughters die or marry or receive other income equal to the dividends on the residue of the trust money, then the said residue is to be equally divided between his five sons – including JCC this time! His household furniture and appurtenances go to his daughters. It seems odd, when John was the son who had housed his father in his declining years, to omit him at one point and yet include him later on – had they not seen eye to eye in some way, over John's religious zeal maybe? Father's personal estate and effects turned out to be less than £100 – presumably this does not include the trust money?]

The Pellatts

* Information from JCC's original books, not in present text. No information on order of birth of the offspring, save that Sarah and Emily are the youngest of the sisters; assumed that Aspley (Jr) is the eldest of the eight.

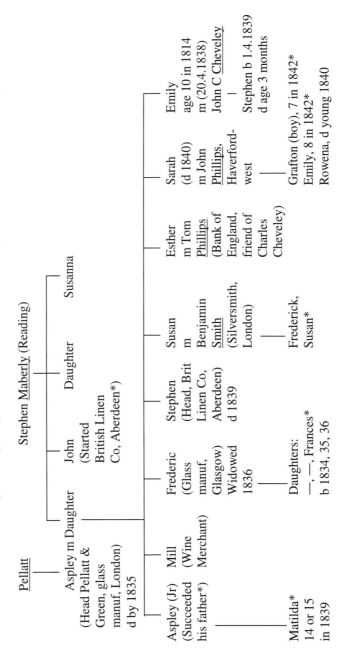

Pellatt

Aspley m Daughter — Stephen Maberly (Reading)

Aspley m Daughter (Head Pellatt & Green, glass manuf, London) d by 1835

Children: John (Started British Linen Co, Aberdeen*) — Daughter — Susanna

- Aspley (Jr) (Succeeded his father*)
- Mill (Wine Merchant)
- Frederic (Glass manuf, Glasgow) Widowed 1836
- Stephen (Head, Brit Linen Co, Aberdeen) d 1839
- Susan m Benjamin Smith (Silversmith, London)
- Esther m Tom Phillips (Bank of England, friend of Charles Cheveley)
- Sarah (d 1840) m John Phillips, Haverford-west
- Emily age 10 in 1814 m John C Cheveley

Matilda* 14 or 15 in 1839

Daughters: —, —, Frances* b 1834, 35, 36

Frederick, Susan*

Grafton (boy), 7 in 1842*
Emily, 8 in 1842*
Rowena, d young 1840

Stephen b 1.4.1839 d age 3 months

Some family pictures: camera lucida black shade profiles – some have been preserved, along with JCC's books. By far the best are these of his two sisters, Margaret (left) and Mary Letitia (right). (Courtesy Mrs J. Cheveley)

PART 16

Second Marriage, 1838-46

A New Era

After an extremely severe winter, the time came for me to bring home my wife. As we were to be married by a different process than that observed in England, I required a testimonial from my minister of my good conduct and respectability. By the way, supposing only the well-conducted and respectable were allowed to marry, what would become of the others? – a point I stayed not to debate.

About April 15th, I was to take the steamer for Glasgow, but the weather proved most unpropitious, March roaring instead of sweet April's smiles and tears, a Liverpool north-wester dead against us. I waited a day or two, hoping it would moderate, and a lull encouraged me to proceed. We left the Mersey about 2 in the afternoon; all was pretty right for the first hour, but as we got further out, the gale came on again. Proud of my sea experience, I saw passenger after passenger succumb, until I was the last on deck, feeling somewhat puffed up. Alas, the ship began to lurch most violently, going right through a head sea in the very teeth of the gale, impossible in sailing ships and never experienced by me before. Down into the wave, sea all over from head to stern; another plunge or two; up flew the heels of the men at the wheel, and – well! I will not say what came up, but my disposition to brag went with it, and I dived ignominiously below. Tea was served to the very few who could partake of it, and we soon sought our births for the night.

It was truly a relief next day to get into smooth water in the Firth of Clyde, and a curious sight to see the passengers, one by one, appear and put on airs of experienced navigators, quite able to play a good knife and fork at dinner. At Finnieston, Emily and her brother received my account of the cause of the delay somewhat incredulously, in a way not complimentary to my courage and gallantry; she had no idea of flinching for any such considerations.

[A hard matter-of-fact Puritan radical who made no allowances for anybody – JCC II.]

On April 20th 1838 [a Friday], in Frederic's dining room, we were united according to the summary and simple Scotch fashion by the Rev Greville Ewing, of the Independent persuasion, our names having been three separate times 'proclaimed' in the parish church. The company consisted of F. Pellatt and his three daughters, aged 4, 3 and 2, who sat in a row on the sofa with their nurse and witnessed the ceremony with wondering eyes, the governess, and two maidservants. It could not be said that ours was an ostentatious or extravagant wedding. [Seems surprising it wasn't in a church; one wonders why?]

A carriage and pair conveyed us to Hamilton, where we took the outside of the coach for Lanark, and visited the falls of Clyde. Next day to 'Auld Reekie', which we entered after dark; as we drove down Princes Street, I thought I had never seen any sight so striking as the innumerable lights gleaming from the towering houses in the Old Town, tier above tier, rising from the valley which separates Old Town from New. We visited Roslin Castle and Chapel, going by omnibus to Loan-head village, 2 or 3 miles distant, over such a monotonous flat of fields that it was difficult to persuade oneself that anything so romantic as Hawthornden or Roslin could come out of it. We stayed in Edinburgh at the Black Bull 4 or 5 days, and went to Stirling, intending to go on to Callender through the Trossachs, but to our dismay, the conveyances were not yet laid on for the season. There were no railways in Scotland then, even between Edinburgh and Glasgow. [There were in fact one or two minor lines; E & G opened 1842.] So we had to be content with distant views of the Bens.

After a few days it was time at the week's end to return to Glasgow. There the three little girls were 'wearying' for Auntie; I question if dear Emily did not almost begin to waver in her allegiance to her new affection when she saw how these little motherless things were bound up in her; I felt like a thief who had stolen a best treasure, and our departure was trying for those dear little children's sakes. [How about his own motherless three? – JCC II.]

Now began another era, so strangely brought round and unlooked for, and so favorable to my future comfort and well being that I have often been filled with admiration of the mercy extended to me and so suited to my exigencies. During all my somewhat chequered life, I have been brought through all my difficulties and trials by a way opened up for me by a Hand unseen. Now, through a long season, I was to have the blessing of a loving and devoted wife and mother, and a well-ordered household; although putting it to rights took many weeks.

Emily soon marked out her own path in society. It had always been understood that we would be free to frequent our respective places of worship; she selected the Independent Chapel, lately erected in Everton Crescent, while I continued at St George's Everton with the children. They were now all at home, and attending school at Mrs Ashe's morning and afternoon. They had been running too wild during the interregnum, and required great good management to bring them into quiet orderly habits, which Emily laboured for with untiring patience and affection without scolding or snubbing. [So far as my father knew; I could tell a different tale – JCC II.] I felt my home had become a very happy one, founded on the only sure basis, well-directed and steadily sustained.

Following Father's death, my sisters vacated William Henry Street and came to Rose Vale until I married, when they intended to visit friends in London and Essex and afterwards take a house elsewhere in Liverpool. At Rose Vale, they and I became acquainted with our next door neighbors, kind and friendly, but certainly very peculiar: three maiden ladies, all well passed the meridian of life, and their younger bachelor brother. I have often observed that four will pair off, but 'sisters three' are not harmonious, two pair off and one is left. The eldest was the 'speckled bird', who seemed to have a rule not to harmonize with the rest, and to live in perpetual suspicion of a plot of some kind. She went about her own business; the other two, equally independent, kept house. They kept no servant, as none could come up to their ideas of what one should be; but they had a dog 'Snap', an ill-favored white half-terrier half-pug, who snarled at all who noticed him. [Very good friends with me, would follow me to church &c. – JCC II.]

We also knew another 'peculiar', the accountant Mr Bartholomew Prescot, much-respected for his unswerving Christian integrity and uprightness. His white head, thin pallid face and cold grey eye gave the idea of a subdued spirit; but his thoughts ran on somewhat wild subjects, such as the restoration of the Jews and the rebuilding of Jerusalem, of which he had drawn out a plan. He had a system of astronomical science and the Universe to upset all modern theories, Sir Isaac Newton's included, substituting Scripture phraseology taken literally, demonstrating very much to his own satisfaction that the Earth was the centre round which the whole of the heavens revolved: on which he had written a large volume and sent a copy to every peer of the realm and the Lord Chancellor. Poor dear old Prescot was an intense bore on his favorite topics. He was a Greek and Hebrew scholar, of which he gave a startling indication when he came to see me after my marriage. Mrs Ashe happened to be present, and he said 'Sir, I wish you joy of your deliverance.' What could he mean but getting rid of the former mistress of my household? She looked awful, and I did not know which way to look, till he explained that in Hebrew, 'Pellatt' meant deliverance.

Two Brides for Two Brothers

Now we began to hear more of the disaster at Mazatlan. Feelings had intensified; to exculpate himself, the agent laid the blame on George of having brought the ship too near the shore, which was proved to be his own doing contrary to George's expressed desire and opinion. When George arrived, therefore, he was coldly received, and his wages refused on various grounds: First, the great expense of repairs and outfit, which was Mr Willis' own fault for buying a ship without knowing the state she was in. Next, the length of the voyage, which he could not help. Then, laying his ship too near the shore. Finally, what most surprised me, that he had paid the men their wages up to the time of the loss, though they had earned them and the ship had delivered her cargo. I had, for the first time in my life, a battle to fight with Mr Willis, which I much regretted, but I *did* fight it, inch by inch, because I felt that George was badly treated. He was an irritable man, so I did all I could to prevent a collision by undertaking to fight for him, which I was enabled to do by the exercise of right feeling and temper on both sides: so far that Mr Willis expressed his respect for my defence of my brother, although he differed from me. At length we brought it to an adjustment, but I believe George was not pleased I had done so by some little compromise.

After this, George joined his wife and family at Belfast. With what he had earned on his voyage, and a few hundreds from Father's death, he resolved to begin business on shore, as an auctioneer, which did not appear to grow naturally from what he had followed so many years. However, he commenced; but all at once, a new project came up, which was more in his own line and promised advantages. A landed gentleman near Lough Neagh proposed to establish a steam conveyance over the Lough, to shorten the way to Belfast. George was appointed captain and superintendent of the steamer's construction, which was to be on the lake side. It promised to be prosperous; but did not, as we shall see, fulfil this expectation.

During this summer, we saw several of Emily's relatives, including her brother Apsley, and Mr and Mrs Benjamin Smith from Blackheath; Mrs Smith (Susan) was my wife's sister, and her husband an eminent manufacturing silversmith in Duke Street, Lincoln's Inn. [Emily's niece Maria was very kind to me, gave me music lessons. It is singular that I got on with all my stepmother's relatives but not with her herself – JCC II.] But of all our guests, no one surprised me more than one whom I had not seen for nearly 20 years, our old friend Abraham Johnson the millionaire of Messing, who had unexpectedly sought me out. He died not many years after and left about £200,000 to a cousin: not thinking of me on *that* occasion. His contemporary millionaire, the whimsical John Griggs of Messing, also died soon after this period, leaving about £100,000 to a clergyman Mr Eden [the then Vicar of Messing], thus disappointing the expectations of friends and distant relatives.

News from Essex this autumn rather surprised us: My sisters, having gone to stay with our comical little old cousin Billy Brathwaite, just in time to see the last of his old bachelor uncle Robert Stammers, still vigorous for his years, had captivated two brothers, Thomas and William Rayner, young farmers at Hedingham, and were likely to proceed to a double union. So their settlement in

Liverpool, as they had purposed, was set aside by this unexpected turn. However, as their goods and chattels were stowed in our house, it was agreed they come to us at the beginning of the year.

Sadnesses – and Some Happiness

In January 1840, a fearful gale in Liverpool did immense damage: vessels in the river went down at their moorings, and chimneys were blown down in all directions, scarcely a street without 3 or 4 pitched through roofs causing death and destruction in many families. [He is in fact a year out: 'The Great Hurricane' (mentioned in *An Everyday History of Liverpool*, Scouse Press) began on Sunday evening January 6th 1839, and a pamphlet about it was given gratis to the purchasers of the Liverpool Journal of January 19th. The wind was fresh all day; about eleven on Sunday night, it veered to the south-west and increased. At midnight it became a fierce gale, at one it stood due west, augmented in fury and became a complete hurricane, continuing during the whole of the dark hours. From two to five o'clock, the gusts were tremendous, chimney-pots and slates swept away like chaff, chimney-stacks falling in and carrying down intervening floors to the cellar. The alarm was as universal as the destruction; thousands rose from their beds, unable to rest. When morning broke, the tempest was still sweeping from the west, and fragments flying from the housetops so as to render walking in the streets perilous. So extensive has been the devastation that we know not where to begin enumerating the disasters – Losses of life and property have been very great, multitudes are recounting narrow escapes, and several vessels were lost.]

On April 1st 1839, a little boy was born to us, who appeared healthy at first, but he did not thrive, and was taken to Heaven after about three months in the world. We called him Stephen after his mother's brother: who too died this year, a further trial on Emily. He was the most gifted of her family, of indomitable application to everything he took in hand, and might be said to have worn himself out at a comparatively early age. Eventually it was arranged that his widow take charge of Frederic's household and little family in Glasgow, a measure of mutual satisfaction and comfort. Emily's sister Sarah (Mrs John Phillips) invited her to Haverfordwest, to meet her sister Esther and her husband Thomas Phillips from London. As Emily was greatly shaken by the loss of her little boy, this change was very desirable, and was facilitated by my sisters being with me. She started by the steamer *Mountaineer* for Milford Haven; six long weeks passed, and I began to think I had been dreaming of being married.

A few months after, arrived the time for Margaret's wedding, which I proposed should take place in Liverpool, where she could be patronized and matronized by self and wife. Letitia's swain was not yet ready, as it was necessary he first get a farm. So Mr Tom Rayner claimed his bride, and [on January 2nd 1840] they were buckled to at St Augustine's church in Shaw Street [This is curious, neither his own church (St George's) nor, it seems, his sisters': he said earlier 'My father and sisters settled on St Andrews, Renshaw Street, as their place of worship.' Admittedly this was 1829, ten years before, but he does not mention any change in their church, unless it was on a page that was cut out in the original.] Sometime in 1840 [September 7th] Letitia entered married life with Mr William Rayner, the ceremony being performed at Castle Hedingham, the theatre of their strivings and thrivings being Mills Farm, Stisted, near Braintree.

The summer brought sad tidings from Haverfordwest: severe illness of Emily's sister Sarah from a dangerous inflammatory attack. Emily would have flown to her at once, but the boat was not going till the following week. The doctor pursued the old-fashioned plan of profuse bleeding to reduce the inflammation, and she rapidly sank under it. It was a sad blow to all; she was beautiful in mind and person, and very dear to Emily, as being the two youngest sisters, they had been fondly attached. She left three children, a boy Grafton, Emily, and Rowena, a sweet little girl who died soon after, very young. Emily went to do what she could for the family, and returned in about a fortnight, during which I had no-one to look after me save two servant girls.

John now went to Mr Edmund Chalmer's, a pretentious man who bestowed more thwacks than learning on the boys: a rough lot who led John such a life that I took him away, and sent him to the High School of the Liverpool Institute, Mount Street. For dear Fanny, who was getting beyond Mrs Ashe, Emily selected Mrs Skerret's school at Mason Street, Edge Hill. Letitia eventually went to Mrs Cover and Miss Barlace in Netherfield Road North, Everton. [Awful brutes; so was old Chalmer – JCC II.]

During this year, Mr Willis discovered that we could not get on without books; as Collard was (as they say at sea) hull-down astern, there was no hope of his fetching up and going ahead at the same time, so a second bookkeeper was engaged to go on with new books while Collard worked at the old. By this time he had possession of the private office (which the Willises vacated), as the public office was 'too noisy' and 'hindered him', though Mr Phillips, the new bookkeeper, managed to get on with *his* work. Collard could go in and out by a side door to pursue his own schemes unheeded, setting all work, and expostulation from me, at defiance.

The end of it was that he was found to have been appropriating things and moneys to his own use, for which, and other delinquencies, he was taken into custody; but the rogue had so contrived matters and implicated the cash-keeper, that other evidence failed, and a clever counsel got him off. It however finished him, and he never got employment again. So Mr Phillips worked away at both sets of books; he proved a valuable blessing, and soon put things on a comfortable footing. The office was now at peace, but I had reason to repent my introduction of Collard and letting my feeling for his family override my knowledge of his character, though I had not suspected him of gross dishonesty. I have learned that a recklessly extravagant man cannot be honest. I felt Collard's conduct the more acutely because Mr Willis seemed to blame me, although I had repeatedly warned him and urged dismissal.

About this time, Mr Prescot came to me, to say that a respectable firm had applied to him for a principal clerk, and asked if I was moveable. I was very loth to entertain such an idea, as I was much attached to Mr Willis, who was really a kind friend, but as a third more salary was offered, I did not think I should pass it by. It elicited from the Willises an expression of friendly feeling (which I was scarcely prepared for) and unwillingness to part with me. They regretted that the state of business would allow an advance of only half the difference between my present salary and that offered by the other house, and urged that I should be throwing myself into an entirely strange connection, which at my time of life might not end pleasantly. On the whole, I determined to remain with them, at the advanced salary of £250. At this time I was able to save them the expense of a Spanish clerk, whom they had hitherto employed to conduct a commission business in Yucatan, Mexico. I had begun to study Spanish a few years before, Mr Willis having paid for lessons for such of the young men wishing to learn, and by now I could supply the place of the Spanish clerk, who left us. [An argument for a further salary increase?]

Messing Revisited

In 1841, as I had a little money to spare, we planned a month's holiday, visiting London and Essex when the midsummer holidays commenced in June, taking the children with us. We set off by train at 6 o'clock, reaching the Euston station at 4 or 5 in the afternoon, 10 hours being then thought good travelling, though the distance is now covered in 5 or 6. We first stayed at Clapham with the Phillipses in Wandsworth Road, the two girls lodging with Uncle Charles; we visited Aunt Smith at Blackheath, and saw the sights of London. I took the children to Castle Hedingham, between which and Stisted they passed their time with their aunts.

While at Stisted, we visited Messing, as I wished to shew them my birthplace, of which they had heard so many stories. As Mr Wm Rayner and my sisters went with us, we created quite a sensation; the 'oldest inhabitants' flocked out and surrounded us. What a change in five-and-twenty years! Old Mother Richardson who made the exquisite gooseberry pies, John Freeman the shoemaker, and Pattie Matthie the patient husband, no longer living; her son Bill, who married our cook Betty Messent, with grown-up family and hammering away at the lapstone and stitching soles assiduously to support them. Wheelwright Cooper could just manage to trundle in and out of the public house, unfit for work or any good thing; poor John Tibball the blacksmith, no longer able to smite, reduced to poverty and glad to accept a shilling for auld lang syne. The whole village seemed in a state of decrepitude and poverty.

Messing Village, present day: view up The Street from the 'Old Crown'. The second building along, with the bow windows, is the former 'Queen's Head', the church is on the left round the corner. Harborough Hall Road is off to the left, Lodge Road, the Easthorp road, off right. (Author)

We went to the church. Externally, the wooden tower and its turret with ball and elaborately-worked vane (which I had portrayed in colour and gilding in my youthful days) was swept away for an ugly brick tower, which completely altered the character of the village. Internally, it had been transformed into high-churchism by Mr Eden, the late Vicar, John Griggs' legatee, who had left a marble tablet commemorating his liberality and munificence, and a hatchment setting forth his arms and achievements. A transept with galleries had been added, and such alterations that I did not recognize the scene of my youth till I came to the chancel, where the splendid East window with its six compartments representing Matthew 25 35:–

I was an hungred & ye gaue me meate
I was thirstie & ye gaue me drinke
I was a stranger & ye tooke me in vnto you
I was naked & ye clothed me
I was sicke and ye visited me
I was in prison and ye cam vnto me

– and the cherubim on the wainscoat puffing their cheeks and extending their wings, brought me back to childhood instanter; and the lions' heads on the Luckyn hatchments recalled brother Dick's face when he was naughty, and the boys crying in the gallery when old Isaac Harvey switched them with his hazel rod. Seating myself in our old pew in the chancel, I was lost in a dream of early days. [Rev Eden (in fact a curate) built the brick tower in 1840 as a thank-offering, along with the transepts and other alterations; the north transept was badly damaged in the 1884 Colchester earthquake and demolished. The three bells and 1805 clock were retained and are still present.]

I was roused by a functionary who showed me a great curiosity which the Vicar had discovered in the chancel wall behind the wainscoat, where he had to his joy found the 'Sedilia' and 'Lavatory', and which he had appropriated as a 'Credence' or depository for the holy things previous to their consecration and placement on the altar, contriving a panel to open like a door. I did not show the looked-for satisfaction at this [understandably, followed by a snide comment about the people being led backward to Popery].

We proceeded round Mother Richardson's corner, past Cooper's Cottages and Mother Scopes' cottage, Margaret and I noticing how the road had been denuded of all its fine elms and oaks, by where the Hall Gate had stood, swept away with its willows, nothing but the poplar as dreary sentinel over the Hall Pond, to my old home. And is this Messing Lodge, so bare of trees, neglected and forlorn? – the garden overgrown and scraggy; the pretty and productive vine swept away; the kitchen garden greatly curtailed and the fruit trees on their last legs: all worn out and uncared for.

We were kindly received by the Moore family, who had 25 years ago taken the farm over our heads, and had brought up a family on it,

East Window in Messing Church, all six panels.
(Courtesy Mr R.C. Brunning)

262

East Window in Messing Church, detail of top right panel.
(Courtesy Mr R.C. Brunning)

evidence that it had been well cultivated. They showed us over the old house, not forgetting the Nursery of so many infantine experiences of weal and woe. Internally, the same meagreness: in short, all that we had cherished of the pleasant and the picturesque had fallen under the one object of making the most of the land, pursued undeviatingly by its present occupant, who in that respect had been wiser than us. Our old dining-room looked sadly come down in the world, a bit of carpet, a table and a few wooden Windsor

Messing Lodge, present day; from Lodge Road. No information about the stone archway in front of the building. (Author)

chairs for the furniture. I sat in my poor dear father's favorite place in the bow window looking up to the village: what a tide of recollection of days forever gone bye – but what had those 25 years wrought! Mercies and blessings for time and eternity which I never dreamt of, called and wondrously led through grace out of darkness into marvellous light, unto this day.

It cost us *something* to get clear of the poor old people who had known us as children. What a change on the Tiptree road! The pleasant old mansion and grounds, Fitz Place, where the Rand family had flourished for centuries and the Cock family lived and benefitted the neighborhood, swept off the face of the earth by the ruthless hand of their near neighbor and friend John Griggs; who took the earliest opportunity after the departure of its next occupant, Sir John Tyrrell, to buy the property and pull the house down, to gratify a whim to increase the paddock round his own very insignificant premises, which, of the two, he had much better have pulled down. But his object, of making himself a name, was quite defeated, as his legatee Mr Eden left the village and let off the house to a stranger, leaving nothing but a marble tablet to celebrate John Griggs. We rode nearly over the spot 'where once a garden smiled', nothing but a few straggling fir trees to remind us of where we had passed many of our youthful days.

We came to Tiptree Heath, famous for Mr Mechi's farming experiments (abhorred by all tenants as putting nonsense into landlords' heads), and with him and other experimenters becoming, like many other things, improved off the face of the earth. Brook House was all going to wrack like Messing Lodge. And so back to Stisted. [Changes are of course inevitable: moral, perhaps, keep memories unspoiled and never go back.]

Next day, on by coach to Colchester, where Richard met us for St Osyth. The children were in great favor with Aunt Richard, who let them run about everywhere and do as they liked. [Always most kind to me after poor Uncle Richard's death – JCC II.] St Osyth, that World's End of Essex, was all unchanged since I visited it before; but a spiritual ray of light proceeded from a little obscure wooden chapel, the Way of Truth expounded with a clearness, simplicity and fervour quite remarkable in a man whose daily business was to drive an omnibus between Colchester and Wivenhoe. We stayed a week, then departed to London and thence home.

Soon after our return, we had a visit from Emily's aunt Mrs Langford and her husband; they lived at Wymondly House, near Hitchin, and we had stayed with them during our recent holiday. She had been Miss Susanna Maberly, third daughter of Mr Stephen Maberly of Reading, Emily's maternal grandfather. With them was our [= Emily's] brother Apsley Pellatt: all on their way to Glasgow to visit Frederic.

Good Works

So we fell into our places again. At the office, work had accumulated; but a most acceptable change, the London mail now coming in in the morning and going out at 6 in the evening [the effect of mail carriage by railway?], and thus we were relieved from evening work, after 15 years drudgery as far as I was concerned.

Emily's household engagements were somewhat more onerous, as we were now reduced to one servant girl, besides the weekly district visiting connected with her Chapel duties.

I had a little time to give to useful measures, and consented to go on the committee of the Liverpool Town Mission. Mr Glyn, the missionary [at Crescent Chapel?] had collected ragged children whom he found about the streets, and had them into a room in Richmond Fair near Everton Crescent where he and a poor bricklayer taught them on sabbath mornings; but as they increased to upwards of an hundred, he applied to me for help as a Superintendant, an appeal I could not resist. Emily enlisted young people from the Chapel as teachers, and we soon organized classes and reduced these rough materials to something like order. This altered our plans at home: the children went to sabbath classes at Crescent Chapel with the servant (when she did not give us the slip, which she frequently did), and Emily and I came to Richmond Fair school morning and afternoon, shutting up the house and leaving the pot or kettle to boil till we came back [not boil dry we trust!]. I am inclined to think this movement of ours in Liverpool anticipated the Ragged School system which soon after was organized in London.

The Liverpool District Provident Society was a large system of banking and relief for the poor, carried on by visiting from house to house all over the city. I had been a visitor for Everton District under Mr Buddicom, and now I undertook to act as one of the Treasurers, for someone who was going to India; but I gave it up eventually, as I felt the responsibility too great.

An unpleasant matter gave me some trouble and uneasiness. Mrs Pattinson's youngest daughter Frances had been left sadly unprotected by her mother, and although Miss McGhie [always most kind to us children – JCC II] had hitherto made a home for her, she had met with reverses and could no longer do so. An old West India lady friend of her mother's, who lived at Everton, took the girl in as a sort of companion; but she was growing superannuated and the girl was giddy and thoughtless and fast running into mischief. Mr Buddicom informed me, and he and I raised money to send her out to her mother; a shipowner whom I had known in Demerara offered a passage, charging only for her provisions. I was glad she was

For the first few months, Mr Phillips and I had to oscillate between Bates' place of business, at the other side of town in Seel Street, and our own at the end of George's Dock: an immense waste of time and trouble. Bates inclined to settle at his own place, but eventually I persuaded them to fix at ours. I soon began to see into Bates' character. He was in good credit with the bankers, but his mercantile transactions were all of the shabbiest kind, and his business arrangements invariably so loose, that he had a loophole to creep out at if he found it convenient. His young men were constantly relating instances of his sharp practice and laughing at the way he had *done* this person and that. All his people served him with fear, not with respect or regard. His whole system was, as Mr Phillips expressed it, artificial. Mr Willis soon revived the business at Mazatlan, which had failed under George's unlucky voyage; then a house at Calcutta, and one in China, were set on foot, but I soon saw there was no bottom in them. The manufacturers in Lancashire did not give the support looked for, and Bates' visage began to fall. A great fat brother came home from Bombay, and they fell out about accounts: both were dishonest. Another brother at Halifax, the family residence, was an unprincipled ruffian, and in using this very strong term, I do not exaggerate. For the present we leave these discordant materials to ferment.

George returned the latter end of the year from his Mediterranean voyage, and some dispute [oh no, not again!] with his owners or agents about a freight home was the result, so he was again adrift. Harriet and their little Fanny, a nice child of 10 or 11, came over from Ireland to meet him. He afterwards obtained command of an East Indiaman, *Ganges*, for Aden with a cargo of patent fuel, and on to Bombay for cotton home. Poor fellow, he and his crew were thrown down by terrible illness arising, it was thought, from the fuel vapour, of which coal tar was a large proportion, and all hands were so debilitated he could scarcely get the ship worked; he himself was laid up nearly the whole time at Bombay.

Letitia's Illness
It was now 1844 and time to see about Fanny's finishing school. Emily's object was to get her placed as an 'articled pupil', or pupil

teacher, so that she might both learn for herself, and instruct in the school: giving her experience in teaching, while lessening the expense of her own *[tuition? Here a sheet is cut out]...*

I felt her departure as much as she, for I loved her dearly. I could not go with her, feeling insecure as to the effect on Mr Bates of a request for leave, but the Driffields were sending their daughter to school, and they went together. Fan's mother received her in London, and she was installed as a pupil teacher at Miss Turk's. I had also to dispose of John, whom after much research I placed with an old Demerara friend who was in partnership as a colonial broker, but he did not take to it. His ideas ran on chemistry or mechanics; an engineering friend gave me no encouragement, and engineering firms were so immoderate in their demands for money and time, for the privilege of working for them, that I saw no chance in that direction. Eventually John was fixed for 5 years with John & Samuel Johnson, chemists and druggists in Church Street, where I thought he would see some manufacturing chemistry: which resulted in ladling out fish oil and pounding drugs in a huge iron mortar. We must leave him to bruise away for the present. I ran up to London for a few days before Emily returned [so you *did* get leave after all!], and saw Fan at the school, as happy as she could be away from dear home.

A new trial proved lengthy and severe. Soon after Fanny's departure, poor Letitia shewed symptoms of ill-health, and complained of excessive internal pains; but our medical man, after attending for some time, seemed as much at a loss as we were. Her sufferings became excessive, she had little rest day or night, and frequently lay shrieking with pain at intervals during the entire night; nothing seemed to alleviate it. It was a fearful time, and her state was so alarming that we called in Mr Robert Bickersteth, a surgeon of great eminence: who pronounced it ulceration of the bladder, and gave us no hope it would ever be cured; on the contrary, he said it was more likely to spread. After visiting for some time, he said 'I can do no good, I grieve at what she will have to endure; there is nothing for it but palliatives, we must knock down the pain with opium.' Small doses of acetate of morphia were begun, and increased as appeared to be needful to lull the pain and produce repose; but the disorder itself did not abate.

For months she continued a sad sufferer, entirely confined to her bed, tenderly and unweariedly watched and nursed by her mother, who scarcely ever left her, and whose concern for her spiritual welfare was intense; yet this dear child remained for a long time insensible to spiritual subjects, which were evidently distasteful to her. She was reduced to skin and bone, it was impossible to imagine a human being thinner, to be alive. The morphia had been increased till it amounted to something fearful, 14 grains in 24 hours! equal to half a cup of laudanum in potency, but the medical men said she would bear it and must have it, as she could not otherwise endure the pain, and nothing else would keep it down.

My position with Bates & Willis was not one of much comfort. I was head of the office establishment, and had much negociation out of doors as well as supervision within. [He makes it into the Liverpool Directory for 1844, which, however, describes him as: Bookkeeper, 26 Clarence Street, Everton Road.] We had a large staff, for whom I found it difficult always to find employ; none were left of the old lot but myself and Mr Phillips. He was methodical, neat and correct, which did not suit Bates' slapdash ideas and loose dealing, with holes to creep out at: what his young men called 'chiselling'. I found some of his behests revolting to my better feelings, but I went the straightforward way as far as I could, and left the dirty part to him. He frequently asked me home to dine, and treated me with Yorkshire hospitality – which means feed your friend sumptuously at the dwelling house, and chisel him at the counting house. [I would assure you, as one myself, that not all Yorkshiremen are like this! – CCT.] I also began to discover that Mr Bates and Mr Willis did not go on amicably (how could they?) and I foresaw a rupture.

In 1845, George returned after his long and trying Bombay voyage; his health was broken, but his spiritual state had benefitted. The owners had other plans for *Ganges*; George had, through a friend, a prospect of a command in the City of Dublin Steam Packet Co, and he and his wife staid with a friend in Dublin many months over this negociation. I was exceedingly disappointed when it fell through after all, and poor George had still employment to seek on shore, as he was getting unfit for roughing it at sea. [Something about the Driffield family mentioned here; Edward, the youngest son, came to him at Bates Willis.]

Fanny came home for her midsummer holidays; we longed to see her, and so did poor Letitia, the violence of whose fearful disorder had abated under the immense quantity of morphia she took daily. It greatly neutralized the pain, but, strange to say, did not affect her injuriously, as with opium eaters, although it produced drowsiness. Reducing the dose did not seem possible at present. Dear Fanny rushed into her room the moment she got into the house, and the meeting between the sisters, who had been separated twelve months, was of extreme joy. She cheerfully devoted her time to the companionship of her suffering sister, and passed most of her hours in her room. Fanny was much grown, now in her 17th year, and looking womanly. She had cultivated French, German, drawing, and music, and her mind was opening to the acquisition of knowledge both secular and divine; her bent was intellectual, and she had no taste for the light and frivolous amusements which captivate girls of her age. It was a great trial when her visit came to a close, especially to the poor invalid and the uncertainty whether they might meet again on earth.

Our servant was now a clever Welch girl, a very plucky wench, as they say in Lancashire. One day she caught a thief in the parlour, the back door being carelessly left open; she manoeuvred him with great courage and adroitness, coaxing him out into a public house, then transferring him into the arms of a policeman, thence to the magistrate, who gave him 'three months' for his household investigation.

Trouble at the Office

Matters did not improve at the office; great dissatisfaction between the two ill-matched partners was too apparent in their conduct towards each other. Bates considered he had been misled as to Mr W's capability to promote a large business, and hinted his intention to bring matters to a crisis. He purchased cheaply a cotton mill at Stockton-on-Tees, on his sole account, and devoted much of his time to it. Mr Willis on his side began to suspect a gradual withdrawal of funds, a disinclination to advance anything for general business, and throwing cold water on our Mexican connection, which required such advances.

Things dragged on uncomfortably towards the close of 1845, when I saw clearly the two parties were preparing for conflict. Mr W was aware of Bates' treacherous designs to get all the funds into his own power, but he had the wrong man to deal with and I hinted as much to him; and as I knew Mr DW, I recommended fair and friendly representation of his views. Bates however worked on in his own thoroughly crooked way. He found he could not detach me, and ceased to treat me with confidence, which I was very glad to find. A couple of lads at his devotion in the office acted as spies: one seemed to have been specially indoctrinated to thwart Mr Willis; he was in fact discovered at the beginning of 1846, when Bates went to Stockton without communicating with Mr Willis or leaving any business directions, to have been taking the letters up to Bates' private house, instead of bringing them to the office.

Bates' brother from Halifax, a rough unscrupulous fellow, now appeared, and I suspected some new move. Mr Willis was impressed with the same opinion, and as a precaution gave the Postmaster a notice to deliver the letters at the office; hitherto we had adopted the plan, usual amongst merchants, of going for our letters, which were sorted into lockers or boxes. This brought out brother Benjamin, who had the assurance to ask Mr Willis by what authority he did this: who retorted by asking by what authority he was there, to which he replied 'by his brother's.' So this man had actually been sent to overrule Mr Willis during Bates' absence, and shewed himself well-fitted for it. He gave the brokers orders to sell this and that, and when Mr W put a stop to it, abused him grossly in most low and vulgar terms. He told me I was not to send out some orders; vainly Mr W in his gentlemanly way told him he had no authority and must not interfere. The matter grew to such a height, and this man assumed such a bullying attitude, that I feared personal violence. He told me again not to send out the orders: I told him they were gone already – Then', he said, 'I dismiss you from my brother's service'. I laughed and said he was joking; he intimated I should soon find it was no joke if I trifled with him. One evening he threatened Mr Willis with personal violence, and after much brutal language and conduct, went out. As we were all leaving for the night, he reappeared with two or three strange-looking men, who on seeing us come out, retreated: but we felt little doubt of some act of violence had we been upstairs in the office.

Next morning we could not get in to the office; the warehouseman said that Mr Joseph Bates was come home, and had ordered that no-one be let in. After some time we were admitted, and took our places. Bates sent for me, and said he understood there had been some unpleasant proceedings during his absence. I said there had been some very shameful ones on the part of his brother, and that if he wished to separate from Mr Willis, such plans as these would not do. He then read me a lecture, told me I was not to be trusted, as I had let Mr Phillips overdraw his salary, and gave me a month's notice to leave: which I told him was a very harsh return for 20 years in one employ. After this, a scene between him and Mr Willis nearly ended in violence. I took Bates' notice for granted, and told Mr Willis I had better look for other employment, in which he could but acquiesce. There were one or two appointments vacant, and a friend and Mr Willis kindly exerted themselves for me; but I was unfortunately past age.

An Opening in London
However, I had not long to deliberate. Emily had written to her brother Frederic telling him how matters were, and he now had a prospect of something in London. He had moved from Glasgow some 4 or 5 years since, after ill success in the glass trade there, and was managing a new electroplate business, carried on by Messrs Elkington & Co at Birmingham as the manufacturers, and my brother-in-law [by marriage] Benjamin Smith in London.

I took the train to London, and staid with Charles overnight. It was late evening, of course candlelight, and I caught a glimpse of a young lady, neatly and simply dressed, looking very blooming, who came to embrace me – my own dear Fan! A surprise prepared by her aunt, and much delighted I was at her loving reception. I met Frederic next morning. He was about to join his brother Apsley in the old glass manufactory and business at Holland Street, Blackfriars; the proposal he made was that I succeed him in managing Elkington's London business, which was carried on at 45 Moorgate Street and 22 Regent Street. I felt this unexpected opening was too visible an interposition of Providence to admit of hesitation; I had some diffidence of my ability in a position so unlike what I had been accustomed to, but this was overruled by both Frederic and Mr Smith, who did not doubt that my long experience would be adequate, as their manufacturing and selling officials would carry on that necessary part, under my supervision. My salary was liberal, and they wished that I be ready to fill my new post by March 1st; it was now early February. At once I wrote to Emily with the news, and followed my letter next day. When I arrived, I found she had stuck bills in the windows, 'House to Let', and engaged a packer to pack our furniture for removal.

At the office, Mr Willis was surrounded with troubles, at war with his amiable partner. He was glad at my success in London; the great drawback was that we must separate after twenty years, and under such painful circumstances for him. I respected him highly as a worthy benevolent man and kind friend, from whom I had ever received sympathy and support; it grieved me to leave him in this season of trial, in a comfortless position with that crafty and unprincipled man. However, he had consulted his solicitor, and I placed myself at his disposal to assist in bringing his case forward. It was recommended that arbitrators hold the funds of the firm until all the rights and wrongs should be investigated and decided. Bates struggled to get clear of this, and many were the scenes of violence and disorder with him and his brother, who was at length taken before a magistrate for an assault on Mr Willis and bound over. Bates, finding that chicanery and violence would not serve, consented at length to the decision of the arbitrators. He had written in the most reckless way to everyone who had been sent out to Calcutta, China, and Mexico, to say the affair was ended and making Mr Willis bear the blame. Thus this ill-advised alliance, which had dragged on for three years its unsuitable and unhappy existence, came to a discreditable termination.

Farewells

Since the summer, Letitia had improved, and although excessively weak, her Mama succeeded by perseverance in getting her to sit up, then to walk a little, and then taking her out of doors in a garden-chair; this was a great help, and contributed much to her regaining strength. By the beginning of the year, the violence of the disorder had wonderfully abated, though not eradicated, and the doses of morphia were considerably reduced, giving us hope she might outgrow it. Providentially, we could now hope to convey her to London with comparative ease and safety; otherwise, a fearful predicament. Miss McGhie came to visit us; I felt much respect and regard for her for past kindnesses, and my children were much attached to her with recollections of their earliest pleasures. We parted with regret; poor thing, we learnt later that her mind had given way and she had died in an asylum. Emily and I visited Prescot: I was not to see it again. In a few years the scene changed, and another came to minister there who knew not the Lord. [Mr Driffield in fact died December 1847, though a Lancashire Directory for 1850 still has him as the incumbent; clearly they had not been diligent in updating their information.]

We began to pack our things to be sent on before us by railway, a formidable operation. At this juncture, who should appear but George, en route for London to become Secretary of the new 'Ramoneur Company', for sweeping chimneys by a new process with a patented flexible expanding and contracting broom. It lasted some months, but fell through in the end, and he was again at an uncertainty.

The Crescent Chapel expressed their high esteem of Emily, and gave her an unexpected testimonial, articles of silver for a tea service. From Richmond Fair school, I received a valuable edition of Bagster's comprehensive Bible, which I prize to this day. We took leave of Mr Ewbank at St George's. I had given up my pew there after about two years of his ministry, for many considerations, especially the children, whose spiritual welfare, so much bound up with their mother, I wished to strengthen by an undivided house: which we had been for about 8 years, and at length had determined to coalesce. Mr Ewbank was very liberal, and could appreciate my views and feelings. [Referring back to JCC II's earlier note, 'My father abandoned the church of his fathers at the instigation of my puritan stepmother Emily Pellatt, an arrant bigot': He may have a point; doubtless a wife would usually follow her husband as head of the household, but maybe Emily refused to do so.] At this time, the Evangelical Alliance was being formed, with Liverpool the great centre. I had written some letters in the Liverpool Courier, in answer to Puseyite virulence in the Liverpool Mail; these letters attracted the attention of the Alliance, and I was recommended as its Secretary, but owing to the other offer, it fell through. [E.B. Pusey was leader of the 'Oxford Movement' which wanted to move the Anglican church towards Roman Catholicism.]

It was now February 25th. Our house was cleared and all our furniture sent off, and we took a small lodging for two days. We arranged for John to board and lodge with a friend, Dr Roach, as he must necessarily remain at Liverpool: although he was not over-comfortable with Johnsons, neither was it quite what I had wished for or anticipated, but was the best I could do, and I hoped to mend matters in time. We took leave of Mrs Ashe; the three maiden sisters and their brother next door in Rose Vale; Mrs Cearns; and eccentric old Bartholomew Prescot. Last but not least, my good kind old master, Mr Daniel Willis. His benevolence had greatly outweighed the many years of toil in his service, and I never could think of him but with affectionate regard. Thus we left Liverpool, which I had known for 25 years and lived in for 20: a period of many trials and cares, but mixed with many mercies.

Addenda – Liverpool Directories
Entries in two of them confirm many of his people and places.

1821:
Edward Cearnes [sic], tailor & draper, 92 Paradise St [off Lord Street].

John Pattison [sic], merchant, 3 Juvenal St; John Pattison & Co, counting house 27 Drury Lane.

[JP's will, see 'The Beginning of the End', confirms that JCC's inclusion of the N is correct.]

Bartholomew Prescot, accountant, 17 Houghton St, office 16 Castle St.

Rowland Roscow, broker, Gt Mersey St, office 34 Drury Lane.

Daniel Willis, merchant, Toxteth Park; Willis Latham & Gair, Willis Place [!], Wapping.

1844:

Mrs Jemima Ashe, ladies' school, Oxton, Birkenhead.

Bates Sons & Co, merchants, 18 Seel St.

Rev Edmund B. Chalmer, A.B., Crosby [no further address].

Joh Harrison & Samuel Johnson, chymists, 7 Church St.

Mechanics' Institute, Mount St. [between #6 and 8. In JCC's reference to it (see 'Sadnesses ...') he crossed out 'Mechanics' and substituted 'Liverpool'].

Bartholomew Prescot, accountant, 31 Castle St; house 36 Roscommon St.

William N. Skerrett, agent, 24 Mason St. [Name with two t's, wife or school not mentioned.]

Daniel & Thomas Willis, merchants, 5 Georges Dock Gates North; houses, Daniel, 4 Rake Lane, Wavertree Road; Thomas, Hurst House near Prescot.

9 Netherfield Rd N: Mrs Mary Ball, Mr Edward Lister, Janet Cover, Boarding School [No #11 – omitted in error? Name Barlace not mentioned].

Rose Vale: The sisters three and brother, name Foster, were at #7, so JCC must have been at #5 or #9.

– Coaches, Trains

London directories indicate that the coach to Prescot and Liverpool (no name given) ran from the Swan-with-two-necks, Lad-lane; departures in 1815 aft. 4½, in 1820 mrn 11½, aft 7½.

In 1834, the coach from Liverpool to London, The Umpire (no 'royal' qualification stated), left the Saracens Head, Angel, and White Horse Inns, every day ¼ before 12, route Warrington, Knutsford, Newcastle, Stone, Lichfield, Tamworth, Lutterworth, Northampton, Newport-Pagnell, Woburn, Dunstable, and St Albans. To Prescot, The Umpire (again) left the Legs of Man, London-road, every aft at 5. There was also an Omnibus from the Grapes, Lime-st, every afternoon, no time given!

John refers to the opening of the Grand Junction and London & Birmingham railway routes (see 'Proposal ...' and 'Father's Homecoming'). The former, between Birmingham (Vauxhall) and Warrington (for Liverpool and Manchester), described as the world's first 'trunk' line, opened July 4th 1837; the first train consisted of 8 first-class carriages, one named (interestingly) 'Umpire'. It was built in conjunction with the other, which opened throughout September 17th 1838 between London (Euston) and Birmingham (Curzon Street). The GJ was soon extended to the latter terminus, with a limited service of first-class through carriages between Lancashire and London from October 1st 1838; all services were transferred from Vauxhall to Curzon Street from November 19th 1838. The GJ, the L&B, and the Liverpool & Manchester merged July 16th 1846 to form the London & North-Western Railway. A short extension westwards to the present city centre site at New Street opened June 1st 1854, and Curzon Street was relegated to freight. The original Vauxhall terminus was a little way north of the present Duddeston station ('Vauxhall & Duddeston' until fairly recently), adjacent to which is the still-extant original locomotive shed, latterly a wagon repair works but now disused. The Aston - Duddeston - New Street section now forms part of the heavily-used electrified 'Cross-City' suburban commuter line. What is commonly called 'Curzon Street Station', in fact the former station hotel, still exists, and is now a 'listed' building, its historical importance recognized as being the only remaining original from the L&B, following the official vandalism that wantonly destroyed the Doric-style 'Euston Arch' when the London end was modernised in the 'brutalist' 1960s style.

– Ships

The table shows some of the vessels that John and brother George were concerned with, typical of the kind engaged in trade at that time; those that 'passed in the night' on his China / India voyages are not covered. The data are taken from Lloyds Register of Shipping (LR), spellings exactly as therein, and generally confirm what JCC says; there is insufficient information to identify exactly some vessels that he mentions. LR gives no age or build date for American-built vessels – maybe unknown or no way to verify any stated age? Note that the term 'ship' can refer to any reasonably-large sea-going vessel, but it also has the more specific meaning of one particular type of vessel.

There are (confusingly) two editions of LR from 1800 to 1834, apparently the result of a disagreement between shipowners (SO) and underwriters (UW), who then published 'rival' volumes in each of these years. Both contain some misprints and the occasional inconsistency, but the latter appears somewhat more reliable factually. The SO have some supplementary tables giving, for example, the annual sailings of the East India Company, including the voyages referred to in Vol. 1. The place of build of some Company vessels is given simply as 'River', which means one of the yards on the River Thames in London. They were known as 'HCS', Honorable Company Ship.

Prior to the 1870s, only vessels inspected by Lloyd's appeared in the Register, which may account for why no *Fox* with Capt Cheveley in 1834-35, nor schooner *Friendship*, were located (A schooner has 2 or more masts, all fore-and-aft rigged.). To give some idea of the physical size of these ships, the famous HMS *Beagle*, built 1820 with two masts (a third mizzen added later), weighed 235 tons and was 90ft 4in long, 24ft 6in wide.

LR may provide more information than is shown here, such as timber of which built, quality class of vessel and material, when last surveyed, and recent repair history:

Table of Vessels with which John and George were involved

[Key to column headings follows]

(1)	(2)	(3)	(4)	(5)	(6)	(7)	(8)
Monarch * 1818	Lutey S sC	365	Nwcstl	12	Johnson	16	Lo Calctt
Thalia 1821	B Simpson Sw sC PIC	202 SDB	Sndrld	1817	J Felt (Fell 1820)	13	Li Demra
Sir John Cameron '22	W Lilly (SO) S/Bg D Lilly (UW) sC	264 SDB	Scotl'd	1815 7	Wilson &c	15	Li Demra
Ann 1821	Straughn S sC	250	SP 05	1802	Gladstone	14	Li Demra
Ardent 1821	Patterson Bg PIC	246 SDB	Wrktn	1804	Crosthwte	14	Li Cnada
Cornwall 1822	T Robbs S sC PIC	380 SDB	Whtby	1798	Gldstn &C	17	Li Demra
Eleanor 1824 *	J Young Bg sC	366 SDB	Quebc	3	Dunbar &	15	Li Dm'ra
Anna * 1823	Rogerson / Bg sC G Chevely PIC	147 SDB	Amer	Pr	J Fell (SO) Patt'n(UW)	12	Li Demra
Glenbervie 1823 *	J Jones Bg sC	391 SDB	Pt Glsg	1815	Douglas	16	Gr Dmra
William Wise	J Winder	213	Wrktn	1815	Peele &Co	15	Li

(1)	(2)	(3)	(4)	(5)	(6)	(7)	(8)
1824	Bg	SDB					Demra
W'm Salthouse 1824 Suppt	J Garness / Bg sC PIC	251 SDB	Liverpl	New	Salthouse	15	Li Demerar
Jess & Flora 1824 *	J Pattison / S sC PIC	261 SDB	Amer	Pr	J Fell	15	Li Demra
Lancaster 1826	J Cannell / S sC	353 SDB	Lncstr	12	Barton &C	17	Li Brbds
Britannia 1825	R Grayson / Bg sC	170 SDB	Sndrld	15	Russell &	12	Li Berbice
Gazelle 1828 *	T Benn / Bg Chevly sC PIC	240 SDB	Whtvn	1826	R & G Benn	14	Li Jamai
Pantaloon * 1831	P Inglis / Bg Chevely sC PIC	121 SDB	Dougls	4	T Murray	10	Li Demra
Isabella * 1832 Suppt	G Chevely / Bg sC	238 SDB	Belfast	New	Wilson & Co	14	Be N Brnswk
William * Mulvey 1836	T Jones / Bg	161	Chestr	1829	Moss & Co		Li St Dmg
Ganges 1844 *	Cheveley / S	614	Qubec	1843	Johnson &		Li N.Y.

* See 'Notes about Particular Vessels' following

Key to Column Headings
1 Name, date of LR volume
2 Captain, type of vessel: Bg = Brig, 2 masts, both square-rigged
   S = Ship, 3 or more masts, all square-rigged, with topsails and yards
   Sw = Snow, like a brig with a supplementary trysail mast (small fore-and-aft rigged)
   sC = Sheathed with copper
   PIC = Has 'proved iron cable' (as opposed to hempen ropes)
3 Tonnage, number of decks (presumably internal, below the main deck): None stated = 2, SDB = Single deck with beams
4 Place built; SP = Spanish prize, Amer Pr = American Prize
5 Date built (SO) or age (UW)
6 Owner
7 Draught when loaded (feet)
8 Surveying port: Be = Belfast, Gr = Greenock, Li = Liverpool, Lo = London
   Destination of latest voyage – may be in previous year to the volume year.

Notes about Particular Vessels
For ease of reference, the vessels are listed in alphabetical order.

Anna. Some repairs 1822; Repairs, new deck and upper works 1824. Continues 1824-26 (UW):

| 1824 | G Chevely | Pattisn & | Be, Jamai |
| 1825, 1826 | G Chevely | Pattison & | Li, Pernm |

(Pernambuco, extreme E of Brazil. SO have her as still owned by J Fell!). Not recorded 1827 (did not exist!).

Eleanor. In 1823, 270 tons, built Quebc – presumably '366' in 1824 is misprint for 266

Monarch. Has Captain Lutey again 1819 (confirming JCC's note that he sailed again), but changed to Capt. McDougall 1820

Ganges. 1845, captain Cheveley / Smith; 1846, voyage Calcutta (via Aden and Bombay?).

Gazelle. Continues (UW): 1829-30, Capt H Chverly, voyage MtVid (Montevideo, bottom of Uruguay, facing Buenos Aires across R. Plate); 1831, Capt H Chverly / Borbidge.

Glenbervie. JCC says 'Barque', but LR 1821-24 has Brig.

Isabella. 1833, Capt Cheveley – spelt correctly at last! Different captain 1834.

Jess & Flora. Presumably captain and owner reversed in error.

Pantaloon. 1832, Capt Chevely / D Smith, voyage Gr, Demra (SO have tonnage as 170!).

William Mulvey. Same in 1837, not in 1838. Captain and owner do not correspond with JCC. (St Dmg, Santo Domingo, Dominican Republic).

– Elkington's

A book *Victorian Electroplate* (S. Bury, Country Life 1971) says something about the firm, though it deals more with products than personnel. Two cousins, George Richard Elkington and Henry E. Elkington of Birmingham were the pioneers of electroplating; they became partners between 1829 and 1836. Plating means the deposition of a thin layer on an object; the similar process of electrotyping forms a much thicker layer, with the original object no longer present. Serious research on electroplating and electrogilding was well under way in 1839, but progress was slow. The Elkingtons took out patent #8447 on 25.3.1840 (some 35 years after the idea was first discovered!) for their processes, which killed off 'Sheffield Plate' within a decade and changed the face of the silver trade worldwide. Their policy was to recruit the best chemists, take out as many patents as possible at home and abroad, buy up their rivals, and neutralize inventors by employing them: ie. create conditions to sweep the board. They licensed many other firms to use their processes. To finance their large-scale activity, they took on a third partner in 1842, the wealthy pen-maker Josiah Mason, to form Elkington Mason & Co, based in Birmingham; Mason left about 1859. After patenting, the Elkingtons made agreements with the London silversmith Benjamin Smith, Duke Street, Lincoln's Inn Fields (the son of Benjamin who had worked for Rundell Bridge and Rundell, the Royal goldsmiths), that he would set up electroplate workshops in Moorgate and a shop in Regent Street, both in their name. He also had to supply designs for their wares, which cost them very little. It ended in tragedy: see later.

– London Directories

As with Liverpool, so likewise with London directories (1846/47/54):

Elkington & Co, Patentees, Electroplaters, gilders, manufacturers and retailers of electroplated and gilt articles of every description. 20-22 Regent St (West End), 44-45 Moorgate St. (also in 1876). [Not Moorgate itself, which is very short.]

Charles Elkington, Electrometallurgical artist and fine art manufacturer, gilder, plater and general electrotypist, and manufacturer of electroplated spoons, forks, and every description of electroplate wares. 14 Hall St, City Rd. (1854 only).

Evans Lescher & Evans, Wholesale Druggists, 60 Bartholomew Close, London.

Benjamin Smith, silversmith, 12 Duke St, Lincoln's Inn Fields (1846 only).

Miss Eliza Turk, Ladies' Boarding School: (1846) Clayton Place, Kennington Road;

(1854) Alfred House, Larkhall Rise (Rectory Grove). [Thurlow Terrace adjacent.]

The Pellatt glassworks has a long history, the entry varying as time goes by:

1808, 1815 Pellatt & Green, Potters and Glass Manufacturers to the King, 16 St Paul's Church-yard.

1819, 1820 Manufacturers and Exporters of glass, china and earthenware …

1828 … and patentees of the glass illuminations and incrustations.

1833 Pellatt & Co, … Holland Street, Great Surrey St.

1840 Pellatt Apsley, maker of all kinds of glass, patentee of glass illuminators, incrustations, intagliated engraving on glass; Manufactory Holland St, Blackfriars Rd, late 16 St Paul's Churchyard.

1841 … Glass manufacturer to Her Majesty, patentee … , manufacturer of improved vials, new renaissance chandeliers, dealer in tea, table and dessert china; Falcon Glassworks, Holland St.

1847, 1854 Pellatt Apsley & Co (late Pellatt & Green), Glass manufacturer to Her Majesty and dealers in tea, table and dessert china, chandeliers, &c, wholesale and retail; Falcon Glassworks, Holland St, Blackfriars Road; 58 Baker St; 5 King St, Portman Sq. ['Pellatt Apsley' is one person, not two – these listings can be ambiguous.]

1876 Still there, as Pellatt & Co.

Also:

1833-34 Pellatt Apsley, Treasurer to Ecclesiastical Knowledge Society, Fenchurch St. [Before he succeeded to the glassworks on his father's death.] And: Pellatt Henry, Attorney, also Clerk to the Ironmonger's Co, 118 Fenchurch St. [Presumably an uncle of Apsley jr?]

1846 Pellatt Mill, Wine merchant, see Nicholls & Pellatt.

PART 17

London, etc., 1846-1870

Arrival

George met us at Euston, and we took a cab to a lodging in Wandsworth Road, Clapham, as we did not wish to burthen our friends with all our traps. At Dunsany Place [part of Lark Hall Lane?] we found Charles and wife, who had provided everything for our refreshment, and we were glad and thankful to place our dear invalid child in comfort, who had borne the journey far better than we had anticipated. Next day, house-hunting, without result; and the following day, Sunday, Fan spent with us.

Thus I began my new life in London. I had entered most unexpectedly on a new stage of existence; a revolution had threatened my means of living, help had come, and I now found myself in circumstances of much comfort. The late turmoils of Liverpool were happily exchanged for what seemed to be a future of quiet employment for me, and success for the promoters. I promised myself, too confidently I fear, remaining years of comfort and peace, but I had yet to learn many lessons in the school of experience: with much to prove to me, if proof were needed, that here was not to be my rest.

Monday March 2nd I appeared at Moorgate Street. The officials were principally Mr Packer the chief salesman, very complaisant and assiduous, devoting all his energies to sales and Wesleyanism, and in high favor with Mr Smith and Mr Pellatt. Mr William Lee the bookkeeper was equally devoted to his prosaic duties. Mr Hind and Mr Webster, two young men, completed the sales staff. At the back was a factory for replating old articles by the new process, presided over by Mr James Napier, a Scotch chemist. After being initiated into some of the mysteries of my new calling, we adjourned to the West End establishment 22 Regent Street, a smart-looking place with three smart young sales men, Clarke, Wildsmith and Fuller. Mr Lee was about to vacate, and I undertook to keep the books, with the assistance of a collector, Mr Barton, to get in the money: no trifling matter at the West End.

Having surveyed the situation, I begged a week's respite to assist Emily in arranging home matters. Truly there was much to do. We thought we had secured a house in Larkhall Rise, but after our expense of cleaning and sweeping chimnies, the landlord let it to another tenant, nor could we get the slightest compensation from either. Eventually we found a house in a new row in Larkhall Lane, Thurlow Terrace, where we thankfully received our furniture with scarcely any injury. The adjustment of our household took a considerable time. Our landlord was as great a screw as usual: there was the bran-new house, but not even a peg to hang a hat on, or a doorplate to keep his paint clean, or a window blind to keep the sun out. Then we had the London workmen! Of all tedious beings, the most tedious, coming to put up a blind, away to their beer at 11, and no more of them for a day or two: gone to finish another job or begin a new one! The never-ending puzzle of smoky chimneys, which being young and inexperienced, had to be drilled, coaxed and educated into civilized habits; and last but not least, that greatest of all trials, 'servant gal-ism'.

I left most of this to Emily's patience and skill, and took refuge during my leisure hours in my new garden. How pleasant to see fresh green turf, bright gravel, expectant flower-beds, the young grape vine on the back of the house, Virginia creeper and clematis on the bit of trellis, and laurels and ivy promising soon to conceal the bare walls of the inclosure, all sprouting hopeful during the remarkably fine and genial spring, a contrast to smoky dingy coal black Liverpool. [The 1851 Census gives his address as 4 Thurlow Terrace, and Emily's birthplace as Middlesex; they had a servant Mary Capel, then aged 34, from Burnham, Somerset.]

Our first summer was singularly hot, for many months almost tropical. John visited us in June, and my anxieties were a good deal awakened, as it was evident he was not suitably placed: his employments were anything but 'practical chemistry' as he had expected. Johnsons intimated that if I could form an engagement for him in London, they would be willing to give him up for the remaining two years of his five-year term. I advertised, and had a multiplicity of applications from various 'chemists' and druggists in the West End: on whom, in the midst of my own new occupations, I had to call, almost worn out daily with fatigue and the disappointment at finding they were not such as I could place him with. I began to fear he must go back to Liverpool, and was at my wits' end when my dear ever ready practical counsellor said she had a scheme, though I did not understand how she was going to work it.

She betook herself to Mr John Relf, a grocer in Gracechurch Street, whose wife my wife knew and highly esteemed, more than she did him, who was devoted to money-getting; a more unpromising subject for promoting our object could scarcely be imagined. Now the Relfs were frequenters of a chapel, and it had entered Emily's imagination that if she could discover a pious druggist in their congregation, she might work on his Christian feelings to take John or recommend some respectable party. It happened that Mrs Relf was not at home, but Emily, who never left a stone unturned, resolved to tackle Mr Relf himself, and dived into the shop.

She found the subject on whom she had to work in the worst possible state; as it was Saturday afternoon, he was busy with customers, and she had to follow him up and down the shop. However, the name of Barkley was at length elicited, who knew that a wholesale house, Messrs Evans & Lescher in Bartholomew Close, were in want of assistance. Emily found her way there, and saw a junior partner, Mr John Evans; on Monday morning, to my great joy, John was approved. So Emily's scheme, unpromising, chimerical, and impracticable, was amply successful. Thus ladies ofttimes rush in and succeed where their Lords would fear to tread. Letitia had improved in health since her residence at Clapham, and was apparently well enough to go to Miss Knight's school near us at the corner of Manor Street. Fanny was still at Miss Turk's: and there for the present stood our domestic arrangements.

My New Employ
By the second week in March, Frederic Pellatt had resigned the conduct of affairs into my hands, though I felt somewhat at a loss in

being left to preside over matters so thoroughly new to me. It only remained for us to visit Elkington Mason & Co in Birmingham. Mr George Richard Elkington was remarkably bright and intelligent, full of energy and business talent, very prepossessing in appearance; his partner and cousin Henry was little, quick and rough, not I thought polished or ceremonious. Mr Mason I did not then see; he had his own business in the steel pen trade, in which he had worked up a large fortune, part invested in electroplate manufacture. He was proud of having raised himself, and boasted of a very low origin with a donkey and hamper of greens as his stock in trade! [His name is perpetuated (inter alia) by the Mason Cottages in Orphanage Road, Erdington, Birmingham, itself named after an institution, now demolished, that he founded.]

I gave myself to matters of cash and accounts, as my most proper and useful province, and oscillated daily between Moorgate and Regent Street. The West End mainly required my care, as I soon found out that the bookkeeper had good reason to absent himself; the books were in confusion owing to his irregularities, and the cash account was deficient, which caused me much trouble to unravel. At Moorgate Street, things were much more regular. Packer was the prime mover; both Mr Smith and Frederic Pellatt placed unlimited confidence in him, and I was taught to do the same, aided by my own observation of his care, and his high professing character and standing amongst the Wesleyan body. [Awful bosh, a thorough rogue – JCC II.] Eventually my confidence was sadly misplaced and shamefully abused.

Almost from the commencement, one thing struck me as very puzzling. Mr Smith my brother-in-law did not give me much time or advice; his mind and attention appeared to be greatly occupied by some subject not connected with the business. James Napier the clever Scotch chemist [ha! ha! – JCC II] who was superintending the replating department when I arrived, was soon withdrawn, and was corresponding with Mr Smith from some place in the country, leaving an ignorant brother who did the work very badly. I ventured some questions, but could elicit no reply; evidently a mystery. In course of time James Napier reappeared; I was anxiously seeking all the information I could obtain on electro and chemical matters, and was desirous of seeing him, but I found he rather shyed me. One day he said 'The fack is that Mester Smith does na want me to let out about the copper'; and it soon transpired that Napier had discovered a new method of smelting it from the ore, which promised the most extraordinary profit, and to which Mr Smith's energies were intensely given. [The whole thing came to grief – JCC II.]

Patents were taken out to secure the invention, and the various great copper smelters were applied to, to join the new system which promised great things if all would act unanimously: which hitherto they had done, under a sort of federal monopoly of which they were excessively jealous. This new intrusion created great alarm and indignation, and the object was to crush it, although they amused Mr Smith for some time by a shew of negociation. Mr Smith now had recourse to influential people in the City; eventually companies were started abroad, and another at Spitty near Swansea, in the thick of the old smelters. So here was war to the knife, as the smelters considered their immense resources would enable them to starve the new attempt out. Calculation, proved by small scale trial of the new system, certainly shewed a large profit margin over the old one, and the advantages were sufficiently obvious to induce influential London men to embark on shares in these undertakings, which were in due time set a going with large

Postscript

And right there, at the end of the fragment of his last book, at the bottom of a page, in the middle of a sentence – he stops. Maybe whoever removed these pages did not realize that some writing had been left behind and any succeeding sheets were subsequently lost. However, in another book his own material is followed by three pages 'Written by John Castelfranc Cheveley the younger, son of J.C.Cheveley, the author of this Autobiography, at 4 Warren St. Tenby, 1883.' He says:

'An Autobiography is necessarily incomplete. No man can give an account from birth except from hearsay; and nobody can finish it, for the hand of death must needs arrest his pen suddenly. Where my father left off, when he was thus overtaken, was at the point of Mr

Benjamin Smith's [*sic*] discovery of a new mode of copper-smelting. Mr Smith had reckoned on realizing a future; and after a short career of extravagance, became bankrupt. …

'In 1855 [in fact 1854] my sister Mary Letitia died at Adelphi Place, Cold Harbour Lane, Camberwell. In 1858 I married, and in 1863 [in fact 1861] my sister Frances died at Chapel Place, Cold Harbour Lane, Camberwell. My father died at Linton House, Bohemia Road, Hastings in April 1870 [the 9th]; and his widow at Grafton Square, Clapham, November 22nd 1878. All were buried in my father's grave at Norwood Cemetery. In 1851 I left Messrs Evans Lescher and Evans in Bartholomew Close, London, and entered the London and County Bank in Lombard St. After spending a few years, partly at the head office, and partly at their Woolwich Branch, I engaged with Messrs. Dennis [?] & Wylie, Shipping Insurance Brokers, at 19 Birchin Lane, London, continuing with them about 11 years, and afterwards with Mr. Arthur Oates Wilkinson in the same line of business at Threadneedle St. In 1869, owing to delicate health, I left London and went to reside at Wilmington, near Lewes, Sussex, and afterwards at Cowes, Isle of Wight, at Southampton, at Hastings and St. Leonards, Folkestone and Penzance. My wife Elizabeth died here in 1881 and was buried in my freehold grave at Madron [close to Penzance]. In 1882 I left Penzance and went to Tenby. In May 1883 I married a second time. My son George was born April 5th 1884.'

But oh dear me, John, you disappoint us! A third of the little you have written is taken up with Mr Smith, who is of no real interest to us at all, and not a word about what really is, your father's last two decades, but instead something about yourself – how *could* you! Or did you intend to complete his story in your 'Family Memoirs'? Subtitled 'The Narrative of John Castelfranc Cheveley (the Elder), from my father's MS written in 1865; Condensed and edited by John Castelfranc Cheveley (the younger)', addressed at 3 St Julian's St, Tenby, datelined November 1891, these comprise two extant volumes: Book 2 ('bought of C Farley, High Street, Tenby') covers the China and India voyages, and Book 3 the present 'Down in Demerara' – but (oddly) it omits any mention of arguably the most significant event in his father's life, his 'conversion to God' at

Prescot; maybe a sore point? Probably the missing Book 1 covered Messing Lodge, and Book 4 was intended for Liverpool and London – if it was ever done; or as he died only a year later, did the Reaper's hand arrest his pen too (like his father's) before completing his task? He tends to paraphrase the original, but does give a little extra information:

Refers to George's water treatment for fever in China (Vol. 1 p. 134) as the first anticipation of later hydropathic institutions such as Ben Rhydding, near Ilkley, in Yorkshire.

Confirms JCC's arrival in London from his India voyage (Vol. 1 p. 184) as November 9th.

Referring to hammocks (eg. 'Plantation le Destin'), he has 'As Londoners say 'hung out' without knowing the origin of the phrase.'

Another name for Seltzer or Spa water, Nassau water ('Home Thoughts from Abroad').

He comments that Miss Susan Morris ought to have been Mistress William Pattinson [Which she already was, of course, in another sense!], and states clearly that they had two children (see 'Struggling On').

The Rest of his Life – Work
What else can be pieced together about JCC's life? Unfortunately, not a great deal has emerged. From his 'too confident promise of comfort and peace' and what he said about Packer and Smith, one a rogue, the other with mind elsewhere and becoming bankrupt, it seems a reasonable guess that his business life in London (as before) turned out badly; and 'here was not to be my rest' suggests that the job was no sinecure, or that he might have had to move on from Elkington's to other employment elsewhere.

A little of him survives in the Elkington records in the 'Archive of Art and Design' of the Victoria and Albert Museum: some 8 letters written by him 1846-49, none thereafter, largely to do with Elkington Mason, Birmingham (It seems odd then that they are held in London rather than the Birmingham reference library. The whereabouts of any records of Elkington & Co, London, are unknown.). In 1848, 'this unfortunate year', an acrimonious correspondence with G R Elkington develops. JCC complains that after agreeing a price with customers, Elkington then increased his own costs, thereby removing London's profit margin: 'If terms are to be altered whenever you find you cannot fulfil your engagements, what certainty is there in business at all? What in the world are we to do if in making our arrangements with customers, we cannot depend on you? What we require in a word (surely it is perfectly fair) is a price named and no afterclaps – These are my views and I believe them to be based on sound business principles.' But no clue is given as to why his confidence in chief salesman Packer was 'sadly misplaced and shamefully abused'.

Bury's book (see 'Addenda – Elkington's') and the Elkington papers confirm Smith's delinquency, that he was much occupied with his own concern in Duke Street. G.R. Elkington took over in 1849 and drove Smith to bankruptcy the next year: from which ignominy he was relieved by dying May 1850 after 7 months' illness.

– Domestic

JCC appears to have remained in the same district of London throughout, though with some changes of address. The element of sadness in his life returned in 1850 with the death of brother Richard; daughter Letitia followed on November 8th 1854, the cause 'Phthisis, 7 years': maybe something to do with her long period of ill-health? (see 'Letitia's Illness'). By this time they had moved from Thurlow Terrace to 2 Adelphi Place. Brother George died on May 29th 1857.

A brighter spot was the marriage of his son on August 10th 1858 at St Matthew's, Brixton, to Elizabeth Smith, age 25, daughter of William Smith (Labourer). John was described as Merchants Clerk (the same as his father) and as age 28!, though in fact he was nearly 31, almost the same age as his father at his first marriage. Frances' death on November 28th 1861 comes as a surprise: the cause is given as Paralysis 3 years, Exhaustion 7 days. She is 'daughter of John Cheveley, Silversmith' – must be an error, surely you cannot be trained up in just three years, but it does suggest he was still working for Elkingtons. JCC was still at Adelphi Place in the 1860 Post Office Directory and in the 1861 Census on April 7th, but had evidently now moved again, though not very far, to 3 Chapel Place.

Incidentally, his four children died in reverse order, the youngest first.

JCC's niece Clara Jane Rayner, his sister Margaret's daughter, was sadly deaf and dumb from birth in 1848. Nevertheless she went to school in her village, learned to write, and could say one or two little words. When she was about nine (1857), it was arranged she should go to a special school in London, before which she stayed with JCC for three months, where she was very happy. Sadly, she was only at the school a week or two when she was taken ill; everything was done for her, but in vain, and she died December 3rd 1857 at the Deaf and Dumb Asylum, Southwark; the cause of death was given as 'brain fever' (probably meningitis). She was interred in Norwood Cemetery; her name is also inscribed on the tomb at Little Yeldham where her mother was buried. She was much loved by all her relatives, and a lengthy poem 'To the Memory of Little Clara', attributed to JCC but equally possibly written by her mother, has survived.

Some evidence survives about places he visited. In Vol. 1, p. 56, he mentions 'when I visited Layer Marney in 1856', when he would have been 61, and one wonders why he returned to this rather out-of-the-way spot, and at that particular time – unless perhaps his family had expressed a wish to see it and they all went together, or he was visiting brother George in Colchester. The building would certainly have deteriorated further in the 40-plus years since his own childhood, as its restoration did not begin till 1869. Some of his pencil sketches have survived, initialled and dated as: Watersmeet, Lynmouth 1855; Chagford Mill, Devon 1865; Broadstairs 1866; Longfield (Kent?) 1868.

– Last Years

There is internal evidence for when he began his writings, when he states 'I have given above what I committed to paper some years ago (1852) for a lecture', referring to his India voyage. His supplementary British Guiana book appears to have preceded the others, possibly also as lecture material, the part on the insurrection being then copied more or less verbatim into its correct sequence with everything else. He began on his full autobiography in 1864, and

Broadstairs: Pencil Sketch by JCC, dated 1866. (Courtesy Mrs M. Timmington)

presumably fairly late therein, for after only some 120 pages of book 1 he says 'this January 20th 1865'. He would then be age 69 and retired from work, so did his writing form a means of occupying himself, particularly during bad days and long dark evenings in winter? The existing material, and maybe his son's encouragement, might well have provided the necessary spark for him to start, though it is sad that his own spark was extinguished before he could finish his task. In his last notebook, he says 'now (1869)', which fits with what JCC II says about when he stopped writing.

Flyleaf inscriptions in the books include addresses 14 Gresham Place, Coldharbour Lane, Brixton and Linton House, Hastings, and Lark Hall Rise, Clapham, Surrey (in what looks like his own hand). Others have simply 'Cheveley, Clapham'. One book at least was bought in Hastings – labelled C.J. Murphy, Account Book Manufacturer, Printer, Binder & Stationer, Hastings, Priced @ 1/6d. The Gresham Place address is curious: JCC was at Chapel Place in 1861 (see above), and he (and Emily) were still there latterly (see his will in the Appendix); did they move out and then back again? And why brother Charles' address Lark Hall Rise? However, what does seem clear is that he was staying at the seaside for at least part of the last few years of his life; was it to escape the smoky London winters by reason of health? His remark that he 'unhappily became acquainted with the terribly insidious disorder of consumption' (see 'The beginning of the end') suggests that he might have contracted it, though his death certificate (which calls him 'Gentleman') states the cause as chronic valvular heart disease (brought on by it?). And why Hastings rather than some other resort? There is a tenuous link via his brother Charles' second wife (see 'Proposal – and Acceptance').

It is unlikely that father and son were ever in Hastings together; John junior did not leave London till 1869, so he would have had to move very rapidly through Lewes, Cowes, and Southampton to be at Hastings by April 1870: and this with a wife and child.

Death and After

Linton House, Hastings, was the lodging-house of the Misses Beverly, one of several in this area. It still stands on the south side of what is now Cambridge Road, the lower part of Bohemia Road, renamed, immediately to the west of steps leading down into Claremont. It was built sometime between 1861 (not in the Census) and 1867 (appears in the town Directory). There, in Hastings Registration District, Sub-District of St Mary in the Castle, he died April 9th 1870; registered the same day by C. Cheveley, who was 'in attendance', residence 52 Lark Hall Rise, Clapham – so one wonders then what Emily was doing latterly: was she with him at Hastings, and if not why not, particularly at the critical time of his death?

John junior says his father was interred in Norwood Cemetery (now known as West Norwood), beside Letitia and Frances, where Emily later joined them, but any memorial for them was either lost by enemy action in the war, or had decayed into illegibility by the 1970s when all surviving inscriptions were recorded. Being Non-conformists, they are in the un-consecrated part of the cemetery, grave #4244 in square 40. (Brothers Charles and Thomas are in the consecrated part, square 86: Charles, buried September 12th 1894 aged 95, his wife Charlotte October 26th 1904 aged 87, grave 25975; Thomas, died February 16th 1887 age 87, and Matilda, April 23rd 1884 age 73, grave 16421, along with Diana Sophia Spurden died July 26th 1877 – her mother?).

JCC's will, dated August 19th 1864, was without doubt written in his own hand – maybe even drawn up by himself? Probate was granted May 2nd 1870. He left everything to Emily, and after her death to his son. Emily died November 22nd 1878, and JCC II December 14th 1892. (See Appendix.)

The 'Cheveley, Clapham' inscriptions in JCC's books could suggest that Charles took care of the books after JCC died, if his son was elsewhere at the time. John junior must have had them in 1881, when he inserted his comments, and presumably retained them to prepare his 'Narrative' in 1891. After his death, it is possible his widow and / or offspring had no interest in them, and passed them all on (along with the black shade profiles) in a 'sideways' move to someone who did (likely, cousin Richard Dodson Cheveley IV, hence the initialling of JCC I's books as 'Read' in 1908, when he was age 20 or 21; which might well have stimulated him to research the full family tree): from whom they eventually came down to their present custodian.

Photograph: JCC himself, date unknown. Original inscribed 'Edward Sims, Tunbridge Wells' – was he staying there when he had it taken? (Courtesy Mrs M. Timmington)

Valediction

And so we bid farewell to John Castelfranc Cheveley the elder. So just who was he? No-one famous, just a respectable lower-middle-class bookkeeper who throughout his life was faced with difficulties and disappointments, though with a faith to support him, but who nevertheless had some adventures and, though he never rose very high, his brief times of status: Midshipman with the Honorable East

301

India Company, and Business Partner in Demerara (what we would call a Company Director), albeit acting as a general factotum. Generally, however, he was insignificant alongside men eminent in their communities: those such as Mr Majendie at Castle Hedingham, shipowner Mr Bonham, Mr Sherbourne of St Helens, the cold-eyed Mr Rainey of Georgetown, or Mr Cearns in Liverpool. But who now remembers anything of them? It is ironic: eminent in life but after death gone and forgotten, yet John Cheveley has endured to become a 'Somebody', simply because, one day late in 1864, he decided to sit down and write an account of his life, a real 'Diary (or rather Autobiography) of a Nobody'.

The great majority of biographies are about people who were already rich and/or famous, simply because that is what they were and their doings are well-documented. However, they tend to give a distorted view of how life was in their times, because they are not typical of the 'ordinary' people, the population as a whole, of whom there are very few biographies, because their lifestyles were so well-known that no-one bothered to write them down. And that is precisely why John's writings are so important: he redresses the balance, with his account of the trials of life for an ordinary man in the pre-social-security era, when there was only the kindness of family or friends to fall back on in hard times.

And yes, John, apropos your comment (Vol. 1 p. 21), you *do* have readers, and a potentially far wider circle of them than I daresay you would ever have imagined. Who or what determined you to take up your pen in 1864, we shall never really know; but we are profoundly grateful both to that unknown agent, and (even more) to you, that you took up the challenge and left behind for us some fifty years of your story – also to those of your relatives who held your notebooks in safe keeping. We all thank you most sincerely, our only disappointment that we can only guess about most of the final part of your life. And we hope for your sake that after your disappointments and hardships in this world, you found peace and happiness in the next.

JCC's Signatures: (a) In his Book 11; (b) On his Will

Appendix – Wills

This is the last Will and Testament of me John Castelfranc Cheveley of Camberwell in the County of Surrey

I direct that all my just debts & funeral and testamentary expences be paid & satisfied by my Executors hereinafter named as soon as conveniently may be after my decease out of such current monies as there may be to satisfy the same and should these not suffice that then sufficient be sold of Stock standing in my sole name in the three per cents consols to make up the amount required. I give devise & bequeath to my dear wife Emily Cheveley all my household furniture & plate but in case of her death before she takes possession then to my Son John Castelfranc Cheveley and the residue of stock standing in my name in the three per cent consols after payment of my just debts & funeral and testamentary expences as aforesaid together with all the rest residue & remainder of my Estate & effects whatsoever & wheresoever both real & personal whether in possession reversion remainder or expectancy   I give devise and bequeath unto my brothers Charles Cheveley and Thomas Cheveley my executors & administrators upon trust to pay the dividends interest & annual produce thereof unto my dear wife Emily Cheveley during the term of her natural life & from & after her decease I give devise & bequeath the aforesaid property & every part thereof unto my son John Castelfranc Cheveley absolutely and I nominate constitute & appoint my dear wife Emily Cheveley & my brothers Charles

303

Cheveley & Thomas Cheveley to be executors & executrix of this my last Will & testament and hereby revoking all former or other wills & testaments by me at any time heretofore made I declare this to be my last will & testament   In witness whereof I the said John Castelfranc Cheveley have to this my last will & testament set my hand this 19th day of August in the year of our Lord one thousand eight hundred and sixty four.

[signed] John Castelfranc Cheveley

Signed by the said Testator John
Castelfranc Cheveley and   William Lee,
acknowledged by him to be his last will   45 Moorgate Street
& testament in the presence of us
present at the same time and subscribed   Edward Barton,
by us in the presence of the said testator   9 Hilldrop Crescent,
and of each other.   Holloway

Probate was granted on the 2nd day of May 1870: The Will of John Castelfranc Cheveley, formerly of Coldharbour Lane Camberwell in the county of Surrey but late of Chapel Place Camberwell aforesaid deceased, who died on the 9th day of April 1870 at Hastings in the county of Sussex, was proved in the Principal Registry of Her Majesty's Court of Probate, by the Oaths of Emily Cheveley of Chapel Place aforesaid Widow the Relict and Charles Cheveley of Larkhall Rise Clapham in the said county of Surrey Esquire and Thomas Cheveley of Upper Tooting in the said county of Surrey Esquire the Brothers of the said Deceased the Executors named in the said Will they having been first sworn duly to administer. Effects under £3,000, No Leaseholds.

Emily's will dated January 1st 1873, with a codicil October 8th 1875, leaves the interest on her estate to her sister Mrs Esther Phillips if Emily predeceases her, and the estate itself equally among her eight nieces, effects under £2,000: No mention of her stepson (or of her late husband's autobiography!). Formerly of 3 De-Crespigny Villas, Coldharbour Lane, Camberwell, she died November 22nd 1878 at 11 Grafton Square, Clapham; one of her executors was one

James Brown Jordan of the same address. Her will was proved December 18th 1878.

John junior's will is very short, written when he was residing in the County of Pembroke and dated June 30th 1892. He appoints his cousin George Rayner as his sole executor, to whom he leaves 'all my estate both real and personal   In trust to pay the income thereof during the lifetime of my Wife either to her or to apply the same for the benefit of my Son George Cheveley as my said Cousin shall in his uncontrolled discretion think advisable   And after the death of my said Wife I direct that my said Cousin shall hold the capital of my estate and all future income thereof In trust for my said Son George Cheveley absolutely.'

The probate grant dated February 20th 1893 describes him as 'formerly of Tenby in the county of Pembroke, but late of No 7 Saint Martins Ash in the city of Chester Gentleman deceased, who died on the 14th day of December 1892 in the said City, and who had a fixed place of abode at the said City'. His cousin renounced the probate and execution of his will, so 'Letters of Administration were granted by Her Majesty's High Court of Justice '… to the said Margaret Cheveley of No 3 Saint Julian Street Tenby aforesaid the lawful Widow and Relict of the said deceased. Gross value of personal estate £201-12-6d, net £170-13-10d.' (Question: why was he in Chester and Margaret still in Tenby?)

– The Family Summarised

(1) Brother George, to whom JCC was closest

Date	Event
Oct 6th 1797	Born Messing Lodge Farm
Feb 1804	Accident with nursery fire
Oct 6th 1809	Ran away
Mar 1816 – June 1817	Midshipman, *Hugh Inglis* (EICo) to China, with brother JCC
Jan 1818 – early summer 1819	Appointed 6th Mate, *Prince Regent* (EICo) to India, but served as Midshipman; did duty as Acting 5th Mate

Date	Event
1820	Actor, very briefly
Spring 1821	To Prescot Vicarage
Early 1822	2nd mate, *Cornwall* (Gladstone's): three voyages to British Guiana
1823	Command of *Anna* (Pattinson Cheveley) to British Guiana, Mate, brother Henry
1823 – 24	To Jamaica, where married Ellen Congreve (probably late 1823)
1824	To Brazil. Growing very stout
Late 1824-25	To British Guiana (Henry now left), St Johns, New Brunswick, British Guiana
November 1825	To Barbados, *Anna* scrapped. In a scrape, to Liverpool as passenger
Mar-Dec 1826	Command to Barbados and St Vincent; no names given, Whitehaven owner
Dec 1826 – spring 1827	To Pernambuco (Hewson Dutchman), no ship name, in dispute; Ellen died during this time
From spring 1827	On shore, Liverpool; Navigation Academy
By summer 1828 – spring 1829	To sea again, no details given
1829	Worked with Latham & Gair, then D & T Willis
During 1830	Command of *Pantaloon* (Murray Bros), Demerara trade
1832	Superintendent of building of *Isabella* (Murray Bros) at Belfast, and command. Married Harriet Welch in Belfast
1835	Resigned from Murrays
1835-36	*Fox* (Newman Hunt & Christopher) to China, returned in dispute
Late 1836 – 37	*William Mulvey* (D & T Willis) to Mazatlan: ship foundered
1838	Auctioneer in Belfast
( )	Superintendent of building and command of Lough Neagh steamer
1842	Promoter welshed, George bankrupted and jailed; sub-editor of newspaper

Date	Event
1842 – late 1843	Command in Mediterranean fruit trade; dispute with owners
1844-45	*Ganges* (owner not given) to Aden, patent fuel, cotton home from Bombay
Feb 1846	Secretary of Ramoneur Co (chimney-sweeping), soon fell through
By 1849	Surveyor for Colchester Mutual Marine Insurance Association – had presumably left the sea for a shore job
1850	Secretary and Surveyor for Colchester Equitable Ship Insurance Society
1853-4	Preacher on Colchester Circuit of Wesleyan Branch Society, Secretary of Colchester Auxiliary Sailors' Society
May 29th 1857	Died at St Johns Street, Colchester, cause Heart Disease; described as Surveyor of Shipping

By 1846 George had six children, though JCC mentions only the eldest, Frances (Fanny), born 1833. She was followed by Richard Dodson III 1836, George Castelfranc 1838, William Stammers Brathwaite 1840, Harriet Matilda 1841, and Emily 1843. Fanny presumably, Richard and Emily definitely, born Belfast. There is then a gap before the seventh, Thomas Welch, Colchester 1850, and the last, Mary Letitia, 1852, died 1853.

He was also a Mason (by 1826, as JCC says – see 'Making Water!'), and was active in local affairs: at a public meeting January 25th 1856, he supported a resolution to remove a row of houses and a small old church, St Ronald's, from the middle of Colchester High Street to enable its widening.

(2) The rest of the family:

Date	Event
1800	Charles born
1801-02	Tom appears. Stillborn son. Christenings
1803	Dick to school

Date	Event
Feb 22nd 1804	Margaret born
Nov 29th 1809	Mary Letitia born
1816	Father rents Brook House, Tiptree Heath
1817-18	Henry and Charles to sea; and return
1819-20	Henry to grocery at Hedingham
	Tom to bookselling
1821	Parents and sisters to farm near Sible
	Richard starts mole plough, and Secretary of Witham Savings Bank
	Charles assists Richard
	Henry grocering at Bocking
1822	Charles to Barber Beaumont at County Fire & Life Office, Regent Street, London
	Richard superintendent of Brookhall Farm, Tiptree Heath
1823	Henry to Mildenhall, disliked it, and to Mate of ship *Anna* under George as Captain
1824	Henry to another employ as Mate
1826 (May)	Tom to Longmans as book collector, after 1-2 yr in Colchester as compositor
	Charles to Bank of England
	Richard marries Elizabeth Vallance
1827	Parents and sisters to Liverpool
1828	Mother dies
	Henry to Captain, drowns in River Plate
1829	Charles marries Elizabeth Rix (14 yr his senior)
	Tom to Bank of England
1834	Father ill with paralytic attack (stroke?)
1837	Mention of Amoore, M.S. of Charles' second wife
	Sisters Margaret and Letitia to start School
	Father's health much improved, but another attack, and dies last day of year
1838	Margaret and Letitia engaged to brothers Thomas and William Rayner (8 and 10 yr their senior), married 1840

– Bank of England

The appointment of John's brothers Thomas and Charles to the Bank of England began something of a tradition of service in the Bank, which developed and continued for well over a century, some 134 (+) years, with a break of only a couple of years in 1901-3; there were briefly (in 1860-1) four Cheveleys in service together. Altogether there were seven Cheveleys, one Rayner, and finally my father, who retired in 1964. He was allowed access to the records, and found the following:

JCC's brothers:

a. Thomas (1801-1887), service 1830-61;
b. Charles (1800-1894), service 1835-71.

JCC says they began earlier, ca.1826 and ca.1830 respectively; this might have been when they entered as probationers, and the service dates above when they were elected to the permanent staff. However, the 1924 date for my father is definitely when he first began as a probationer.

Three nephews of JCC:

a. Son of JCC's sister Margaret (1804-85):
   George Castelfranc Rayner (b ca.1847 d ?)
   In service in 1881 (and 1887?)

b. Eldest son of JCC's brother George:
   Richard Dodson (III) (27.10.1836 – x.x.1920
   Service 12.1854 - 1901: Leeds Branch 18.1.59 – 9.12.1895.
   Then to Treasury cashier, London

   (b.i) RDC III's daughter:
   Margaret Castelfranc (x.x.1885 – x.x.1983)
   Service 1903-10, Woman Clerk: one of the first such in the B of E. At first, she had to use a separate entrance from the men, and take her meals in a screened-off area of the directors' dining room on the top floor.

   (b.ii) RDC III's son: Richard Dodson (IV) (x.x.1887 – 23.2.1983)
   Service 1905-44: Principal, Bank Stock Office

c. Third son of JCC's brother George:
William Stammers Brathwaite (x.x.1840 –??)
Service 1860-72: Leeds Branch 1862 – 27.4.1872. Then to
Manager, Bradford Old Bank (He disappeared around August
1878, having got his fingers burnt on the stock market –
apparently with Bank funds! – and been found out. The skeleton
in the family cupboard.)

(c.i) WSBC's son: George Edward (x.x.1865 – x.x.1951)
Service during 1914-18 War, as Temporary Clerk, presumably in
Leeds Branch

(c.ii) WSBC'S grandson (my father):
Philip Cheveley Thornburn (2.5.1904 - 5.10.76)
Service x.x.1924 – 1.5.64: Clerk, finally Superintendent,
Leeds Branch. (Introduced into the Bank by 2nd cousin
Richard, at a difficult time for employment for young men
fresh out of college; not so different 70-odd years on!)